AF540193

HUMAN RESOURCE MANAGEMENT IN AGRICULTURE

HUMAN RESOURCE MANAGEMENT IN AGRICULTURE

DR. K. SIVARAMAKRISHNA,
Faculty Member
P.G. Deptt. of Industrial Relations & Personnel Management
Sir C.R. Reddy College, Eluru, A.P.

DR. K. RAMESH
Reader
Deptt. of Industrial Relations & Personnel Management
Andhra University, Visakhapatnam, A.P.

PROF. M. GANGADHARA RAO
Department of Commerce & Management Studies
Andhra University, Visakhapatnam, A.P.

DISCOVERY PUBLISHING HOUSE
New Delhi—110 002 (INDIA)

First Published 1995
Reprinted-2011

ISBN 81–7141–270–X

Published by
DISCOVERY PUBLISHING HOUSE
4831/24, Ansari Road, Prahlad Street,
Darya Ganj, New Delhi-110002 (India)
Phone: 23279245 • Fax: 91-11-23253475
E-mail:dphtemp@indiatimes.com

Laser Typesetting by :
Allied Computers,
Karnal

Mehra Offset Press
Delhi

DEDICATED TO

BADRADRI SITARAMULU

Preface

Indian agriculture is the largest sector of economic activity and has crucial role to play in the country's economic development by providing food and raw materials, employment to a very large proportion of the population, capital for its own development and surplus for national economic development.

With the introduction of new technology in 1960s, green revolution has ushered in and the yield per hectare of different crops has considerably increased. Inspite of this, the yield per hectare in India is still below the world average in respect of all the crops. The need of the hour is to increase the agricultural productivity including labour productivity.

The relations between peasants and labourers have become one of the most delicate and complex problem in Indian agriculture sector especially during the last three decades. The relations which were mostly based on traditional caste relations are fast changing in different parts of the country due to the influence of socio-economic and political factors. The agricultural labour who happend to be the down trodden and oppressed sections of the society are increasingly becoming conscious of their rights and are trying to assert their rights. This resulted in frequent conflicts and clashes in rural areas affecting the entire agrarian economy. The country can be longer afford to ignore these clashes. The ameliorative measures like land reforms, tenancy legislation and minimum wages, taken by the government failed in improving the situation.

The cultivator, on the other hand, can no longer afford to function as a grower and harvester merely relying on his instincts, although honed by centuries of experience, but should develop himself into a full scale farm manager endowed with entrepreneurial abilities and negotiating skills.

There have been many studies of the agriculture. Most of these tend to analyse origin the classification of agricultural labour, agrarian structure, income and employment trends of the agricultural labourers. But there is no comprehensive study on agricultural labour, treating them as 'resource'.

Under these circumstances, alternative and effective institutional arrangements have to be made in the direction of comprehensive human resource management in agriculture encompassing all the functions from induction to post-retirement benefits. It has been rightly remarked that the improvement of economic condition and social position of agricultural workers is a prerequisite for the welfare of industrial workers.

The present study of human resource management confines its attention to the selected villages of the State of Andhra Pradesh which is popularly known as 'Granary of South' because of its large surplus in the production of food grains, pulses, oil seeds, Varginia tobacco, chillies and fruits. The role of the agriculture in the economy of Andhra Pradesh is expected to increase further in the years to come. Thus this study of human resource management practices in selected villages of Coastal Andhra, Rayalaseema and Telangana regions of Andhra Pradesh is expected to be useful not only to this State but to all other Indian States where rural scene by and large conforms to the same pattern.

A study of this nature cannot be successful but for the unstinted cooperation extended by several persons and it is our duty to acknowledge their help. At the outset, we are thankful to the respondent farmers and labourers spreadover nine villages of Coastal Andhra, Rayalaseema and Telangana regions of Andhra Pradesh.

We express our hearty sense of gratitude to Prof. B.S. Murthy, Chairman, P.G. Board of Studies and Head of the Department of Industrial Relations and Personnel Management, Andhra University, for his scholastic suggestions to improve the quality of work.

We are indebted to Andhra University, our Alma mater for providing us this opportunity and also in making use of University Library.

We will be failing in our duties if we forget to express our sense of appreciation and hearty thanks to Mr. M. Hema Sundar and Miss. P. Kavitha who helped in tabulation and typing work. We are thankful to Sri. K. Srinivas M.Sc., and Sri. P. Venkateswara Rao for their help in final typing.

Finally, the authors are grateful to their life-partners who suffered silently while they were on this work.

Authors

Contents

1

Introduction

Human Resource Management is the utilisation of human resources to achieve organisational objectives.[1]

An attempt is made in this chapter to present the significance of human resource at macro and micro levels; role of agriculture in economic development; the size and structure of human resource in agriculture; significance of management in light of peculiar features of human resource employment in Indian agriculture.

Human Resource at Macro and Micro Levels

The human resource endowment is a natural gift given to every nation in this world and human resource plays pivotal role in utilising the natural resources in building a strong nation. Thus human resource factor appears to be the most strategic and critical. A country may possess abundant and inexhaustible natural and physical resources, but unless there are men who can mobilise, organise and harness nature's bountiful resources for the production of goods and services, the country cannot make rapid strides towards economic and social advancement.

Arthur Lewis observed "there are great differences in development between countries which seem to have roughly equal resources, so it is necessary to enquire into the difference in human behaviour".[2] It is often

1. W. Arthur Lewis, *The History of Economic Growth* (London : George Allen & Unwin Ltd., 1965), p.iv.

2. R. Wayne Mondy and Robert M. Noe III, *Human Resource Management* (Bostan : Allyn and Bacon, 1990), p.4.

felt that, though the exploitation of natural resources, availability of physical and financial resources and international aid play prominent roles in the growth of modern economies, none of these factors is more significant than efficient and committed manpower. A nation with an abundance of physical resources will not benefit itself unless human resources make use of them.[1] Thus, one of the major tasks of developing countries is the building up of 'human capital'.[2] There is a growing realisation that rapid rate of 'human capital' formation is as important as a pre-condition of economic growth as the rapid rate of physical capital formation.

The growing awareness of the need for and urgency of building human capital for the attainment of accelerated and self sustained economic growth could be ascribed to several factors. First, the belief is gaining ground that economic growth in the advanced countries appears to be attributable to human skills rather than to capital. Second, investment in human resources has directly contributed to economic development and growth. Third, human resource development is not only an essential pre-condition of economic growth, but it is its major objective as well. Fourth, the rapid and spectacular post war recovery of countries, could be ascribed, by and large to the nations' resources in technical and skilled manpower. Finally, in most of the developing countries there are possibilities of raising the general living standards of the population substantially through future and rational utilisation of the surplus manpower particularly in the rural areas and through the development of physical and mental capacities of population.

The significance of human resource at micro level has been aptly summed up by Drucker thus: "managers are fond of saying 'our greatest asset is people'. They are fond of repeating the trueism that the only real difference between one organisation and another is the performance of people".[3] The basic objective in utilising human factor is to obtain a maximum return from human resources.[4] It may be noted that an

1. Leon C. Megginson, *Personnel* (Homewood, Illionois : Richard D Irwin Inc., 1972), p.140

2. 'Human Capital' defined as the sum total of the knowledge, skills and aptitudes of the people, inhabiting the country.

3. Peter F. Drucker, *Management : Tasks, Responsibilities, Practices* (London : William Heimmam Ltd., 1973), p.308.

4. Liver O. Sheldon, *Philosophy of Management* (London : Pitman 1923), p.27.

organigaion's performance and resulting productivity are directly proportional to the quantity and quality of its human resources. Most of the problems in organisational settings are human and social rather than physical, technical or economic. In the words of Sheldon, "no industry can be rendered efficient so long as the basic fact remains unrecognised that it is principally human. It is not a mass of machines and technical processes, but a body of men. it is not a complex of matter, but a complex of humanity. It fulfills the function not by virtue of some impersonal force, but by human energy. Its body is not an intricate maze of machanical devices but a magnified nervous system. Thus no one can deny the fact that a pool of well-informed or trained and highly developed personnel plays the most significant role in the most successful or effective functioning of an organization—industrial, business or any other through whose creative and sustained efforts its overall objective may be fully achieved.

Significance of Agriculture in Economic Development

In the continuum of economic development of any nation, the agriculture plays a vital role-which, however varies from nation to nation depending upon the stage of economic development. The origin of trade and industry itself is because of agricultural activity and its surplus. In a rather fundamental sense, agricultural progress is a prerequisite for industrial development. It not only caters to the food requirements of the population but also fosters the evolution and growth of the industry. In addition to supplying food, agriculture provides many of the raw materials for industry and generates export surplus to earn the foreign exchange. However, agriculture is not only a supplier of goods for domestic and export needs but is also a supplier of production factors such as capital and labour[1].

Indian Perspective

India is one of the important developing countries where the role of agriculture is very crucial for promoting and sustaining economic development, as a vast segment of its population depends on it for its livelihood.

---

1. Charles E. Kellog, "Interactions in Agricultural Development", summary of proceedings on Agriculture of United Nations Conference on the Application of Science and Technology for the Benefit of the Less Developed Areas (Washington : World Food Congress, June 1-18, 1963), p.45.

Agriculture is a way of life in India than a business. It is the backbone to Indian economy and occupies a place of pride. The significance of agriculture in the national economy can be explained by discussion of the role of agriculture under different heads.

Share of Agriculture in the National Income

An important aspect of the role of agriculture can be seen from the large contribution it makes to the country's national income. Even though the contribution of agriculture is declining and the economy is progressing, its contribution to national income is still significant. Thus, while the agriculture contributed 57 per cent of the national income in 1950-51, its contribution stood at 33 per cent in 1988-89. Whereas in developed countries, the agriculture's contribution was only two per cent in United Kingdom, three per cent in U.S.A., four per cent in Canada, in 1983. The more developed a country, the smaller is the share of agriculture in national output. India being a developing country its contribution is declining in total national output.

Supplier of Substantial Food and Foodgrains

Being supplier of 176 million tonnes of food in 1990-91 to 836 million people, besides other necessities of life, the agriculture sector in India is playing an important role in the economy. Not only this, the agriculture is also providing all the food to live-stock whose number runs into several millions.

Agriculture as a Source of Livelihood

Agriculture has a greater role in economic development in less developed countries like India as it provides livelihood to a vast majority of people living in the country. The agricultural sector provides livelihood to about three-fourths of the Indian population. At the turn of the century, 71.5 per cent of the total labour force was engaged in agriculture and this estimation has not changed until now. According to the 1991 census, 70 per cent of the working force was still engaged in the primary sector. This fact reflects the importance of agriculture relative to other sectors of the economy.

Largest Employment Providing Sector

Agriculture dominates the economy to such an extent that a very high proportion of working population in India is engaged in agriculture. In 1951, 69.5 per cent of the working population was engaged in agriculture. In 1991 this percentage had fallen marginally to 65 per cent. However, with rapid increase in population, the absolute number of people engaged in agriculture has become exceedingly large. It has been estimated that since 1971, the labour force has increased by about 35 million; of these, about 25 million have been absorbed in agriculture and 9 million in agricultural activities. This indicates that inspite of rapid industrialisation in the country, the primary sector is still the main sector providing employment opportunities to the majority of the workers and has thus, acted as a big shock-absorber.

Agriculture and Industrial Development

Being the largest supplier of necessities of life, raw materials and consumer of industrial products, it plays a very important role in many dimensions for the industrial development. Cotton and jute textile etc., industries depend on agriculture directly. There are many other industries which depend on agriculture in an indirect manner. Many of our small-scale and cottage industries like handloom weaving, oil crushing, rice husking etc., depend upon agriculture for their raw materials. It has been estimated that the industries which draw their raw material from the agriculture sector contribute nearly 50 per cent of income generated in the manufacturing sector in India. Agriculture also provides a market for industrial products. Since the level of income of Indian farmers and landless labourers is very low, this acts as a constraint on industrial development. As agriculture develops in India and as the income accruing to the rural people increases, the size of market for industrial products in rural areas will also increase.

Agriculture's Role in the International Trade

Indian agriculture is contributing significant foreign exchange to our balance of trade. Agriculture exports constitute a major portion of India's exports and accounted for 50 per cent of our exports, and manufacturing with agriculture content contributes another 20 per cent or so, and the total comes to 70 per cent of India's exports. This reveals the heavy dependence on agriculture and reflects the underdeveloped nature of the economy. But in recent diversification of product, the share of agricultural exports has consistently fallen. The share of agriculture exports in total exports has declined from 41.6 per cent in 1965-66 to 16.5 per cent in 1989-90. Regarding imports, except in certain years, when country faced drought conditions, the imports of agricultural products is relatively low. The agricultural imports in total imports was high at 40.7

per cent in 1975-76, after that it fell considerably to 15.5 per cent in 1986-87. Another important thing about agrcultural exports is that while they earn substantial share of foreign exchange, they do not drain it away through imports.

Agriculture Under Five Year Plans

The above discussion clearly reveals that agriculture is the central core of Indian economy and realising this, development of this sector has been accorded a very high priority in successive five year plans.

During the post independence period, the key role of agriculture in promoting and sustaining a rate of rapid economic development in the country has been a major theme in all Plan documents.[1] Thus, with the initiation of the planning era, development of the agricultural sector has come to be viewed in the broader context of the development of the economy as a whole. Higher and higher outlays have come to be provided for development of agriculture during successive five year plans.

A new strategy for agricultural development was adopted in 1966-67 to facilitate greater application of science and technology for increasing agricultural productivity.[2] The principal elements of the new strategy adopted for increasing agricultural production include - (a) applying a package of practices comprising water management, high yielding varieties of seeds, pest control and a sufficiency of fertilizer application along with good cultural practicies; (b) introducing short term varieties in the major cereals; (c) intensive cultivation of subsidiary food crops and commercial crops.[3] To supplement these efforts, it was proposed to take a programme of multiple cropping in areas having sufficient irrigation potential.[4]

The agricultural situation took a decisive turn for the better after the adoption of the above mentioned measures. The index number of agricultural production for all commodities showed an improvement although the rate of growth in foodgrains was much faster than other

---

1. Government of India, *Agriculture and Community Development and Cooperation* Vide report 1966-67 (New Delhi ; Ministry of Food, 1967), pp.1-5.

2. Ibid.

3. Government of India, *Fourth Five Year Plan : A Draft out line* (New Delhi: Planning Commission, 1969), pp.175-176.

4 Ibid., p.125.

commodities.[1] A study in the changes of area as between various crops after the adoption of the new strategy reveals that in addition to the area diverted from cash crops, all the gains in the gross cropped area in the country were also taken away by foodgrains. On the whole, hopeful beginnings have been made in the direction of the much awaited break through in agriculture. The farmer has responded favourably to the new technology for improving productivity. However, the overall agriculural growth, 2.6 per cent per annum since 1965, has been modest, compared both to performance in other Asian countries and to India's population growth rate of 2.1 per cent per annum. In the same period, "despite major technological breakthroughs, the all India agriçultural growth rate has not accelerated in the past two decades".[2] The World Bank has made it clear that without shifting Indian agriculture to a higher growth path, India will not be able to meet many of its development objectives. According to it, heavy physical subsidies to agriculture are not sustainable.

Human Resource in Indian Agriculture

The Human Resource in Indian Agriculture originally consisted of only cultivators. But due to historical, economic and social factors, labour class has emerged in course of time. Thus human resource in agriculture has come to consist of cultivators (owners/lessees of land) and labour.

The agricultural labour in India can be classified into two categories (i) attached labourers and (ii) casual labourers. "Attached labour" is defined as those who are more or less in continuous employment and are under some sort of contract with employers during the period of employment. Casual labour is defined as workers other than attached workers. They are employed from time to time according to exigencies of work.

The emergence of two groups—employer and employee—gradually subscribing to divergent thinking under the influence of socio-economic and political forces-led to distrubed relations on the rural front.

It is interesting to enquire into the origin of agriculture labour class and their growth in relation to cultivators in India during the post

1. P.C. Bansil, "Production Patterns and Green Revolution", *Indian Journal of Agriculture Economies*, XXVII, No.4, Conference Number, (December, 1972), pp.104-108.
2. "The World Bank, India : Country Economic Memorandum", 1991 - Vol.II, Excepts From the Executive summary of the report, *The Economic Times*, (21st October 1991).

independence period.

Origin of Agriculture Labour Class

The transition of economic stages which is forced by the pressure of physical environment—soil, climate, fauna and flora gives rise to a new economic institution which gradually merge into the social structure.[1] This theory of origin of economic institutions holds good in respect of origin of agriculture labour class. The agrarian history reveals that the agriculture labour class in India is not a primitive institution but it is a socio-economic institution, evolved out of an imperious economic necessity in a closed system of village economy.[2] The evolved agriculture labour class is linked up with the caste system in India.[3]

According to one theory, the genesis of agriculture labour as a class could be traced to the caste system, and the pre-capitalist employer-labour relations in India.[4] According to another theory, the establishment of British rule was responsible for the emergence of a distinct class of agriculture labour[5].

It could be observed from the above theories, that historical genesis of the class lay firstly in the pre-capitalist employer-labour relations. In India a class of propertyless labourers existed as an intergral part of the pre capitalist economy and society:they were in the heriditary servitude to the landed families; were forbidden to hold land and were employed in agriculture productions and certain specific tasks considered to be particularly household servant, in return for their mere subsistence."[6] Their landless slave status was bound up with a specific position in the

1. A.M.Lorenzo M., Agrestic Serfoom - A Tale of Exploitation, *Planning for Labour A Symposim*, The Labour Forum, (Bangalore : The Labour Publication Trust, 1947)p.221.
2. Ibid p.221.
3. Ibid. p.222.
4. Dharma Kumar, *Land and Caste in South India* (Cambridge : Cambridge University Press,1965).
5. S.J.Patel, *Agricultural Labours in Modern India and Pakistan* (Bombay : Current Book House, 1975).

   A.R. Desai, *Social Background of Indian Nationalism* (Bombay : Popular Prakasham, 1976).
6. U. Patnaik, "On the Evolution of the Class of Agricultural Labourers in India", *Social Scientist* Vol.II, No.8, 1983, p.4.

caste hierarchy.[1] The origin of agriculture labour lay secondly and in a large measure in a process of peasant pauperisation, in a situation of falling land-man ratio and insufficient growth of alternative employment owing to the very low rate of industrialisation in the colonial period.[2]

Growth and Structure of Population

Table 1.1 shows growth and structure of population in India during the period 1951 to 1991. While the total population had gone up by 134 per cent, the rural population has gone up by 111 per cent during these four decades. The decennial growth rate had consistently increased from 17.72 to 22.39 during the same period. As could be observed from this table, inspite of increase in urbanisation and migration to urban areas, the percentage of rural population still accounts for three-fourths of the total population in the country as per latest 1991 census. Thus India, even after 45 years of independence, continues to live in villages whose main occupation is agriculture and other related activities.

Table 1.1 : Growth and Structure of Population in India

(in million)

POPU-LATION	1951	1961	1971	1981	1991	DECENNIAL GROWTH RATE 1961 OVER 1951	1971 OVER 1961	1981 OVER 1971	1991 OVER 1981
RURAL	295.00 (82.70)	347.27 (81.74)	421.95 (79.78)	507.61 (76.30)	621.27 (74.26)	17.72	21.50	20.30	22.39
URBAN	61.83 (17.30)	77.56 (18.26)	106.97 (20.22)	157.68 (23.70)	215.34 25.74)	25.45	37.91	47.41	36.57
TOTAL	***356.83 (100.00)***	***424.83 (100.00)***	***528.92 (100.00)***	***665.29 (100.00)***	***836.61 (100.00)***	***19.86***	***24.50***	***25.78***	***25.75***
DENSITY	**108**	**129**	**160**	**202**	**254**	**19.44**	**24.03**	**26.25**	**25.74**

Note : Figures in parenthesis indicate the percentage to column totals.

Soruce : Census of India, 1991, Series-2, Andhra Pradesh, paper-1 of 1991, supplement provisional population totals, Director of Census Operations, 1992.

1. I. Habib, *Agrarian System of Mughal India* (Bombay : Asia Publishing House, 1963).
2. Patel, op.cit., p.14.

Structure of Work Force

The structure of work force in India is given in table 1.2 for the years 1961; 1971; 1981 and 1991. It could be seen from this table, the total agricultural workers consisting of cultivators and agricultural labourers had gone up from nearly 131 millions in 1961 to 185 millions in 1991—an increase of nearly 50 per cent during the 30 years period. The percentage of agricultural labourers to total agricultural workers had increased from 24.03 to 40.30 during the same period and this resulted in decline in percentage of cultivators. Further the percentage of agricultural labourers in total main workers had also gone up from 16.71 in 1961 to 26.15 in 1991. All these figures invariably indicate that the size and proportion of agricultural labourers had increased significantly during the post independence period.

Table 1.2 : Structure of Work Force in India

(in million)

Classification of Workers	1961	1971	1981	1991
Population	424.84	528.92	665.29	836.61
Cultivators	99.51	79.88	92.52	110.59
Agricultural Labourers	31.48	47.49	55.50	74.65
Total Agricultural Workers	130.99	126.67	148.02	185.24
Non-Agricultural Workers	57.43	54.71	74.49	100.19
Total Main Workers	188.42	181.37	222.52	285.42
Marginal Workers	--	--	22.09	29.48
Total Workers	188.42	181.39	244.61	314.90
Percentage of Cultivators to total Main Workers	52.81	43.65	41.58	38.75
Percentage of Agricultural labourers to total main workers	16.71	26.18	24.94	26.15
Percentage of total Agricultural workers to toal main workers	69.52	69.84	66.52	64.90
Percentage of non-agricultural workers	30.48	30.16	33.48	35.10
Percentage of agricultural labourers to total agricultural workers	24.03	37.49	37.49	40.30
Percentage of agricultural workers to toal workers	69.52	69.84	60.52	58.82
Percentage of agricultural workers to total population	30.83	23.95	22.25	22.14
Percentage of main workers to total population	44.35	34.29	33.45	34.12
Percentage of total workers to toal population	44.35	34.29	36.77	37.64

Source : Statistical Abstracts of India, Directorate of Economics and Statistics, Ministry of Agriculture and Rural Development, Government of India, New Delhi.

Sex Wise Distribution of Cultivators and Labourers

The sex wise distribution of cultivators and agricultural labourers in India shown in Table 1.3 indicates that the percentage of females had declined in respect of both cultivators as well as agricultural labourers. As per the latest 1991 census, while female cultivators accounted for 21 per cent; the female agricultural labourers accounted for 39 per cent.

Table 1.3 : Sex-wise Distribution of Cultivators and Labourers in India

(in million)

CLASSIFICATION	1961	1971	1981	1991	DECENNIAL GROWTH RATE		
					1971 OVER 1961	1981 OVER 1971	1991 OVER 1981
CULTIVATORS:							
MALE	66.41	66.91	77.59	87.72	5.28	10.00	13.05
FEMALE	33.10	9.27	14.93	22.87	–72.01	61.15	53.17
TOTAL	99.51	79.18	92.52	110.59	–20.43	16.86	19.53
AGRICULTURAL LABOURERS :							
MALE	17.31	31.70	34.73	45.82	83.09	9.58	31.91
FEMALE	14.17	15.79	20.77	28.83	11.45	31.49	38.83
TOTAL	31.48	47.49	55.50	74.65	50.85	16.87	34.50

Note : Figures in parenthesis indicate the percentage to column totals.

Soruces : Census of India, 1991, Series-2, Andhra Pradesh, paper-1 of 1991, supplement provisional population totals, Director of Census Operations, 1992.

Structure of Indian Agrarian Economy

The Human Resource Management in agriculture is very much influenced by the structure of agrarian economy. It may be noted in this connection, the Indian agrarian structure consisting of land use pattern; croping pattern; investment in agriculture; source wise irrigation; consumption of fertilisers; area coverage under HYV, use of agricultural machinery and implements; yield per hectare and quantum of production of principal crops - has been changing rapidly during the post-independence period. Several factors—industrialisation, population pressure, land reforms, green revolution, new technology relating to agricultural development etc., are responsible for the changes in agrarian structure. These changes in agrarian structure has its impact on human resource management through :

a) Quantum and quality of labour required
b) Wages and benefits available to agriculture labour
c) Attitudes and values of agricultural labour
d) Unionisation of agricultural labour
e) Farmer-labour relations
f) Govt. policies and programmes concerning agricultural labour etc.

It is true that these changes in Human Resource Management in Agriculture had their effect, in turn, on Indian agrarian structure. Thus, the changes in Indian agrarian structure and the changes in HRM in Indian agriculture are interdependent. It is relevant, in this context, to mention that this relationship had been studied for the first time by the Thorner[1] in 1956. Subsequently, realising the significance of this relationship, many studies by different scholars from time to time have been made on this issue.[2]

In view of the impact of the structure of agrarian economy on human resource management as indicated above, it has been thought appropriate to present the changing agrarian structure at all India level and at State level in the following few pages.

Land Use Pattern

The total geographical area of the entire country was 328.73 million hectares by 1985-86[3]. But the total reported area according to village papers for land utilisation purposes was only 304.32 million hectares by 1985-86. This reported area had increased during the last three and half decades (1950-'51 to 1985-'86) by 20 million hectares. The area under forest had increased from 40.48 million hectares to 66.75 million hectares - that is by more than fifty per cent. Inspite of this, the net area sown had gone up from 118.75 million hectares to 141.00 million hectares, a growth of nearly twenty per cent during the period under study. The total cropped area rose from 131.89 million hectares to 177.33 million hectares—an

1. Daniel Thorner, *The Agrarian Prospects in India* (Bombay : Allied Publishers, 1976).

2. Details of the different studies are given in the review of literature.

3. Directorate of Economics and Statistics, Ministry of Agriculture, Government of India, New Delhi.

increase of above 30 per cent during the period of three and half decades. The percentage of net area sown to total reported area had gone up from 41.77 in 1950-51 to 46.33 in 1985-86. While this was so, the per centage of total cropped area to reported area had increased from 46.39 to 58.27 during the same period. Thus the increase in total cropped area was more than the increase in net area sown during the period under study—indicating thereby the practice of adopting intensive cropping pattern.

Cropping Pattern

A study of the cropping pattern in India during the period 1950–51 to 1990-91 shows that rice is the major crop which is raised in 39.6 million hectares in 1990-91 followed by wheat with 24.0 million hectares[1]. The area under both the crops has steadily gone up during the period under study. The area under cereals has increased from 78.2 million hectares in 1950-51 to 103.1 million hectares in 1990-91. The acreage under the pulses has also increased from 19.1 million hectares to 24.4 million hectares during the period. More than cent per cent increase in area was observed in respect of oil seeds. The crops like cotton and sugarcane had registered a marginal increase in their area. The following further observations emerge made from a close study of cropping pattern. i. Food crops account for nearly three fourths of the total cropped area, ii) a large proportion of area under foodgrains is occupied by cereals accounting for more than 82 per cent and iii) among non-foodgrains, oil seeds form an important group covering 24 million hectares.

Human Resource Employment in Agriculture : Peculiar Features

Agricultural Employment in India has certain peculiar features as compared to that of industrial sector. These features profundly influence the nature, structure and the process of human resource management in agriculture.

i. The environmental relationship between agriculture and human energy is immediate and direct; while in industry this relationship is distant and indirect. While natural factors govern the employment of human labour in agriculture; economic factors govern the employment of human labour in industry. Problems of economic and social welfare concerning the man power engaged in agriculture and industry emerge, therefore, from divergent planes (i.e., natural and cultural

3. Directorate of Economics and Statistics, Ministry of Agriculture, Government of India, New Delhi.

respectively.)

ii. Agriculture in India is not only an economic activity but also a way of life. Since business family life are intimately connected with and intertwine in farming, the general welfare of the agricultural community is a prior consideration for any improvement directed to strengthen the agriculture.

iii. The out standing feature is that for millions of persons born in rural areas, agricultural career becomes an inescapable career. Thus while industry makes a selective recruitment the agriculture invites all the candidates who want to join it. It has been rightly commented that agriculture "fills the thankless role of acting as a great population insurance system of the world"[1].

iv. While the employment in agriculture is seasonal in character; the employment in industry, with the exception of the seasonal type, is more or less continuous throughout the year. While the peak periods offer maximum employment to agricultural labourers, for the rest of the year, they have to be continuously in search of other avenues of employment. Thus they may remain unemployed or under-employed for the rest of the year.

v. Like employment, the working day of the agricultural labourer shows considerable variations. During the peak seasons of agricultural activity, the working days are longer, while they are shorter during weeding or preparatory opertion. The hours of work of women labourers particularly are shorter in operation - weeding, transplanting etc., in which they are usually employed.

vi. Agricultural labourers mainly consist of two components - attached labourers and casual labourers. While attached labourers are mostly employed on contract basis for a year or so, their wage employment is greater than that of casual workers, whose opportunity for employment is determined by seasonal needs.[2] As against this, most of the recruitment in industry is made on permanent basis and very few employees will be hired on daily wage basis.

---

1. Howard Louise. E., Labour in Agriculture, Quoted in Report of Agricultural Labour Enquiry : Vol.I, All India, Ministry of Labour, Government of India, 1954.

2. Report of Agricultural Labour Enquiry: Vol.I, All India, Ministry of Labour, Government of India, 1954, p.27.

vii. Three fourths of land holdings in India are either marginal or small; they are un-economical in size; their paying capacity is limited and they are subjected to the vagaries of natural calamities. Whereas in industry, most of the units are started having in mind the optimum size and they normally are not subject to vagaries of natural calamities.

viii. The number of employers in agriculture is as much, if not greater than, the number of workers and the former is not better than the latter. The uneconomic holdings and seasonal nature of work also result for widespread underemployment and unemployment among both farmers and labourers.

ix. The relationship between farmers and labourers is peculiar. Attached workers are dependent on their employers in a variety of ways. They are bound by the ties of debtor-creditor, landlord-tenant, proprietor-sharecropper, etc. The employer-employees relationship becomes subservient to these other relationships. So far as casual labourers are concerned, they have to change employers quite often and this makes it difficult to develop any long term relationships and to have any obligations and aspirations arising therefrom. With the exception of casual labourers, we do not find these problems in industry.

x. The agricultural labourers are by and large unorganised, scattered over a large area; and are illiterate and ignorant. They do not have sufficient and effective leadership. The industrial labour are organised to a large extent and their unions play an important role in influencing human resource management in industry.

Significance of Human Resource Management in Agriculture

Human Resource Management has become one of the most delicate and complex problems to Indian agricultural sector especially during the last three decades. With the changes in attitudes, values and with the growing aspirations, the agricultural labour 'who happened to be the downtrodden and oppressed sections of the society are increasingly becoming conscious of their rights and are trying to assert their rights. As they assert their rights and fight against the injustice and exploitation, the feudal interests in the country-side and other reactionary, obscurantist elements get enraged and try to suppress this new awakening among them with increased brutality. Consequently, the violence and social oppression against scheduled castes have increased in recent years in almost all parts of the country. The growing class consciousness, the rising wages, increasing educational standards, changing career patterns and greater mobility among agricultural labour have all contributed to influence the nature and process of human resource management. In some parts of the country like Kerala, West Bengal, they have organised their own trade unions and thus acquired a bargaining power which enabled them to give a tough fight to their employers to establish their rights. In these states, the government had also to step in and play an important role in protecting the interests of agricultural workers and thereby to establish harmonious agrarian relations.

Human Resource Management in Agriculture in Different States

Agrarian conflicts have become a common feature in India especially in the past few years. The land ceiling and tenancy legislations have not resulted in the benefit expected of them. Further, due to new agricultural strategy, agricultural productivity has no doubt registered an upward trend. But, the fruits of this strategy are enjoyed mainly by the rich and prosperous farmers and the disparity between them and the landless agricultural labourers had increased. This increased disparity led to a sense of deprivation on the part of the poorer agrarian classes and in turn to violence.

The study of state-wise break-up of the agitations reveals interesting facts. While no state was free from the problems of agrarain unrest, the two states with the largest number of agitations (against the landed) were Bihar and Madhya Pradesh, both relatively backward. In Punjab, there were only few small and mild agitations despite its well developed and modernised agriculture.

The point of interest is that while agrarian tensions were prominent in some states, they were dormant in other states. Agrarian unrest had been a characteristic feature in Kerala[1], Uttar Pradesh, West Bengal, Madhya Pradesh, Bihar[2], Haryana, Punjab and Assam[3]. In the case of the

1. Joan P Menchar, "Agrarian Relations in the Two Rice Regions of Kerala", *Economic and Political Weekly,* Annual Number (February 1978), p.349.
2. This is confirmed by the Observations of Central Team of Planning Commission, *Economic and Political Weekly,* Vol.XVII, No.33, (14th August, 1982).pp.1307-8.
3. S.S.Gill and U.C. Singh, "Emergence of Agricultural Labour and its impact on Labour Relations in Punjab Agriculture", *Indian Journal of Labour Economics,* Vol.XXV, No.4, (January, 1983), pp. 121,129.

other states, even though agrarian relations are not very much strained, much attention is felt necessary to strengthen these relations[1]. Otherwise, the problem may reach its peak on any day in the changing environment of the rural areas.

Need of Effective Human Resource Management

It is an established fact that human resource management will have a profound impact on agricultural productivity—productivity per hectare and productivity per worker employed. Indian agriculture is characterised by miserably low per hectare productivity and per labour productivity compared with many countries. In fact the yield per hectare in India is below the world average in all the crops. It is true that green revolution had its impact on increasing the productivity but it is still low compared with international standards. Also, productivity per worker in agriculture was the lowest compared to productivity in non-agricultural sector.

There are many reasons for this low productivity like overcrowding in agriculture, illiteracy, ignorance, superstitions and conservatism in our peasants; inadequate non-farm services, size of holdings, pattern of land tenure, poor techniques of production, and inadequate irrigation facilities. On top of all these, one important factor which has been causing grave concern is ineffective human resource management and gradual deterioration in the relations between peasants and workers. Several steps have been taken to make improvements in respect of the earlier factors but nothing has been done nor even there is an awareness among official circles about the existence of the latter problems[2]. With the result, Indian agriculture has been in doldrums especially during the last two decades. Attempts to rejuvenate it were made number of times in so many different forms but without any spectacular success. The introduction of the new agricultural strategy which goes with the name of the Green Revolution was held as an important step but this hope was only shortlived. Despite five Five Year Plans and three Annual Plans since 1950-51 India has failed to solve its basic and number one problem i.e., the feeding of its teaming millions. This problem will become much more severe and intense in the years to come particularly with the tremendous growth of population which is expected to touch 1,000 millions before the end of

1. V.B. Auti, "Farm Labourers' Strike in Kopargaon" *Economic and Political Weekly,* Vol.XVI, No.33, (August 15, 1981), pp.1338-39.

2. M. Gangadhara Rao, Agrarian Relations in Andhra Pradesh, Unpublished Report of U.G.C. Major Research Project, UGC New Delhi, p.30.

this century. According to Prof. V.K.R.V. Rao, India requires a minimum growth rate of 4 per cent in food grains and 6 per cent in non-food crops during this century to meet the basic requirements of the economy for food and agricultural raw materials. But the rate of growth in agriculture has been only 2.9 per cent between 1967-68 to 1988-89. So the most important challenge to the Indian agriculture is how to push up agricultural production in the shortest possible time so as to catch up with mounting demand for agricultural goods. The solution, undoubtedly, lies in developing effective and efficient human resource management in agriculture and thereby bringing about the cordial relations between peasants and labourers.

Further, a study and understanding of the history of the development of nations should convince anyone that unrest among large numbers of agriculturists and labour from rural areas has been the starting point of national turmoils and revolutions which had brought about the collapse of existing structures relating to economic, political, social and cultural conditions of a country and the creation of a new order. The French, Russian and Chinese revolutions are examples of recent memory. The current agrarian unrest in India compounded with widespread economic destress, unemployment and unprecedented escalation in price of essential consumer goods could provide the spark to ignite big explosions.

2

The Present Study

A brief review of research studies already made on different aspects of agricultural labour has been presented in this chapter to highlight the gaps and to establish the need for the present study. This chapter also deals with the geographical area of the study, objectives, methodology and sampling of the study. Finally the limitations of the study are given.

Review of Research Studies

Human Resource Management in agriculture is a very complex phenomenon influenced more by social factors than by economic factors. Agricultural labourers, predominantly belonging to the lower castes are bereft of any ownership rights and have been living for the past several centuries at the mercy of an exploitative system based on caste and operated by a combination of coersion and intimidation.[1] The study of changing agrarian structure, agricultural labour and labour relations in India has developed into one of the most important themes of social sciences research. Several research studies have been carried out on this theme during the last three decades. It is thought appropriate to present a brief review of the research studies undertaken on some of the aspects of human resource management in agriculture.

Origin and Growth of Agricultural Labour

Many research studies have been carried out on the origin and growth of agricultural labour; but, they differed in their conclusion. While one group traces the origin of agricultural labour to the establishment of British rule, the second group stress the caste structure prevalent

1. Ani Lukose, *Labour Movements and Agrarian Relations* (Jaipur : Rawat Publications, 1991), p.VII.

in the society right from times immemorial responsible for the existence of a distinct class of agricultural labourers. While the first group consists of Patil[1], Malaviya[2],Ghose[3], Jacks[4], Mathai[5], Mukharjee[6] and Thomas[7]; the second group consists of Kumar[8] Mukharjee[9] and Joshi[10].

Classification of Labour

A few studies have been made on classification of labour. The studies of first agriculture labour enquiry[11]; the second agricultural labour enquiry[12] Thorner and Thorner[13], Pranab Bardhan and Ashok Rudra[14] dealt with this aspect.

---

1. Surendar J Patel, *Agricultural Labour in Modern India and Pakistan* (Bombay : Current Book House, 1952).
2. H.D. Malaviya, *Land Reforms in India,* 2d ed. (Delhi : All India Congress Committee, 1955).
3. Kamal Kumar Ghose, *Agricultural Labourers in India; A Study in the History of their Growth and Economic Condition* (Calcutta : Indian Publications, 1969).
4. Jacks, "Study of Faridpur District of East Bengal", quoted in *A Survey of Research in Economics* (Bombay : Allied Publishers, 1975), IV.174.
5. John Mathai, "Study of Village Communities in India', op.cit., p.174.
6. Radha Kumud Mukharjee, "History of Village Communities in Western India", op.cit., p.174.
7. P.J.Thomas, "Resurvey of some South Indian Villages", op.cit., p.174.
8. Dharma Kumar, *Land and Caste in South India - A Study of Agriculture Labour in the 19th Century* (Cambridge : Cambridge University Press, 1965).
9. Ramakrishna Mukharjee,"Rural Class Structure in West Bengal" quoted in *A Survey of Research in Economics* (Bombay : Allied Publishers, 1975), IV 174.
10. V.R. Joshi, "Growth of Agricultural Labour with Special Reference to Uttar Pradesh", *Indian Journal of Labour Economics,* (April - July, 1958).
11. Government of India, *Agriculture Labour Enquiry 1950-'51 : Report on Intensive Survey of Agricultur Labour, Employment, Underemployment, Wages and Levels of Living* (New Delhi : Ministry of Labour, 1954) I - All India.
12. Government of India, *Second Agriculture Labour Enquiry 1956-57* (New Delhi : Labour Bureau, Ministry of Labour and Employment, 1960), I - All India.
13. Danial Thorner and Alice Thorner, *Land and Labour in India* (Bombay : Asia Publishing House, 1962).p.177.
14. Pranab Bardhan and Ashok Rudra, "Types of Labour Attachments in Agriculture, Results of a survey in West Bengal - 1979", *Economic and Political Weekly,* (August 30, 1970).

Agrarian Structure

The agrarian structure which has its profound influence on human resource management in agriculture has been considered as an important topic for research by several scholars. The agrarian structure in India is such that the upper castes are the main land holding castes and the lower castes (particularly Scheduled Castes and Scheduled Tribes) are the one who provide agricultural labour. In some parts of the country, while the landlords in villages are from higher castes, the actual cultivators are from middle castes and the labourers are from lower castes viz., Scheduled castes and Scheduled tribes. The studies made by Thorner[1]; Thorner and Thorner[2]; Warriner[3]; Sundarayya[4]; Bateille[5]; Alexander[6]; Mencher[7]; Sachidananda and Mandal[8]; Mishra[9] are to be noted in this context.

Income and Employment Trends

Research on two important aspects—income and employment trends of the agricultural labourers was initiated on a systematic basis with the launching of the first Agricultural Labour Enquiry 1950-51[10], Prior to this, a few studies were made by Lorenzo[11], Danthwala and

1. Daniel Thorner, *The Agrarian Prospects in India* (Delhi : University Press, 1956).
2. Daniel Thorner and Alilce Thorner, op.cit.
3. Doren Warriner, *Land Reform in Principle and Practice* (Oxford : Clarendon Press, 1969).
4. P. Sundarayya, *Telangana People's Struggle and its lessons* (Calcutta : Communist Party of India (Marxist) 1972).
5. Andre Betille, *Studies in Agrarian Social Structure* (New Delhi : Oxford University Press, 1974).
6. K.C.Alexandar, "Changing Labour - Cultivator Relations in South India", *In Changing Agrarian Relations In India* ed. by V.R.K. Paramahamsa (Hyderabad : National Institute ofCommunity Development, 1975), p.21.
7. Jone P. Mencher, *Agriculture and Social Structure in Tamilnadu* (New Delhi : Allied Publishers (P) Ltd., 1978).
8. Sachidananda and B.B. Mandal, "Agrarian Relations - a Case Study of Purnea area in Bihar", *Man in India,* Vol.63, No.1, 1983, pp.3-20.
9. G.P. Mishra, *Some Aspects Of Change In Agrarian Structure* (New Delhi: Sterling Publishers (P) Ltd.,1977).
10. Government of India, *Agricultural Labour Enquiry 1950-51,* op.cit.
11. A.M.Lorenzo, *Agricultural Labour Conditions in North India* (Bombay New Book Company,1959).

Desai[1], Sukla[2], Moore[3], Das[4] and Mishra[5]. In the post independence period, a number of village and area studies were conducted to reveal the living and working conditions of the agricultural labourers. In this context the studies conducted by Agro-Economic Research Centres of different universities deserve to be mentioned. Apart from these, four all India Surveys of Agricultural Labour, Viz., First[6] and Second[7] Agricultural Labour Enquiries 1950-51; 1956-57 and First, Second[8], Rural Labour Enquiries 1963-65, 1974-75 were under taken. Besides, some rounds of National Sample Survey (NSS) have thrown valuable light on the conditions of the agricultural labourers[9]. A few other studies utilising the published data on agricultural wages have also come out to discuss the conditions of agricultural labourers. The Studies of Krishnaji[10], Rao[11] and Sahoo[12] are to be mentioned in this context.

---

1. M.N. Danthwala and M.B. Desai, *Report of the Hali Labour Enquiry Committee of 1948* (Bombay : Government of Bombay, 1949).
2. J.B. Sukla, *Life and Labour in a Gujarat Taluka* (Bombay : Longmans Green and Co. Ltd., 1937).
3. C.J. Stevanson Moore, *Report on the Material Condition of small Agriculturists and Labourers in Gaya* (Calcutta : Bengal Secretariat Press, 1898).
4. R.K. Das, "Plantation Labour in India", quoted in *A Survey Of Research in Economics* (Bombay : Allied Publishers, 1975), IV 181.
5. S.Mishra, "Agricultural Wages in relation to Rural Cost of Living", *Indian Journal of Economics,* (July, 1948).
6. Government of India, *Agricultural Labour Enquiry 1950-51* op.cit.
7. Government of India, *Agricultural Labour in India,* "Report On The Second Agricultural Labour Enquiry", 1956-'57. op.cit.
8. Government of India, *Rural Labour Enquiry, 1963-65", Final Report* (Simla : Labour Bureau, Department of Labour and Employment, 1973).
9. Government of India, *Rural Labour Enquiry 1974-75 : Final Report on Wages and Earnings of Rural Labour House-holds* (Chandigarh : Labour Bureau, Ministry of Labour 1979).
10. N. Krishnaji, "Wages of Agricultural Labour", *Economic And Political Weekly*, (September 25, 1971).
11. V.M. Rao., "Agricultural Wages in India - A Reliability Analysis", *Indian Journal of Agricultural Economics,* (July 1972).
12. B. Sahoo, "Trends in Wages and Earning of Agricultural Labour in India Since 1950", *Indian Journal Of Commerce,* (September, 1969), pp. 37-38.

The wage differentials have also been studied by scholars like Bardhan[1], Mehtha[2], Nayar[3], Mandal[4], Parthasaradhi[5], Sarthi[6], Bhardwaji and Mishra[7], Joshi[8], Joseph[9], Myer and Paul[10], Parmar[11], Pandey and Others[12], Chandra[13], Singh[14], Renu[15], Ajit Kumar[16]; and

---

1. Pranab Bardhan,*Labour and Rural Poverty - Essays in Development Economics* (New Delhi, Oxford University Press, 1984).
2. Sushila Mehta, *A Study of Rural Sociology in India* (New Delhi : S. Chand and Company, 1980).
3. P.K.B. Nayar, "Emerging Pattern of Agrarian Movement in India", *Kerala Sociologist,* Vol.IV, No.2, (December, 1970).
4. Gc. Mandal, "Share of Agricultural Labour in National Agricultural Product -An Exercise", *Economic and Political Weekly,* (December, 1983), Review of Agriculture p.A-151.
5. G. Pardhsaradhi, "Employment, Wage and Poverty of Hired Labour within Indian Agriculture", Evidence on selected Issues from Micro Surveys in West Godavari District, Andhra Pradesh, India in *"Hired Labour in Rural Asia",* ed. by S.Hirashima (Tokyo : Institute of Developing Economies, 1977).
6. Acharya Sarathi, "Agricultural Wages in India, A disaggregatedAnalysis", *Indian Journal of Agricultural Economics,* 44(2) (April-June, 1989), pp.121-39.
7. J.L. Bhardwaji and C.S. Mishra, "Raising Trends In Wage Rates of Agricultural Labour : A Study", *Kurukshetra* 34(4) (January, 1986), pp.34-35.
8. A.V. Joshi, "Agricultural Wages in India", *Economic and Political weekly,* (Supplement) 23(20) 29 (June, 1988, p. A - 46-58.
9. K.U. Joseph, "Raising Agricultural Wage Rates; A sign of Kerala's Economic Prosperity", *Indian Labour Journal* 29(4), (April, 1988), pp.549-50.
10. R.M. Myer and R.R. Paul, "An Analysis of Wage Trend and Wage structure of agricultural labour in Pubjab", *Man Power Journal* 19(1) (April-June 1983), pp.71-86.
11. B.D. Parmar, "Trend in Agricultural Wages in Saurashtra Region", *Indian Journal of Industrial Relations,* 21(4) (April, 1986), pp.479-489.
12. R.K. Pandey and Others, "Agricultural Field Wages In Orissa : An Economic Study", *Margin* 21(1) (October - December 1988), pp.72-78.
13. Ramesh Chandra, "Minimum Wages in the Eastern Region", *Administrator* 34(2), (April-June 1989), pp.57-60.
14. Ranabir Singh, "A Study of Income and Expenditure of Rural Labour House-holds in Different Regions of the Country", *Man Power Journal* 22(2), (July, September, 1985), pp.1-17.
15. Renu Sen Gupta, "Employment and Wages of Agricultural Labourers", *Rural India,* 47(9-101), (September-October 1984), pp.148-150.
16. Ajitkumar Singh, "Economic Conditions of Agricultural Labour in Uttar Pradesh : A Study based on Agricultural Rural Labour Enquiry Reports", *Journal of Labour Economics* 27(4), (January, 1985), p.334-46.

Srivastava[1], Jeemol[2], Jose[3] and Parmar[4].

Agricultural Labour *vs.* New Strategy of Agricultural Growth

The adoption of new agricultural strategy (using high yielding varieties, scientific fertilisers and irrigation facilities) is a significant development in Indian agriculture. This strategy, in certain areas, has changed the production profile in a remarkable way and ushered in green revolution. It has its own impact on the employment, income and relations of agricultural communities. Several studies have come out revealing the role of new strategy in ushering an era of fuller employment and adequate incomes in the country side. Studies conducted by Agro-Economic Research Centres of different universities, Second Agricultural Labour Enquiry, Muthaiah[5], Lahiri[6], Shah and Singh[7], Byres[8], Billing and Singh[9], Ashok Rudra[10], Bardhan[11],

1. D.C. Srivastava, "Minimum Wages in Agriculture : A Critique", *Administratior,* 34(2), (April-June, 1989), pp.1-20.
2. Jeemol Unni, "Agricultural Labourers in Rural Labour House holds, 1956-57 to 1977-78; Changes in Employment, Wages and Incomes", *Economic and Political Weekly* Supplement 23(26), (29th June, 1988), p. A - 59-69.
3. A.V. Jose, *Agricultural Wages in India* (New Delhi : Asia Employment Programme, 1988), p.72.
4. B.D. Parmar, *Regional Development and Agricultural Wages* (Bombay : Himalaya Publilshing House, 1986).
5. C. Muthaiah, "Agricultural Labour Problems in Thanjavur and the New Agricultural Strategy", *Indian Journal of Agricultural Economics,* (July-September, 1970), pp.15-23.
6. R.K. Lahiri, "Impact of HYVP on Rural Labour Market", *Economic and Political Weekly,* (September 26, 1970), pp A - 111-114.
7. S.L. Shah and L.R. Singh, "Impact of New Agricultural Technology on Rural Employment in North-West U.P.", *Indian Journal of Agricultural Economcs,* (July-September, 1970, pp. 29-33.
8. T.J. Byres, "The Dialectic of India's Green Revolution", *South Asian Review,* (January, 1972), pp.99-116.
9. H. Martin, Billings and Arjan Singh, "Mechanisation and Rural Employment : With Some Implications for Rural Income Distribution", *Economic and Political Weekly* (June 27, 1970), pp.A-61-A-72.
10. Ashok Rudra, "Employment Pattern in Large Farms of Punjab",*Economic and Political Weekly,* (June, 26, 1971), pp.A - 89-94.
11. Pranab Bardhan, "Green Revolution and Agricultural Labourers", *Economic and Political Weekly,* (July, 1970), Special No.1, pp.1239-46.

Frankel[1], Wills[2], Hanumantha Rao[3], Chatopadhyaya[4], Page[5], Joshi[6], Pardhasaradhi and Prasad[7], Alexandar[8], Aggarwal[9], Singh and Singh[10], Sen[11] Bhalla and Chadha[12], Betille[13], Vysa[14] are to be mentioned in this context.

---

1. F.R. Frankel,*Economic Gains and Political Costs*, (Bombay : Oxford University Press,1971), pp.197-98.
2. Ian R. Wills, "Green Revolution and Agricultural Employment and Incomes in Western U.P.", *Economic and Political Weekly,* (March 27, 1971), pp.A-2-A-10.
3. Ch. Hanumanth Rao, "Green Revolution and the Labour's Share in Output, *Agricultural Situations in India,* (August 1971), pp.283-85.
4. M. Chatopadhyaya, "Note : Role of Female Labour in Indian Agriculture", *Social Scientist,* Vol.10, No.7, pp.43-54.
5. V.S. Page, "Changing Agrarian Relations in Maharashtra", in *Changing Agrarian Relations in India*, ed. by V.R.K. Paramahamsa, (Hyderabad : National Institute of Community Development, 1975), p.120.
6. V.H. Joshi, "Some Observations on the Changing Agrarian Relations in Two Villages of Gujarat", op.cit. p.102.
7. G. Pardhasaradhi, and D.S. Prasad, "The New Technology within Agriculture and Changes in Agrarian Relations, Case Study of Delta Village in Andhra Pradesh", op.cit., p.168.
8. K.C. Alexandar, "Changing Labourer-Cultivator Relations in South India", op.cit., p.21.
9. P.C.Aggarwal, "Some observations on changing Agrarian Relations in Ludhiana, Punjab", op.cit., p.111.
10. Daulat Singh and V.K. Singh, "Changing Agrarian Relations in Uttar Pradesh : Some Observations", op.cit.p.97.
11. Sen Bhavani, *Evolution of Agrarian Relations in India,* (Delhi : People's Publishing House, 1962).
12. G.S. Bhalla and G.K. Chadha, "Green Revolution and Small Peasants - A Study of Income Distribution in Punjab Agriculture - I and II", *Economic and Political Weekly,* XXVII, No.20 and 21, pp.826-832 and 870-871.
13. Andre Betille, *Studies in Agrarian Social Structure,* (Delhi : Oxford University Press, 1974).
14. D.V.S. Vyas, "Institutional and Development Implications of Green Revolution - A Perspective and Policy Guidelines; in Report on the Asian Regional Services on Contribution of Rural Institutions to Rural Development particularly Employment, Geneva, 1972.

Agricultural Labour Markets

Attempts towards an understanding of the structure and functioning of agricultural labour markets consisting of supply of labour; demand for labour; wage rates; labour markets are of very recent origin. The studies of Chatterjee[1], Donde[2] are the two important studies on supply of labour.

On the demand side, the work is some what more comprehensive. Studies have been made on the estimational aspect as well as on the diagnostical aspects of the demand. The studies of Rao[3], Ghosh[4], Goswamy and Bora[5], Sharma[6], Mishra and Das Gupta[7], Agarwal, Rao and Singh[8] are worth mentioning in this context. The studies of Ghosh[9], Dutta[10]

---

1. Boudhayan Chatterjee, "Studying the Labour Market in Agriculture—Some Methodological Issues", *Indian Journal of Agriculture Economics,* (October, 1961).

2. W.D. Donde, "Rural Labour in Konkan : A Study in Socio-Economic Environment", Unpublished Ph.D. dissertation, Department of Economics, Bombay University, 1951.

3. V.M. Rao, "Labour Requirements in Agriculture in India in 1981", *Indian Journal of Agriculture Economics,* (April - June, 1963).

4. D. Ghosh, "The Agricultural Labourer : 1950-51 - 1956-57", in *Agricultural Labour in India,*ed. by V.K.R. V. Rao, (Bombay : Asia Publishing House, 1952).

5. P.C. Goswami and C.K. Bora, "Demand for Labour in Rural Areas of Assam : A Case Study in Nowgong District",*Indian Journal of Agricultural Economics,* (July-September, 1970).

6. A.C. Sharma, "Man Power Requirements on Punjab Farms", *Man Power Journal,* (October, 1965 - March, 1966).

7. B. Mishra and H.K. Das Gupta, "Employment of Agricultural Labour in Dindigal Taluk of Madras State", *Indian Journal of Agricultural Economics,* (July- September, 1970).

8. R.C. Agarwal, M. Dinakar Rao and Singh, "A Study of the factors effecting the Demand of Rural Labour in Agriculture", *Indian Journal of Agricultural Economics,*(July - September, 1970).

9. Kamal Kumar Ghosh, "Agricultural Labourers in India, quoted in *A Survey of Research in Economics,* (Bombay : Allied Publishers, 1975), IV.196.

10. K.L. Datta, "Report on Causes of Rise in Prices in India", quoted in op.cit.

Suresh Chandra[1], Gough[2], Soni[3], Agarwal[4], Sinha[5], Kurve[6] are to be mentioned in the regard.

Among the studies carried out to present an integrated view of the demand-supply conditions of the agricultural labour and to find out the impact of these on wage levels, mention may be made of Ramakrishnan[7], Mishra[8] and Krishna[9].

Factors Influencing Agricultural Labour Market

Apart from the basic factors of supply and demand, there are other factors which influence the functioning of the agricultural labour markets. All these factors are grouped into three major categories[10]. They are 1. Governmental actions; 2. Workers' Organisations and; 3. Rural-Urban Migration. Many systematic attempts have been made to understand these factors or to examine their impact.

---

1. Suresh Chandra, "Agricultural Wages : Rates of Wages and Methods of Payment in Western Districts of United Provinces", *Indian Journal of Agricultural Economics*, (April, 1948).
2. James W. Gough, "Agricultural Wages in Punjab and Haryana : A Note", *Economic and Political Weekly,* (March 27, 1971).
3. Rabindranath Soni, "The Recent Agricultural Revolution and the Agriculture Labour", *Indian Journal of Agricultural Economics,* (July- September, 1970).
4. G.D. Agarwal, "Agricultural Wages and Systems of Payment in the United Provinces", *Indian Journal of Agricultural Economics,* (April, 1948).
5. L.P. Sinha, "Agricultural Wages and System of Payment in Bihar", *Indian Journal of Agricultural Economics,* (April, 1948).
6. P.S. Mavin Kurve, "Agricultural Wages and Systems of Payment in Bombay, Karnataka", *Indian Journal of Agricultural Economics,* (April, 1948).
7. K.C. Ramakrishnan, "Labour in Agriculture-Supply and Demand", *Indian Journal of Agricultural Economics,*(January, 1948).
8. V.N. Mishra, "Labour Market in Agriculture : A Study of Gujarat Districts", *Indian Journal of Agricultural Economics,* (July - September, 1970).
9. Jai Krishna, "Labour Market in Rural Areas",*Indian Journal of Agricultural Economics,* (October -1970).
10. V.S. Vyas and H.V. Shivomaggi, "Agricultural Labour : A trend Report", *A Survey Research in Economics,* IV, Agriculture Part II (Bombay : Allied Publishing, 1975), p.214.

Among the governmental measures, the most important one is the passing of Minimum Wages Act, 1948. The studies of Das[1], Majumdar[2], Sahilendra Jha[3], regarding the fixation of minimum wages and their implementation deserve to be mentioned.

Agricultural labour all over the country faces unemployment and under-employment depending upon the duration of the slack season. The Third Five Year Plan envisaged rural works programme which could harness the surplus rural manpower for economic development. A number of research workers as well as official and non-official agencies have studied the progress of rural work programme. The studies made by Directorate General of Employment and Training of the Ministry of Labour and Employment[4] Dandekar[5], Vyas[6] are to be mentioned in this context. A series of land reforms have been undertaken with a view to provide land to landless labourers. The studies of Palit[7] and Page[8] deserve to be mentioned.

Workers' Organisations

Trade unions and labour cooperatives constituted the two important workers' organisations which seek to strengthen his economic position

---

1. Arvind Das, "Toward A Theory of Agrarian unrest", *National Institute Bulletin,* (April, 1977).
2. N.A. Majumdar, "Rural Unemployment : Measurement for what?", *Economic and Political Weekly* (4th September, 1971).
3. Shailendra Jha, "Agricultural labour in the district of Munger : A Case Study", *Rural India*, 53(2) (February, 1990), pp.39-41.
4. Privendra Bahadur, "Utilisation of Idle Rural Manpower in Selected Countries - Organisation and Planning", *Indian Journal of Labour Economics*, (January, 1967).
5. V.M. Dandekar, "Utilisation of Rural Manpower", *Economic Weekly,* (February, 1962), Annual number.
6. V.S. Vyas, "Use of Rural Manpower for Development", *Economic Weekly,* (June 19, 1965).
7. S.K. Palit, "Resettlement of Landless labourers - A Case Study", *The Indian Journal of Economics,* (October, 1961).
8. V.S. Page, "Changing Agrarian Relations in Maharashtra", in *Changing Agrarian Relations in India*, ed. by V.R.K. Paramahamsa (Hyderabad : National Institute of Community Development, 1975), p.92.

and thereby his bargaining capacity. The studies of Thakur[1], Muthiah[2], Oommen[3], Parthasaradhi[4], Alaxander[5], Nitish[6], Suman Sarkar[7], Anderson[8], Beteille[9], Shah[10], Aziz[11], Lipset[12], Gough[13], Kats and Kahn[14]; Kennedy[15]; Dayal[16] Agarwal[17]; Fonseca[18],

---

1. S.N. Thakur, "Trade Unions in the Rural Sector", *Indian Journal of Labour Economics,* (October-1968, January, 1969).
2. C. Muthiah, "The Agricultural Labour Problems in Tanjavur and the New Agricultural Strategy", *The Indian Journal of Agricultural Economics,* XXV, No.3 (July-September, 1970).
3. T.K. Oommen, "Impact of Green Revolution on the Weaker Sections", in *Changing Agrarian Relations in India,* ed. by V.R.K. Paramahamsa (Hyderabad : National Institute of Community Development, 1975), p.151.
4. G. Parthasaradhi, "Agricultural Cooperatives", *Madras Journal of Cooperation,* (June, 1971).
5. K.C. Alaxander, "The Dynamics of Peasant Organisations in South India", *Social Action,* 28, No.1 (January-March, 1981).
6. R.Nitish, De., "Indian Agrarian Situtation : Some Aspects of Changing the Context", in *Agrarian Relations in India,* ed. by Aravind Das (New Delhi: Manohar Publications, 1979).
7. Suman Sarkar, "India's Agricultural Development-An Alternative Path", *Economic and Political Weekly,* XXI, No.19, (May 10, 1986), pp.825-36.
8. Anderson A. Walfred, *Society* (London : D. Van Nostrand Company, 1964).
9. Andre Beteille, "Peasant Associations and the Agrarian Class Structure", *Contributions to Indian Sociology,* No.IV, (December, 1970).
10. Ghanshyam Shah, *Protest Movements in Two Indian States,* (Delhi : Ajanta Publications, 1977).
11. Abdul Aziz, *Organising Agricultural Labourers in India : A Proposal* (Calcutta : Minerva Associates, 1980).
12. S.M. Lipset, *Political Man* (Bombay : Vakils, Feffer and Simons, 1959).
13. Kathleen Gough, "Changing Agrarian Relations in Thanjavur 1952-1976", *Kerala Sociologist,* IV, No.2, (December, 1976).
14. V.D. Kennedy, *Unions, Employers and Government* (Bombay : Manaktala and Sons, 1966).
15. Katz and Kahn, *The Social Psychology of Organisation* (New Delhi : Wiley Eastern Pvt. Ltd., 1966).
16. Sahad Dayal, *Industrial Relations System in India* (New Delhi : Sterling Publishers, 1980).
17. R.D. Agarwal, *Sociology in India* (Bombay : Popular Prakashan, 1972).
18. A.J. Fonseca, *Wage Determination and Organised Labour in India* (London : Oxford University Press, 1964).

Phelps[1], Crouch[2], Giri[3], Johri[4], Shiva Kumar[5] are to be mentioned in this context.

Agrarian Relations

The term "Agrarian Relations" refers the relationship between different classes of people involved in the agricultural production process. As already mentioned, there are basically two distinct class groups - land owners/cultivators and agricultural labourers. Frequent tensions and conflicts between cultivators and labourers foment class hatred; disturb mutual relations and damage the agrarian economy and hence it is absolutely essential to develop harmonious relations between two groups not only in their own interest but in the larger interests of the nation as a whole. In this context, a few important studies are Mencher[6], O'brein[7], Nayar[8], Nitish[9], Sunil[10], Varghese[11], Mukhopadhyay[12], Menon[13],

1. O.W. Phelps, *Introduction of Labour Economics* (New York : McGraw-Hill Book Company, 1955).
2. Harold Crouch, *Trade Unions and Politics in India* (Bombay : Manaktala and Sons, 1966).
3. V.V. Giri, *Labour Problems in Indian Industry* (Bombay : Asia Publishing House, 1958).
4. K.K. Johri, *Unionism in a Developing Economy* Bombay : Asia Publishing House, 1967).
5. S.S. Shivakumar, "Aspects of Agrarian Economy in Tamil Nadu : A Study of Two Villages", *Economic and Political Weekly,* XIII, No.18, (May, 1978).
6. J.P. Mencher, "Agricultural Labour Movement in their Socio-Political and Ecological context : Tamil Nadu and Kerala", *In Culture and Society,* ed. by Balakrishna Nair (New Delhi : Thompson Press, 1975).
7. George O'Brein, *Labour Organisatios* (London : Mathews and Company, 1921).
8. K.P.B. Nayar, "A Case Study of Two Peasant Organisations in Palghat District, Kerala", *Journal of Kerala Studies,* IV Part II and III, (June-September, 1977).
9. R. Nitish, De., "India's Agrarian Situation : Some aspects of changing the context", in *Agrarian Relations in India,* ed. by Aravind Das (New Delhi : Manohar Publications, 1979).
10. Sunil Sen, *Agrarian Relation in India 1879-1947* (New Delhi : People's Publishing House,1979).
11. T.C. Varghese, *Agrarian Change and Economic Consequences* (Bombay : Allied Publications, 1970).
12. R. Mukhopadhyay, "Role of Caste in Agrarian Relations", *Social Scientist,* XIII, No. 9,(1980), p.42.
13. Saraswathi Menon, "Historical Development of Thanjavur", *Economic and Political Weekly,* XIV, Nos.7 and 8, (August, 1979).

Panday[1], Oommen[2], Alaxander[3], Page[4], Muthiah[5], Singh[6], Joshi[7], Aggarwal[8], Prasad[9], Chatterjee[10], Prasad[11], Bhaskara Rao[12], Atchi Reddy[13], Sengupta[14]

Need for the Present Study

The foregoing review of literature concerning research studies on agricultural labour clearly demonstrates that no attempt has been made so far on a comprehensive study of all the aspects relating to human resource management in agriculture either at all India level or pertaining to the State of Andhra Pradesh. It may be noted, in this context that the

---

1. S.M. Panday, "Organisation of Agricultural Workers : An Indian Case Study", *Indian Journal of Industrial Relations*, 12, No.4, (April, 1977). pp.470-506.
2. M.A. Oommen, "Land Reforms and Agrarian Change", in Kerala Economy Since Independence, ed. by M.A. Oommen (New Delhi : Oxford and IBH Publishing Company, 1979).
3. K.C. Alexander, "Cultivator Relations in South India", in *Changing Agrarian Relations in India;* ed. by V.R.K. Paramahamsa (Hyderabad : National Institute of Community Development, 1975), p.21.
4. V.S. Page, "Changing Agrarian Relations in Maharashtra", op.cit., p.29.
5. C. Muthaiah, "Development of Landless Labourers-Role of Group Bargaining Power", op.cit., p. 49.
6. Daulat Singh and V.K. Singh, "Changing Agrarian Relations in Uttar Pradesh", op.cit., p.97.
7. V.H. Joshi, "Some Observations on Changing Agrarian Relations in Two Villages of Gujarat", op.cit., p.102.
8. Partap C. Aggarwal, "Some observations on the Changing Agrarain Relations in Ludhiana, Punjab", op.cit. 111.
9. D.S. Prasad, "The New Technology within Agriculture and Changes in Agrarian Relation : Case Study of a Delta Village in Andhra Pradesh", op.cit., p.168.
10. Bishwa B. Chatterjee, "Disparity and rural Conflict", op.cit., p.175.
11. Pradhan H. Prasad, "Production Relations : Achills' Heel of Indian Planning", op.cit., p.191.
12. V. Bhaskara Rao, *Agrarian and Industrial Relations in Hyderabad State* (New Delhi : Associated Publishing House, 1985),p.146.
13. M. Atchi Reddy, "Labour Relations in Andhra Pradesh Agriculture 1881-1981", *Indian Journal of Labour Economics*, 26(3) (October, 1983), pp. 160-87.
14. Debjani Sengupta, "Khet Majdoor Movement : A Case Study in West Bengal 1974", *Social Scientist* 15(7), (July, 1987), pp.30-53.

term "Human Resource Management", as already mentioned in Chapter-I, is a comprehensive term covering all the aspects—right from the stage of human resource planning to the stage of post retirement welfare programmes. The studies carried out so far dealt with only a few aspects of human resource management and no effort is made to present an integrated picture covering all the aspects of human resource management. It is to be emphasised that these different aspects of human resource management influence, individually and collectively, the ultimate objective of goal congruence to the best satisfaction of both the farmer and labourer. In industry,a few studies have come out during the last three decades following an integrated approach of human resource management. But in agriculture, which provides livelihood to two thirds of total population and which generates more than 40 per cent of the national income, it is high time that such studies are to be made to present a total picture of the situation instead of analysing and understanding only a part of the total scene. It is true that the agricultural sector is very much unorganised; no records of human resource management are available either from the farmers or the labourers or from the government offices. Inspite of this, it is worth making an effort to build up the picture from the memories of farmers and labourers and their leaders through direct interview supported by information collected from secondary sources.

The study also assumes significance from the followig points of view :

i. Of late, it has been realised the need for designing a new development strategy in which more and more labourers will be absorbed rather than replaced. They can be employed more productively in agriculture and their services can be utilised for capital construction. This prevents costly migration process from rural to urban areas and the non-agricultural sectors also will be benefitted through increased supplies of agricultural output; increase in the purchasing capacity of rural population and they will be relieved from the burden of supporting the population migrated otherwise from rural to urban area. In view of the urgent need for implementation of this new development strategy[1] a comprehensive study of human resource management in agriculture is very much essential.

1. Anne Booth and R. M. Sundaram, *Labour Absorption in Agriculture* (Delhi: Oxford University Press, 1984), pp.5-12.

ii. The attitudes and aspirations of agricultural labour have changed substantially during the past three decades and are fast changing in different parts of the country due to the influence of socio-economic political factors. The agricultural labour is no longer quiescent[1]; it is aware of its position; and aware of the unity and in some cases it has been violent. The country can no longer afford to ignore the position of agricultural labour and instead of making piece-meal studies, a comprehensive study of their management with a view to find out the steps so as to match their aspirations is urgently called for.

iii. There has been an increasing awareness among the industrial communities about the need for scientific human resource management and more and more industrial units in India, in course of time, are coming forward to adopt sophisticated techniques of human resource management resulting in benefit to both the employer and employees. The agricultural activity which account for 60 per cent of total economic activity and in which two-thirds of total population are working should also come forward for experimenting in the new techniques of human resource management in its own interest. It is necessary to study the existing position of human resource management practices; how to introduce the new techniques; the role of the government and other agencies in implementing these new practices etc. The agriculture sector cannot continue to work in the same old fashion, but should rise to the occassion to invite the new idea and actions and institutions relating to scientific Human Resource Management practices step by step.

iv. The agrarian relations in the early days in Indian villages which are characterised by the qualities of mutual help, trust and affection; selfless service and contentment are now being replaced by the qualities of mutual distrust; communal hatred, and high level aspirations. This resulted in frequent conflicts and clashes in rural areas. This drastic change of values on the part of farmers and labourers is already adversely affecting the agrarian economy. It is high time that a systematic and

---

1. *Planning for Labour,* presented by Labour Forum, New Delhi on the occasion of The Preparatory Asian Regional Conference of the I.L.O.-1947.

comprehensive study of human resource management in agriculture is to be made to offer possible solutions to the above problems.

v. Certain ameliorative measures like land reforms, tenancy legislation, minimum wages etc., have no doubt been initiated, but in view of the serious loopholes in the implementation of these measures, the desired effect could not be achieved. Consequently the naxalites[1] and other left political parties have started mobilising poor peasants and landless labourers against landlords and the clashes between the two have become very frequent[2]. It is necessary to examine these failures of governmental measures and suggest remedial steps to bring back normal harmony, peace and progress on the rural front.

vi. The present study of human resource management confines its attention to the State of Andhra Pradesh, which is popularly known as 'grannary of South' because of its large surpluses in the production of foodgrains, pulses, oil seeds, virginia tobacco, chillies and fruits. Thus the economy of Andhra Pradesh is predominatly rural and a large majority of its people are dependent on agriculture. The agricultural activities and their output establishes the fact that Andhra Pradesh is one of the leading agrarian states of India. One of the biggest sources of wealth of the State is its produce from land and it contributes not less than 50 per cent of the State income. Andhra Pradesh leads other states in the production of tobacco and caster seed and ranks second in respect of dry chillies, greengram and horsegram and third in respect of jowar, millets and mesta fibre. Though it ranks sixth in respect of the area under paddy, it ranks fourth in respect of its production next to West Bengal, Bihar and Madhya Pradesh. Further, the role of the agriculture in the economy of Andhra Pradesh is expected to increase further in the years to come as could be observed from the figures present in Table

1. R.K. Balagopal, Kodandaram Reddy, "Forever Disturbed" Peasant Struggle of Sircilla-Vemulawada" *Economic and Political Weekly,* XVII No.48, (27th November, 1982), pp.97-190.
2. Ghanshyam Shah, *Protest Movements in Two Indian States* (Delhi : Ajantha Publications, 1977), p.83.
3. Tallur, N.S., *op.cit.*, p. 5

Projected Cropped Area and Irrigated Area of Andhra Pradesh

(In million hectares)

	1990-91	2000	2025
Reporting Area	27.44	27.44	27.44
Net Area Sown	11.01	12.40	13.00
Gross Area Sown	13.19	16.70	17.60
Gross Area Irrigated	5.40	7.30	10.20
	(89–90)		
Percentage of gross irrigated area to gross area sown	40.94	44.00	58.00
Net Area Irrigated	4.29	5.40	7.30

Source : Abridged Report on National Commission on Agriculture, 1976,(New Delhi : Ministry of Agriculture and Irrigation, New Delhi, 1977), pp.233-236.

It could be seen from the table that while the gross area sown is expected to increase by one-third by 2025; the gross irrigated area is expected to increase nearly by cent per cent. Thus the percentage of gross irrigated area to gross area sown is expected to increase from 40.94 in 1991 to 58.00 by 2025. This increase in cropped area and irrigated area will intensify the agricultural operations resulting in employment of more agricultural labour.

In this context, the present study is expected to play a useful role in making a diagnostic analysis of the problem and in offering appropriate suggestions to develop an effective human resource management ushering in a new era in agrarian relations. The observations and suggestions of this study will be useful not only to the State of Andhra Pradesh directly but to all other Indian states where rural scene, by and large conforms to the same pattern.

Geographical Area of the Study—Andhra Pradesh

The State of Andhra Pradesh came into existence through the fusion of three regions—Coastal Andhra, Rayalaseema and Telangana regions with diverse physiogeographical, socio-economic and political background that had conditioned their economic and agricultural development.

The Coastal region consisting of nine districts Srikakulam, Vizianagaram, Visakhapatnam, East Godavari, West Godavari, Krishna, Guntur, Prakasam and Nellore, has fertile delta formed by three major rivers, the Godavari, Krishna and Penna. Most of the paddy and other important food and commercial crops are grown in this area.

The Rayalaseema region comprising the four districts of Anantapur, Cuddapah, Kurnool and Chittoor is long known as the stalling ground of famines. The soil is rocky and unyielding; the rainfall is scanty and uncertain. The region is scarcely populated.

Telangana region comprises of nine Telugu-speaking districts—Mahaboobnagar, Ranga Reddy, Hyderabad, Medak, Nizamabad, Adilabad, Kareemnagar, Warangal, Khammam and Nalgonda of former Hyderabad State. Except the city of Hyderabad, the economy of entire region has remained stagnant and undeveloped due to centuries of feudal rule. The land is mostly dry and its agriculture is confined to growing some dry crops with the help of tank irrigation.

Population and Work Force

a. Growth and Structure of Population

Table 2.1 presents growth and structure of population in Andhra Pradesh during the last four decades. It could be seen from this table that the population of Andhra Pradesh had more than doubled - from 31.12 millions in 1951 to 66.35 millions lakhs in 1991. The decennial growth rate had increased from 15.65 during 1951-'61 to 23.81 during 1981-'91 but the rate of increase in decennial growth rate was declining in the last two decades compared to the earlier two decades as a result of the family planning programme. The density of population per square kilometre had more than doubled i.e., from 112 in 1951 to 241 in 1991. The composition of population shows that the percentage of rural population had come down from 82.60 in 1951 to 73.15 in 1991 during the same period. This shift in population must have been caused by increase in migration from rural to urban areas in search of remunerative livelihood.

b. Structure of Work Force

An enquiry has been made into the structure of work force in Andhra Pradesh. As shown in table 2.2, the number of total workers (including marginal workers) had increased by 63 per cent - from 18.66 millions in 1961 to 29.44 millions in 1991. But their percentage to population had declined from 51.86 in 1961 to 44.37 in 1991. Agricultural

Table 2.1 : Growth and Structure of Population in Andhra Pradesh

(in million)

POPULATION	1951	1961	1971	1981	1991	DECENNIAL GROWTH RATE 1961 OVER 1951	1971 OVER 1961	1981 OVER 1971	1991 OVER 1981
RURAL	25.70 (82.60)	29.71 (82.56)	35.10 (80.68)	41.06 (76.68)	48.54 (73.15)	15.62	18.10	16.99	18.00
URBAN	5.42 (17.40)	6.27 (17.44)	8.40 (19.32)	12.49 (23.32)	17.81 (26.85)	15.76	33.90	48.61	42.98
TOTAL	***31.12 (100.00)***	***35.98 (100.00)***	***43.50 (100.00)***	***53.55 (100.00)***	***66.35 (100.00)***	***15.65***	***20.90***	***23.90***	***23.81***
DENSITY	113	131	157	195	241	15.93	19.85	24.20	23.59

***Note*:** Figures in parenthesis indicate the percentage to column totals.

***Soruces*:** Census of India, 1991, Series-2, Andhra Pradesh, paper-1 of 1991, supplement provisional population totals, Director of Census Operations, 1992.
Statistical Abstracts of Andhra Pradesh, Directorate of Economics and Statistics, Government of Andhra Pradesh, Hyderabad.

workers constituted nearly two-thirds of total workers. The total number of agricultural workers which stood at 12.82 millions in 1961 rose to 19.45 millions in 1991. As already agricultural workers consisted of two main components namely cultivators and agricultural labourers. While the proportion of agricultural labour in total agricultural workers was increasing during the last four decades, the proportion of cultivators in total workers was declining. The agricultural labourers who constituted 41.63 per cent only in 1961 rose to 59.49 per cent by 1991 in total agricultural workers. It is also reported that this phenomenon had occurred with a remarkable uniformity in all the districts of Andhra Pradesh.

Further it is also observed that the proportion of agricultural labourers in the main workers was the highest in Andhra Pradesh among all the states. Both put together, the cultivators and agricultural labourers constitute 80.80 per cent of the main workers in the rural population as per 1991 census as against 80.40 per cent in 1981 census. All this shows that the percentage of population which directly depends on agricultural sector had gone up. With the population having increased by 24 per cent in the latest decade (1981-'91) and the process of migration to the urban

Table 2.2 : Structure of Work Force in India

(in million)

Classification of Workers	1961	1971	1981	1991
Population	35.98	43.50	53.55	66.35
Cultivators	7.48	5.79	7.41	7.88
Agricultural Labourers	5.34	6.81	8.33	11.57
Total Agricultural Workers	12.82	12.60	15.74	19.45
Non-Agricultural Workers	5.84	5.41	6.97	8.94
Total Main Workers	18.66	18.02	22.69	28.89
Marginal Workers	--	0.86	1.88	1.04
Total Workers	18.66	18.87	24.57	29.44
Percentage of Cultivators to total Main Workers	40.10	32.16	32.64	27.75
Percentage of Agricultural labourers to total main workers	28.60	37.79	36.69	40.76
Percentage of total Agricultural workers to toal main workers	68.70	69.95	69.30	68.51
Percentage of non-agricultural workers	31.29	30.40	30.69	31.49
Percentage of agricultural labourers to total agricultural workers	41.63	54.02	52.93	59.49
Percentage of agricultural workers to toal workers	68.70	66.77	64.01	66.08
Percentage of agricultural workers to total population	35.62	28.97	29.37	29.31
Percentage of main workers to total population	--	41.42	42.38	42.79
Percentage of total workers to toal population	51.86	43.39	45.88	44.37

Source : Statistical Abstracts of Andhra Pradesh, Directorate of Economics and Statistics, Ministry of Agriculture, Government of Andhra Pradesh.

Census of India, 1991 series 2, Andhra Pradesh, paper 1 of 1991, Supplement provisional population totals, Director of Census Operation, 1992.

areas slowing down in recent years, the continuous dependence of such a large proportion of population on the inelastic resource of land should cause concern. This unmistakably emphasises the need for effective human resource management in agriculture.

c. Sex Wise Classification of Cultivators and Labourers

As shown in table 2.3, the percentage of female cultivators had come down from 38 per cent in 1961 to 28 per cent in 1991. The percentage of female agricultural labourers had declined from 54 per cent in 1961 to 51 per cent in 1991. Thus these figures show that although the percentage of female agricultural labourers was on the declining trend, they are still in majority as per 1991 census.

Table 2.3 : Sex-wise Distribution of Cultivators and Labourers in India

(in million)

CLASSIFI-CATION	1961	1971	1981	1991	DECENNIAL GROWTH RATE 1971 OVER 1961	1981 OVER 1971	1991 OVER 1981
Cultivators:							
Male	4.65	4.78	5.71	5.65	2.81	19.29	–1.02
Female	2.83	1.01	1.70	2.23	–64.38	68.48	31.18
Total	7.48	5.79	7.41	7.88	–22.61	27.86	6.37
Agricultural Labourers :							
Male	2.46	3.55	4.11	5.63	44.73	15.56	37.17
Female	2.88	3.26	4.22	5.94	12.98	29.58	40.84
Total	5.34	6.81	8.33	11.57	27.58	22.27	39.03

Note : Figures in parenthesis indicate the percentage to column totals.

Soruces : Census of India, 1991, Series-2, Andhra Pradesh, paper-1 of 1991, supplement provisional population totals, Director of Census Operations, 1992.

Role of Agriculture in State Economy

The state of Andhra Pradesh is essentially an agricultural State where more than 70 per cent of the population depend upon agriculture and the contribution of agriculture to State's income is nearly 50 per cent. An attempt is made in this sub section to study the specific ways in which agriculture is playing a vital role in the economy of Andhra Pradesh.

The agricultural sector meets the increasing needs for foodgrains on account of rise in incomes and also increase in population of the states. If the supplies of these goods are not sufficient, the cost/prices go up jeopardising the very process of development of the state. Agriculture also contributes to development of the state through the supply of labour. As such agriculture is the major source of labour for the development of non-agricultural sectors like industry and services.

Agriculture can help the state a great deal in earning foreign currencies. The export requirements can be easily met by adding a crop or two within the existing crop pattern and that too with little incentives and with perhaps no additional capital investments.

In the initial stage of development process, the state needs large capital resources and these could not be generated as the existing capital sector being small. Being a big-size industry, agriculture sector, with rise in production with little cost, it can contribute a lot in generating surplus for industrial development.

In long run, the industrialisation of the state may provide adequate number of high-income jobs to the labour force, but there is the immediate problem of providing more productive work to those who are depending upon this sector. An increase in production and productivity in agriculture will create more jobs and raise the volume of work to be done in agriculture as well as in industry. So both ways employment opportunities can be expanded for larger number than before in the State. Lastly large expansion of agriculture will generate large incomes to rural people of the state which can stimulate industrial growth. Since the State is on the way of development, it is all the more necessary that agriculture development keep pace with the general advancement to sustain it with supplies of wage goods inputs, and demand for manufactured goods.

Structure of State's Agrarian Economy

a. Land Use Pattern :

The total geographical area of the State is 27.44 million hectares[1]. The area under forests had increased from 5.85 million hectares in 1960-'61 to 6.21 million hectares in 1990-'91 largely because of afforestation undertaken by the government. Land put to non-agriculture use had gone up from 1.83 million hectares in 1960-'61 to 2.30 million hectares in 1990-'91 due to the fact that more and more land had come to be used for construction of railways, roadways, canals and for new settlement of people. Inspite of this, net area sown had increased from 10.78 million hectares in 1960-'61 to 11.02 million hectares. The percentage of net area sown to total geographical reported area had increased from 39.30 in 1960-61 to 40.16 in 1990-91. Area sown more than once had more than doubled during the period under study. Thus the total cropped area rose from 11.82 million hectares to 13.19 million hectares in 1990-91. With the result, the percentage of total cropped area to total geographical area had increased from 43.12 to 48.07 during the last 30 years. Thus the percentage of increase of total cropped area was more than the percentage of increase of net area sown reflecting thereby widespread use of intensive cropping pattern in the State during the period under study.

---

1. Statistical Abstracts of Andhra Pradesh, Directorate of Economics and Statistics, Government of Andhra Pradesh, Hyderabad.

b. Size and Distribution of Land Holdings

The size of agricultural holding decisively affects the cost of production and income from agriculture. The ownership or otherwise of land holding and whether it is self-operated or leased out also determine the degree of operators' interest in the land; and income from that agricultural activity. Further the size, tenure and tenancy status of agricultural holdings influence to a large extent the human resource management in agriculture. Hence it is considered appropriate to examine the size and distribution of land holdings in Andhra Pradesh.

A study of the distribution of operational area, number of holdings and average size of holding by major size groups in 1980-'81 and 1986-'87 shows that the area under the smallest size group (viz., less than one hectare) had increased from 18.85 lakh hectares in 1980-'81 to 20.54 lakh hectare in 1986-'87 resulting in increase in the proportion of the smallest size from 13.2 per cent to 14.5 per cent during the period under study. It may be noted here that though this smallest size accounts for more than half of the total holding, their share was less than 15 per cent of total operated area. Further though the number of holdings operated under marginal and small categories account for 75 per cent of the total holdings in 1986-'87, the area operated by them was less than 32 per cent. On the other hand, the large holdings which account for only 1.8 per cent of the total holdings share as much as 16.9 per cent of the total area. But one interesting feature was that the area under large holdings declined from 19.05 per cent to 16.9 per cent during the period under the study. Implementation of land reforms; family partition must have been the important factors for this decline in the area of large holdings. But the marginal and small holdings (upto 2 hectares) accounting for nearly three fourths of land holdings should cause concern and demand for remedial steps with a view to improve the working efficiency of agricultural sector and thereby facilitate effective human resource management in agriculture. It is also to be noted that the average size of holding under all the categories had declined between 1980-'81 and 1986-'87. The State average size holding had come down from 1.94 hectares in 1980-'81 to 1.72 hectares in 1986-'87.

The distribution of land holdings according to tenure and tenancy status in each major group for 1986-'87 is also studied[1]. It could be observed that 99.6 per cent of agricultural holdings were wholly owned

1. Statistical Abstracts of Andhra Pradesh, Directorate of Economics and Statistics, Government of Andhra Pradesh, Hyderabad.

and self operated. The operational area held by these holdings accounted for 99.5 per cent of the total area. This shows that the remaining 0.4 per cent of the number of holdings and 0.5 per cent of the area belonged to all other categories viz., a) partly owned and partly leased in and partly otherwise operation b) wholly leased in and c) wholly otherwise operated. Further in respect of all size groups, the number of holdings as well as the area possessed belonging to wholly owned and self operated category were more than 99 per cent. Among this category, marginal group accounted for 53.9 per cent of holdings and 14.5 per cent of the area. The first two groups viz., marginal and small (less than two hectares) accounted for as many as three-fourths of total number of land holdings; but their area was less than 32 per cent. As against this, large size holdings (ten hectares and above) which account for only 1.8 per cent had 16.8 per cent of area under their control.

c. Cropping pattern

The Study of cropping pattern in Andhra Pradesh shows that the rice was the major crop in the State with 30.59 per cent of total cropped area during 1990-91[1]. Infact the area under rice cultivation had gone up from 2.96 million hectares during 1960-61 to 4.04 million hectares during 1990-91. The increase in acreage under rice was followed by decline in area under jowar, bajra and other cereals and millets. This shift in cropping pattern must have been the result of increase in the habit of rice eating; spread of irrigation facilities and remunerative margin in rice cultivation. However, the area under all foodgrains had declined from 9.14 million hectares in 1960-61 to 7.76 million hectares in 1990-91. This decline in area under foodgrains may be compared with the production of foodgrains. While the production of foodgrains had nearly doubled during the last 30 years, the area had declined by more than 1.4 million hectares during the same period. It is obvious that this increase in production of rice was necessitated by the increase in population and had been facilitated through the introduction of high yielding varieties, scientific manures and use of agricultural mechinery and implements. In conformity with the demand for and the policy of Government of India relating to the production of oil seeds, the acreage of oil seeds had gone up from 1.42 million hectares in 1960-61 to 3.12 million hectares in 1990-91 an increase of 11.61 per cent of total cropped area. The area under cotton had more than doubled during the period under study. But the area

1. Statistical Abstracts of Andhra Pradesh, Directorate of Economics and Statistics, Government of Andhra Pradesh, Hyderabad.

under sugar cane, tobacco and chillies did not register any significant increase during the same period.

d. Plan Expenditure in Andhra Pradesh

The expenditure actually incurred under different heads in respect of each five year plan in Andhra Pradesh is also examined. It could be observed from that the total plan expenditure under the all heads has been increasing from plan to plan[1]. It was 967.80 million in first plan and the same had gone upto Rs.52000 millions under seventh plan—which works out to more than fifty fold increase. Since the economy of Andhra Pradesh is an agriculturally oriented one, major proportion of the total expenditure under each plan was naturally spent on agriculture, irrigation and power. These three heads accounted for 74.40 per cent in first plan; 70.60 per cent in second plan; 75.70 per cent in third plan; 77.90 per cent in fourth plan; 75.90 per cent in fifth plan; 59.02 per cent in sixth plan and 59.98 per cent in seventh plan.

e. Irrigation

The Study of area under irrigation shows that the net area as well as gross area irrigated had increased in the State during the period 1960-61 to 1989-90. The percentage of net area irrigated to net area sown had gone up from 26.98 to 38.62 during the period under study[2]. The information of sourcewise irrigation also shows that the area irrigated with assured irrigation facilities like; canals and tube wells had gone up facilitating technological break through resulting in increasing agricultural production. However, it is a matter of grave concern that nearly two-thirds of net area sown was rain fed area depending upon the vagaries of mansoon. It is needless to mention that the presence/absence of irrigation facility makes a perceptable difference in yield per area, quantum and quality of production; paying capacity of farmer remuneration to agricultural labour and the relations between the farmer and agricultural labour. Research carried out on this issue has amply proved the profound impact of irrigation on agrarian structure and relations.[3]

1. First to Seventh Plan of Andhra Pradesh, Finance and Planning Department, Government of Andhra Pradesh, Hyderabad.
2. Statistical Abstracts of Andhra Pradesh, Directorate of Economics and Statistics, Government of Andhra Pradesh, Hyderabad, 1989.
3. G. Satyanarayana, *Changing Agrarian Structure and Labour Relations* (Jaipur : Rawat publications, 1992), pp.57-89.

f. Use of Agricultural Machinery and Implements

During the last three decades, the machanisation of agriculture had gained momentum due to the initiative and efforts of Government of India; improvement in economic status of the Indian farmer and his realisation of the benefits of mechanization. A Study of the use of agricultural machinery and implements in Andhra Pradesh, during the period 1961 to 1987 shows that the number of tractors had gone up from 1.78 thousands in 1961 to 32.54 thousands in 1987. Consequently, the average net cultivated area per tractor had come down from 6,127.27 hectares in 1961 to 308.76 hectares in 1987. Number of water pumps installed for irrigation purpose had also gone up from 0.51 lakhs in 1961 to 8.90 lakhs in 1987. This spurt in machanisation during the last two and half decades must have had a favourable impact on the yield per acre; time involved in agriculture operations and ultimately on cost of production. However, this trend towards machanization of agriculture must have had an adverse impact on the demand for agricultural labour. Very few skilled labourers will be required to maintain the tractors and pumpsets in place of hundreds of unskilled labour.

g. Yield Per Hectare

A Study of the yield per hectare in respect of different crops for the period 1965-'66 to 1990-'91 shows that the yield per hectare in respect of rice had increased from 1,126 Kg's in 1965-'66 to 2.442 Kg's in 1991—more than cent per cent increase in the productivity of this crop[1]. In respect of other crops also, the yield rates had nearly doubled with the exception of sugar cane. This phenomenal increase in yield per hectare must have contributed to the substantial increase in quantum of production of respective crops.

h. Production of Principal Crops

Data relating to production of principal crops shown that the production of rice had gone up from 3.66 million tonnes in 1960-'61 to 9.65 million tonnes in 1990-'91[2]. There had been spectacular increase in the production of rice by more than 20 lakh tonnes during the last five years. The increase in area under rice and the yield per hectare must have been responsible for this steep increase in the production of rice. The production of groundnut had an impressive growth with nearly one

---

1. Statistical Abstracts of Andhra Pradesh, Directorate of Economics and Statistics, Government of Andhra Pradesh, Hyderabad, 1987.

2. Ibid.

million tonnes during the last five years. Other crops like pulses, cotton, tobacco, chillies had registered moderate increase in their production during the last five years.

Objectives, Scope, Methodology and Sampling

i. Objectives

The present study of human resource management in agriculture is undertaken with the following specific objectives :

i. to present the socio-economic profile of respondent farmers and labourers;

ii. to enquire into procurement and utilisation of agricultural labour and their performance appraisal;

iii. to assess the compensation and inducements available to agricultural labourers;

iv. to analyse the nature of relations between farmers and labourers and the factors contributing there to, and

v. to suggest measures for developing harmonious agrarian relations for effective utilisation of human resource in agriculture.

Since this study is a comprehensive enquiry of human resource management in agriculture, the following aspects are covered under the scope.

1. Socio-economic profile of the respondents - cultivators and labourers.
2. Procurement of labour.
3. Utilisation of labour and duration of employment.
4. Period of leave and Absenteeism.
5. Nature and extent of indiscipline.
6. Wage rates — their determination, differentials and trends.
7. Application of incentives and provision of other benefits.
8. Grievances - nature and their redressal.
9. Efforts of unionisation of agricultural labour-problems involved.
10. Conflicts between cultivators and labourers.
11. Consultation and cooperation between cultivators and labourers.

ii. Methodology and Sampling

It could be observed from the above that a multi -stage sampling technique is used in the study. The region, the district, the village and the household are the stages in the process of selection of sample. The following criteria are observed while selecting districts, and the villages.

1. Geographical location.
2. Presence or absence of irrigation facilities.
3. Implementation of development schemes like I.A.D.P., etc.
4. Degree of economic development;
5. Cropping pattern and their production.
6. Degree of mechanisation and modernisation of agriculture.
7. Nearness to urban areas and spread effects.
8. Awareness movement of solidarity and unionisation among pesants and workers.
9. Cases of cooperation and conflict.

Basing on the number of villages, rural population and households of cultivators and labourers in the three regions of Andhra Pradesh, four villages from Coastal Andhra; two from Rayalaseema and three from Telangana are considered to be the desirable sample size of respective villages from the three regions. The actual selection of villages is made in such a way that the nine villages broadly represent the characteristics of agricultural economy and human resource management in the entire State of Andhra Pradesh.

Selection of Households of Cultivators and Labourers

Since the study is on human resource management, the sample of households is taken in such a way that the cultivators and agricultural labourers are related to each other to the extent possible. Further only one representative—usually head of the family—is taken from each household of farmer or labourer. Thus the selection of household is based not only on the stratified random sampling technique but also on the matched sampling technique. It may be noted, in this context, that this study covers both the categories of agricultural labour—attached labourers and casual labourers. While the duration of employment of attached labourers is usually one year and above; the duration of employment of casual labourers runs into few days. The degree of attachment between farmer and attached labourer is very high compared to that of farmers V casual labourers. Thus, the relations and the factors influencing them and the management practices to be applied differ in between farmer V attached labourer and farmer V casual labourer. Thus the study of agricultural labour and their management will be complete only if both the attached labourers and casual labourers are covered. In view of this, both the attached and casual labourers are selected based on uniform sampling method.

The following statement shows the regions, districts, villages and number of farmers and labourers selected for the study.

SAMPLE SIZE

REGION & DISTRICT	*VILLAGE*	*NF*	*NAL*	*NCL*
COASTAL ANDHRA				
Vizianagaram	Piridi	35	5	35
East Godavari	Vangalapudi	35	5	35
Krishna	Guntupalle	35	5	35
Prakasam	Veerannapalem	35	5	35
TOTAL		**140**	**20**	**140**
RAYALASEEMA				
Cuddapah	Brahmanapalle	35	--	35
Anantpur	Sanjeevapuram	35	--	35
TOTAL		**70**	--	**70**
TELANGANA				
Warangal	Jookal	35	5	35
Nalgonda	Raigir	35	5	35
Nizamabad	Andhra	35	5	35
TOTAL		**105**	**15**	**105**
GRAND TOTAL (ANDHRA PRADESH)		**315**	**35**	**315**

Note : NF—Number of Farmers
NAL—Number of Attached Labourers
NCL—Number of Casual Labourers

Collection of Data

Since this study is primarily an empirical investigation of selected villages, most of the data are collected from primary sources — through direct contact with the cultivators and labourers. For this purpose, two structured qustionnaires are prepared and administered separately for farmers and labourers. Both the questionnaires cover the following aspects:

1. Indentification
2. Socio-Economic Background
3. Employment of Labourers
4. Leave and absenteesim
5. Wages
6. Incentives
7. Fringe Benefits
8. Grievances
9. Discipline
10. Conflicts and Consultations
11. Farm Relations

The questionnaires are pre-tested before they are finalised.

Both the farmers and labourers are informed of the purpose of the study and asked to communicate the time convenient to them. As per the prior appointments, each of them figured in the sample is individually approached and is asked to answer the questionnaire. The researcher himself filled the questionnaire as many of them were illiterates. Adequate precautions are take to ensure the respondents answer the questionnaire on their own without consulting others. Further, on completion of answering the questionnaire, each respondent is interviewed informally and in a casual manner on several other issues. Apart from the questionnaire, notes on the content of the oral interview is prepared for each of the respondent separately. The same is analysed and included in the study.

The data is collected from the secondary sources namely Report on Agrarian Relations in Andhra Pradesh (sponsered by UGC); Population Census; Reports of First and Second Agricultural Labour Enquiries; National Commission on Agriculture; First and Second Rural Labour Enquiries; National Commission on Labour; Yearly Statistical Abstracts of India and Andhra Pradesh; Five-Year Plans; Yearly Survey of Economic Trends and many research studies of individual scholars and institutions.

Limitations of Study

A research study of this nature cannot be carried out without any limitations. Hence it is relevant to mention the limitations of this study.

1. There are about 29,500 villages; 78.80 lakhs of cultivators and 153.73 lakhs of agricultural labourers in Andhra Pradesh as per 1991 census. A study of human resource management in agriculture in Andhra Pradesh would be complete and comprehensive by covering all these villages, cultivators and agricultural labourers. But it is simply impossible for any individual or even to group of individuals to cover within the limited time and resources available. Hence it is proposed to study four villages from Coastal Andhra; two villages from Rayalaseema and three villages from Telangana. While selecting these villages, care has been taken that they represent broadly the characteristics of their respective regions. Further, a uniform sample of 35 farmers and 35 casual labourers and five attached labourers were taken from each village to represent the conditions prevailing in the entire village. Hence the observations and conclusions arrived at represent the situation of the State in general and the nine villages in particular. Inspite of all care taken in choosing the sample, it may have its own limitations.
2. Most of the information in this study is collected directly not from any office records but from the memories of farmers and labourers. Naturally, the correctness of the information depends upon the memory power of the respondents. But, most of agricultural surveys in India depend to a large extent on the memories of farmers and labourers.
3. Most of the information collected in this study is for one to three years only. It is needless to mention that a study of human resource management will be more meaningful by analysing the data relating to at least ten years which brings out the seasonal and cyclical fluctuations. But, it is very difficult to collect data in agricultural surveys for a period beyond three years.
4. It is no exaggeration to say that this study of human resource management in agriculture is first of its kind. This maiden attempt, in the absence of developed techniques and systems, may have certain defficiencies in collection, tabulation and analysis.

5. This study could have been made more effective through meaningful comparisons with the observations arrived at in other studies carried out on some of the aspects of farmers and agricultural labourers of Andhra Pradesh. But, unfortunately the period of those studies is different from this and hence they are not comparable

However every possible effort has been made to evaluate each situation as accurately and objectively as possible.

3

Socio-Economic Profile

Agricultural sector is an important segment of the society and the two important partners—farmers and labourers are drawn from the society. It is needless to mention that in every society, human beings are characterised by manifold differences arising out of sociological conditions, such as religion, caste, maritial status, sex etc., and by acquired economic factors such as ownership of property occupation, income etc. Social differences are thus universal characteristics of human behaviour.[1] As a result of these differences, we find inequalities among the people in the society in respect to status, privilege and prestige.[2] Infact social influences become operative with the first caring and smiling of newly born baby.[3]

As rightly mentioned by Ruth Benedict, most people are shaped to the form of their culture because of the enormous malleability of their original endowment. They are plastick to the moulding force of the society with which they are born.[4] These social influences reinforced by economic influences after some time, continue throughout the lifetime and affect the attitude, personality, behaviour, and the performance of the individual.

---

1. Kurt B. Mayer and Burkley Walter, *Class and Society* (New York : Random House, 1969),p.4.
2. Andre Bateille, *Unequality Among Men* (New Delhi : Oxford University Press, 1977), p.16.
3. L.M. Prasad, *Organisation Theory and Behaviour* (New Delhi : Sultan Chand and Sons, 1984), p.2.135.
4. Ruth Benedict., Patterns of culture as quoted by J.L. Kachroo, in *General Sociology* (New Delhi : Book Hive Publications, 1981). p.37.

It has been rightly remarked that "No man is an Island".[1] Individual and society are inseparable and they have mutual influence on each other.

Thus, in all societies, sociological and economic factors create inequality which prevails as a fundamental feature of the socio economic structure of the society.[2] It may be also noted in this connection, that in a traditional society like India, as rightly observed by Rudolphs, these inequalities are supported and legitimised by the value system.[3] Further, these inequalities are not only legitimised but, even fixed permanently on account of closed status system. They have become an accepted way of thought as pointed by Neale.[4]

As a result of the realisation of inequalities and on account of socialisation of inequalities by means of tradition the groups especially at the lower level unquestioningly accept their low status.[5]

Thus the above discussion clearly shows that inequalities in India have come to stay because of traditional sanction behind them. The inequalities are not only present but they are socialised and accordingly people in India have accepted not only inequalities but even the suppressions and oppressions that accompany these inequalities.

Hence, it is essential to enquire into the socio economic background of farmers and labourers so as to understand the impact of such factors on attitudes, behaviour, performance of the two parties and interaction between them. In this Chapter, it is proposed to enquire into and analyse the various social characteristics namely age, education, maritial status, caste, religion, size of family and economic factors like size and structure of land holdings, cropping pattern, other assets, income, expenditure, surplus and investment of farmers and labourers.

---

1. John Donnes, as quoted by J.L. Kachroo, *General Sociology* (New Delhi : Book Hive Publications, 1981), p.103.
2. Sachidananda, *The Harizon Elite* (Faridabad : Thompson Press (India), 1977).p.37.
3. Lloyd I. Rudolph and Hoeber Rudolph Susanne, The Modernity of Traditions : *Political Development in India* (Chicago : The University of Chicago Press, 1967), p.5.
4. Wallter C. Neale, India : *The Search for Unity Democracy and Progress* (Bireton : Van Nostrand, 1965), p.17.
5. Rajendra Sing, "Culture of Inequality" *Seminar* 255, (November, 1980), p.16.

Social Status

Age

The distribution of population on the basis of the age has an important bearing upon any social phenomena. The presence of excessively large number of people in the dependent age categories of childhood or old age may restrict social activities and as well adversely affect the economic potential of a farm family.[1] Further, rural population which has a higher concentration of people of advanced age are likely to be more conservative and they accept new ideas, less readily than younger people.[2]

Farmers

The agewise classification of respondent farmers shows their length of experience in agrarian sector and in there interaction with agricultural labour. Their opinion on different aspects of agrarian relations and their reactions towards different situations are likely to vary depending upon their age and experience. Table 3.1 provides agewise classification of farmers. It could be observed from this table that slightly more than half of the (52.07 per cent) respondent farmers belong to age groups 30-39 and 40-49 at State level. The same trend could be observed at the regional level also. At village level, certain variations could be observed. While nearly three fourth of respondent farmers of Jookal village were in the above two age groups; only 37 per cent of farmers of Raigir village were in these two age groups. The percentage of farmers belonging to these two age groups in other villages were in between the above two extremes viz., 37 per cent and 72 per cent. This shows that large number of respondent farmers had commenced their active involvement in agriculture sector in 1960s the time by which several factors influencing agrarian relations had come into operation.

The farmers with the age of above fifty constituted nearly 30 per cent in all the three regions as well as at State level. It is only in Rayalaseema, the two extremes—highest percentage of farmers (54.26 per cent) in Brahmanapalle and the lowest percentage (22.85 per cent) in Sanjeevapuram are observed with the age of above 50 years.

---

1. Walter L. Slocum, Agricultural Sociology, (New York : Harper & Brothers Publishers, 1962), p. 30.
2. T. Lynm Smith, *The Sociology of Rural Life,* (New York : Harper & Brothers Publishers, 1953), p.41.

Table 3.1 : Age-wise Percentage Distribution of Farmers

REGION AND VILLAGE	AGE GROUPS IN YEARS					
	20–29 %	30–39 %	40–49 %	50–59 %	60 and above %	Total %
COASTAL ANDHRA						
Piridi	11.43	31.43	22.86	22.86	11.43	100.00
Vengalapudi	5.71	28.57	25.71	17.14	22.86	100.00
Guntupalle	8.57	8.57	42.86	28.57	11.43	100.00
Veerannapalem	14.29	28.57	22.86	20.00	14.29	100.00
OVERALL	**10.00**	**24.69**	**28.57**	**22.14**	**15.00**	**100.00**
RAYALASEEMA						
Brahmanapalle	8.57	28.57	8.57	20.00	34.29	100.00
Sanjeevapuram	11.43	28.57	37.14	5.71	17.14	100.00
OVERALL	**10.00**	**28.57**	**22.86**	**12.86**	**25.71**	**100.00**
TELANGANA						
Jookal	5.71	37.14	34.29	8.57	14.29	100.00
Raigir	17.14	11.43	25.71	17.14	28.57	100.00
Andhra Nagar	11.43	25.71	20.00	25.71	17.14	100.00
OVERALL	**11.43**	**24.76**	**26.67**	**17.14**	**20.00**	**100.00**
ANDHRA PRADESH	***10.48***	***25.40***	***26.67***	***18.41***	***19.05***	***100.00***

Attached Labour

Unlike in the case of farmers, nearly 86 per cent of attached labourers belong to younger age group *i.e.*, less than 40 years. This trend is found in all the seven villages of Coastal Andhra and Telangana Regions where the employment of attached labourers was in vogue, (Table 3.2). The reason for this trend may be attributed to the fact that, it is generally the practice to serve as attached labourers in the initial stages of their career and later to pursue independent activity either as tenants or as casual labourer.

Casual Labour

In respect of casual labourers significant number of them were found in the age groups of above forty, (Table 3.3). The reason being casual labourers serve in the same capacity till their death unless they change their field of employment by migrating to nearby urban areas. Thus, while attached labourers serve for a limited period in their career, the casual labourers work in the same capacity throughout their career. This difference in the duration of their respective employments will have its own effect on the farmer-labour relations.

Table 3.2 : Age-wise Percentage Distribution of Attached Labour

REGION AND VILLAGE	Age Groups in Years				
	Below 20 %	20–29 %	30–39 %	40–49 %	Total %
COASTAL ANDHRA					
Piridi	---	40.00	60.00	----	100.00
Vengalapudi	---	40.00	60.00	---	100.00
Guntupalle	---	20.00	80.00	----	100.00
Veerannapalem	---	----	60.00	40.00	100.00
OVERALL	---	**25.00**	**65.00**	**10.00**	**100.00**
TELANGANA					
Jookal	20.00	60.00	20.00	---	100.00
Raigir	---	---	60.00	40.00	100.00
Andhra Nagar	---	---	80.00	20.00	100.00
OVERALL	**6.67**	**20.00**	**53.33**	**20.00**	**100.00**
ANDHRA PRADESH	***2.86***	***22.86***	***60.00***	***14.28***	***100.00***

Table 3.3 : Age-wise Percentage Distribution of Casual Labour

REGION AND VILLAGE	Age Groups in Years					
	20–29 %	30–39 %	40–49 %	50–59 %	60 and above %	Total %
COASTAL ANDHRA						
Piridi	34.29	25.71	20.00	11.43	8.57	100.00
Vengalapudi	14.29	42.86	34.29	5.71	2.86	100.00
Guntupalle	14.29	17.14	20.00	11.43	37.14	100.00
Veerannapalem	14.29	20.00	25.71	20.00	20.00	100.00
OVERALL	**19.29**	**26.43**	**25.00**	**12.14**	**17.14**	**100.00**
RAYALASEEMA						
Brahmanapalle	20.00	11.43	34.29	22.86	11.43	100.00
Sanjeevapuram	25.71	45.71	20.00	8.57	---	100.00
OVERALL	**22.86**	**28.57**	**27.14**	**15.71**	**5.72**	**100.00**
TELANGANA						
Jookal	17.14	37.14	34.29	5.71	5.71	100.00
Raigir	11.43	20.00	48.57	11.43	8.57	100.00
Andhra Nagar	20.00	11.43	34.29	22.86	11.43	100.00
OVERALL	**16.19**	**22.86**	**39.05**	**13.33**	**8.57**	**100.00**
ANDHRA PRADESH	***19.04***	***25.72***	***30.16***	***13.33***	***11.75***	***100.00***

Religion

Religion is one of the socio-cultural factors influencing the attitude, behaviour, and interaction with other people. The different religious sects follow different rituals so as to express and enforce group solidarity. This ritualism, according to Kamala Chowdhary, has two implications - first, it reduces anxiety; second it prevents the development of the exercise of discretion and the power of decision making in situations of uncertainity.[1]

Farmers

All most all the respondent farmers with the exception of one Christian in Vangalapudi and one Muslim in Andhra Nagar were Hindus in all the nine villages.

Attached Labour

In respect of attached labour 90 per cent of them in Coastal Andhra Villages and cent per cent of them in Telangana villages belong to Hindu Religion. It was only in Guntupalle a few Christian attached labourers were noticed.

Casual Labour

With regard to casual labourers, cent per cent of them were Hindus in Piridi, Vangalapudi of Coastal Andhra, Brahmanapalle and Sanjeevapuram of Rayalaseema, Jookal and Raigir of Telangana regions. In other villages also, with the exception of Veerannapalem, casual labourers belonging to Christanity constituted 54.29 per cent. It is surprising to find Muslims who constitute the second biggest religious group in Andhra Pradesh, were not found significantly among both attached and casual agricultural labourers.

Caste

Caste is a fundamental and unique institution of Indian society. Infact the relationship between caste and Indian society has been so long and so intimate that many have viewed caste and Indian society as inseparable.[2] The relative status of the people and their occupations in Indian society are decided by the caste system. Thus, while the farmers generally belong to upper castes, the labourers mostly belong to sched-

1. Kamala Chowdhary and Sudhir Kakar, *Social and Cultural Factors in Management Development,* (New Delhi : Tata McGraw-Hill, 1971), p.525.
2. L. M. Prasad, *Organisation Theory and Behaviour* (New Delhi : Sultan Chand and Sons, 1984) p.2.150.

uled castes and scheduled tribes.[1] Consequently, the farmer-labourer relations had come to be influenced by the intercaste relationships.[2] Further, certain communities like Kammas, Reddis in Andhra Pradesh have come to be closely associated with agricultural activity and they are regarded as poineers/innovators of agrarian sector.[3] The people belonging to Kamma community occupy the place of pride in this regard.[4] They are followed by Reddy, Kapu and others. Thus, Kamma community must have developed certain attitudes and techniques in carrying out agricultural operations and managing agricultural labourers, which have been emulated by other communities.

Farmers

Table 3.4 shows that nearly 60 per cent respondent farmers are from Kamma community. This dominance of Kamma community is not because of their size in total population of the State, but, because of the selection of sample villages—where most of them are dominated by Kamma community. The exception are Piridi in Coastal Andhra, Jookal and Raigir in Telangana. The other communities represented in the study are Reddy, Kapu, Koppulavelama, Yadava etc.

Attached Labour

The caste of attached labour is an important factor influencing their employment and their relations with the farmers. The reason being that they move very closely with the farmers and the members of farmer's family. An enquiry into the caste of attached labourers reveals that 80 per cent of them belong to scheduled caste in Piridi, Guntupalle, Veerannapalem of Coastal Andhra and Raigir of Telangana. It was only in Vangalapudi in Coastal Andhra, Jookal and Andhra Nagar of Telangana attached labourers belonging to other communities were significant. This reveals that scheduled castes supplied attached labourers to a larger extent in most of the villages. Other communities might have found this employment as not so attractive.

---

1. A.K. Mukhopadhyaya, "Some Reflections On Agrarian Relations in India," in *Changing Agrarian Relations in India,* (Hyderabad : National Institute of Community Development, 1980).
2. K. C. Alexander, *Changing Labour-Cultivator Relations in South India,* Op.cit., p.21.
3. Gilbert Etienne, *India's Changing Rural Scene, 1963-1979* (New Delhi: Oxford University press, 1982). pp.4-5.
4. G. Anjaneya Swamy, *Agricultural Entreprenurship in India* (Allahabad : Chugh publications, 1988) p.71-73.

Table 3.4 : Caste-wise Percetange Distribution of Farmers

REGION AND VILLAGE	Kamma	Reddi	Kapu	Koppula Velama	Yadava	Others	Total
	%	%	%	%	%	%	%
COASTAL ANDHRA							
Piridi	--	--	5.71	74.29	--	20.00	100.00
Vengalapudi	97.14	--	--	--	--	2.86	100.00
Guntupalle	100.00	--	--	--	--	--	100.00
Veerannapalem	97.14	--	--	--	--	2.86	100.00
OVERALL	**73.57**	--	**1.43**	**18.57**	--	**6.43**	**100.00**
RAYALASEEMA							
Brahmanapalle	54.29	34.29	--	--	5.71	5.71	100.00
Sanjeevapuram	94.29	--	--	--	--	5.71	100.00
OVERALL	**74.29**	**17.14**	--	--	**2.86**	**5.71**	**100.00**
TELANGANA							
Jookal	2.86	45.71	8.57	5.71	2.86	34.29	100.00
Raigir	--	17.14	--	--	45.71	37.14	100.00
Andhra Nagar	91.43	2.86	--	--	--	5.71	100.00
OVERALL	**31.43**	**21.90**	**2.86**	**1.90**	**16.19**	**25.71**	**100.00**
ANDHRA PRADESH	***59.68***	***11.11***	***1.59***	***8.89***	***6.03***	***12.70***	***100.00***

Casual Labour

Casual Labourers belonging to scheduled caste account for 72.38 per cent and the balance is more or less equally shared by scheduled tribes, backward castes and others at State level (Table 3.5). It is surprising to find that a large group of casual labourers is drawn from others in Piridi (54.28 per cent) and 42.80 per cent from scheduled tribes in Guntupalle and 34.29 per cent from backward castes in Raigir.

Thus, the above study shows that while the farmers belong to upper castes, the agricultural labourers belong to lower castes and particularly from scheduled castes. This caste structure is playing a significant role in human resource management in agriculture.

Education

The attitudes, perceptions and behaviour of people are very much influenced by their degree of literacy and educational attainments. Further, with the advent of scientific methods of farming and growing complexity of farm labour relations, education has assumed a greater

Table 3.5 : Caste-wise Percetange Distribution of Casual Labour

REGION AND VILLAGE	S.C. %	S.T. %	B.C. %	Others %	Total %
COASTAL ANDHRA					
Piridi	22.86	2.86	20.00	54.28	100.00
Vengalapudi	77.14	--	--	22.86	100.00
Guntupalle	57.14	42.86	--	--	100.00
Veerannapalem	91.43	8.57	--	--	100.00
OVERALL	**62.14**	**13.57**	**5.00**	**19.29**	**100.00**
RAYALASEEMA					
Brahmanapalle	77.14	20.00	2.86	--	100.00
Sanjeevapuram	100.00	--	--	--	100.00
OVERALL	**88.57**	**10.00**	**1.43**	--	**100.00**
TELANGANA					
Jookal	77.14	5.71	11.42	5.71	100.00
Raigir	65.71	--	34.29	--	100.00
Andhra Nagar	82.86	2.86	8.57	5.71	100.00
OVERALL	**75.24**	**2.86**	**18.09**	**3.81**	**100.00**
ANDHRA PRADESH	***72.38***	***9.21***	***8.57***	***9.84***	***100.00***

Note : S.C.–Scheduled Castes. S.T–Scheduled Tribes. B.C.–Backward Classes

significance to farm people.[1]

Farmers

Table 3.6 shows the educational attainments of farmers. It is evident from this table that slightly less than two thirds of respondent farmers were literates, most of them having education of not more than X standard. In Coastal Andhra and Telangana about 10 per cent of respondent farmers were having educational attainments of Intermediate and above.

Attached Labour

The percentage of illiterate agriculture labour is higher than what is observed in respect of the farmers. Cent per cent of attached labourers of Vangalapudi and Guntupalle of Coastal Andhra and all the three villages of Telangana were found to be illiterates. Thus literacy that too upto V standard was found in respect of a few attached labourers in Piridi and Veerannapalem villages of Coastal Andhra.

1. Walter L. Slocum, *Agricultural Sociology* (New York : Harper & Brothers Publishers, 1962), p.33.

Table 3.6 : Caste-wise Percetange Distribution of Farmers

REGION AND VILLAGE	Illiteracy %	I toV Std. %	VI to X Std. %	Interme-diate %	Degree %	Others %	Total %
COASTAL ANDHRA							
Piridi	45.71	14.29	31.43	8.57	--	--	100.00
Vengalapudi	62.86	2.86	20.00	2.86	11.43	--	100.00
Guntupalle	20.00	20.00	48.57	5.71	5.71	--	100.00
Veerannapalem	14.29	34.29	37.14	5.71	2.86	5.71	100.00
OVERALL	**35.71**	**17.86**	**34.29**	**5.71**	**5.00**	**1.42**	**100.00**
RAYALASEEMA							
Brahmanapalle	25.71	40.00	22.86	2.86	8.57	--	100.00
Sanjeevapuram	28.57	51.43	20.00	--	--	--	100.00
OVERALL	**27.14**	**45.71**	**21.43**	**1.43**	**4.29**	--	**100.00**
TELANGANA							
Jookal	54.29	20.00	20.00	5.71	--	--	100.00
Raigir	48.57	11.43	20.00	17.14	2.86	--	100.00
Andhra Nagar	42.86	25.71	25.71	--	2.86	2.86	100.00
OVERALL	**48.57**	**19.05**	**21.90**	**7.62**	**1.90**	**0.95**	**100.00**
ANDHRA PRADESH	***38.10***	***24.44***	***27.30***	***5.40***	***3.81***	***0.95***	***100.00***

Casual Labour

Surprisingly the State of literacy is slightly better in respect of casual labourers compared to attached labourers. The percentage of literates varied between 17 per cent and 38 per cent in Coastal Andhra villages, 3 per cent to 20 per cent in Rayalaseema villages and zero per cent to 10 per cent in Telangana villages.(Table 3.7)

Regional variations in educational achievements of farmers and labourers were perhaps due to the differences in per capita income and level of economic development. There is every reason to strengthen the literacy drive and to improve the educational attainments of farmers in all the three regions. The literacy campaign started in recent years under the title of "Akshara Jyothi" is expected to play a crucial role in educating the farmers as well as labourers.

It is needless to mention that education among both farmers and labourers will help to reduce the mutual suspicion and hatred and promote harmony and cooperation between the two groups.

Table 3.7 : Percentage Distribution of Casual Labour by Education

REGION AND VILLAGE	Illiterate %	Upt V Std. %	V–X Std. %	Total %
COASTAL ANDHRA				
Piridi	65.71	25.71	8.57	100.00
Vengalapudi	82.86	17.14	--	100.00
Guntupalle	77.14	11.43	11.43	100.00
Veerannapalem	62.86	37.14	--	100.00
OVERALL	**72.14**	**22.86**	**5.00**	**100.00**
RAYALASEEMA				
Brahmanapalle	80.00	14.27	5.71	100.00
Sanjeevapuram	97.14	--	2.86	100.00
OVERALL	**88.57**	**7.14**	**4.29**	**100.00**
TELANGANA				
Jookal	91.43	8.57	--	100.00
Raigir	100.00	--	--	100.00
Andhra Nagar	94.29	2.86	2.86	100.00
OVERALL	**95.24**	**3.81**	**0.95**	**100.00**
ANDHRA PRADESH	***83.49***	***13.02***	***3.49***	***100.00***

Marital Status

Marital status of an individual indicates the responsibility to be born by him and influences very much his decision making also.

Farmers

With the exception of four per cent of respondent farmers, the rest were married. More or less the same trend could be observed in individual villages. The fact that more than 90 per cent of the respondent farmers and labourers were married serves as positive factor in farmer-labour relations, since both of them tend to take decisions with maturity, responsibility and stability.

Attached Labour

All the selected attached labourers with the exception of one in Jookal of Telangana Region were married.

Casual Labour

In respect of casual labourers, 87 per cent were married; three per cent unmarried and nearly 10 per cent widowed at State level. At village level more than 90 per cent were married in Piridi, Vangalapudi and Guntupalle of Coastal Andhra, Jookal and Andhra Nagar of Telangana.

Size of Family

Farmers

The standard of living of a farmer and his capicity to pay the agricultural labour mostly depends upon the size of his family. Table 3.8 shows the average size of the family and the number of earning members of family. At village level, Brahmanapalle recorded the largest size of family with 8.48 followed by Piridi 7.48, Raigir with 7.27 and Sanjeevapuram with 6.76. The village, Jookal, had smallest size of family with 4.62 members. The average number of adults was highest in Raigir with 5.42 and in Jookal with 3.22 members. Regarding average number of children in the farmer's family, Sanjeevapuram recorded

Table 3.8 : Average Size of Family and Number of Earning Members of Each Farmer

REGION AND VILLAGE	Average Size of Family	Average no. of Adults	Average no. of Children	Average no. of earning members in the Family	Average no. of earning Adults	Average no. of earning Children
COASTAL ANDHRA						
Piridi	7.48	4.51	2.97	2.73	2.60	0.03
Vengalapudi	5.02	3.71	2.31	1.77	1.77	--
Guntupalle	5.37	3.57	1.80	1.31	1.31	--
Veerannapalem	5.28	3.51	1.77	1.77	1.77	--
OVERALL	**6.03**	**3.82**	**2.21**	**1.89**	**1.86**	**0.03**
RAYALASEEMA						
Brahmanapalle	8.48	5.17	3.31	2.42	2.37	0.05
Sanjeevapuram	6.76	3.34	3.42	2.17	2.17	--
OVERALL	**7.62**	**4.25**	**3.36**	**2.29**	**2.27**	**0.02**
TELANGANA						
Jookal	4.62	3.22	1.40	2.59	2.54	0.05
Raigir	7.27	5.42	1.85	3.00	3.00	--
Andhra Nagar	5.59	3.28	2.31	1.76	1.71	0.05
OVERALL	**5.82**	**3.97**	**1.85**	**2.61**	**2.58**	**0.03**
ANDHRA PRADESH	***6.48***	***4.01***	***2.47***	***2.24***	***2.23***	***0.01***

highest with 3.42 children and lowest in Jookal with 1.40 children. In respect of average earning members of the farmer's family, highest was found in Raigir with three earning members and the lowest with 1.31 was observed in Guntupalle.

Among the three regions, the average size of family was largest in Rayalseema with 7.62 persons which was above the State average i.e., 6.48 persons. The average number of adults were recorded largest in Rayalaseema with 4.25 persons which was higher than the State average of 4.01 persons. Piridi of Coastal Andhra, Raigir of Telangana, and Brahmanapalle of Rayalaseema recorded more than the State average and also their respective regional average. The average number of children was largest in Rayalaseema which was more than the State average i.e., 2.47 children and smallest in Telangana with 1.85 children. Piridi of Coastal Andhra, Brahmanapalle and Sanjeevapuram of Rayalaseema had recorded more than the State average number of children. Vangalapudi of Coastal Andhra, Sanjeevapuram of Rayalaseema, Andhra Nagar of Telangana recorded more than their regional average number of children. In respect of average number of earning members in the family, Telangana recorded largest with 2.61 followed by 2.29 in Rayalaseema which were higher than the State average of 2.24 persons. Piridi of Coastal Andhra; Brahmanapalle of Rayalaseema; Raigir and Jookal of Telangana were having more earning members than the State average of earning members in the family.

Attached Labour

In general, the labourers perceive that more number of family members contribute to enhance their economic status of the family but in real terms it is not so. The large size of the family leads to low standard of living and many times to indebtedness of the labourers. In the two Agricultural Labour Enquiries[1] and two Rural Labour Enquiries,[2] the

1. Government of India, *Agricultural Labour Enquiry, 1950-'51*, Report of Intensive Survey of Agricultural Labour, Employment, Underemployment, Wages and Levels of Living, (New Delhi : Ministry of Labour, 1954), I-All India.

   Government of India, *Agriculture Labour In India*, Report on The Second Agricultural Labour Enquiry, 1956-'57 (New Delhi : Labour Bureau, Ministry of Labour and Employment, 1960). I - All India.

2. Government of India, *Rural Labour Enquiry 1963-'65*, Final Report, (Simla: Labour Bureau, Ministry of Labour, 1973).

   Government of India, *Rural Labour Enquiry 1974-'75*, Final Report, (Chandighar : Labour Bureau, Ministry of Labour, 1979).

main focus was given to the size of the family of agricultural labourers. In this context, it is appropriate to enquire into the size of the family of attached labour and casual labour and the earning members of the family.

Table 3.9 depicts the average size of the family, average number of adults and average number of children and the average earning members of the attached labourers' family. The average size of the family at State level was 4.65 persons whereas in Telangana,the average size of family was 5.00 persons which was more than the State average. Piridi of Coastal Andhra and Jookal, Raigir and Andhra Nagar of Telangana recorded more than the State average. The average number of adults were 2.65 persons at the State level. It is interesting to note that the average number of children at the State level and regions was 2.00 whereas Piridi of Coastal Andhra Raigir of Telangana recorded more than the State and regional averages with 2.60 and 2.20 respectively.

In respect of overall earning members of the family, the State average was 2.24 persons but the Telangana average was more than the State i.e., 2.67 persons and Coastal Andhra was less with 1.80 persons. Piridi of Coastal Andhra and Jookal and Raigir of Telangana recorded more than the regional average number of earning members. Regarding

Table 3.9 : Average Size of Family and Number of Earning Members of Each Attached Labour

REGION AND VILLAGE	Average Total family members	Average no. of Adults	Average no. of Children	Overall Earning members of Family	Average no. of earning Adults	Average no. of earning Children
COASTAL ANDHRA						
Piridi	5.20	2.60	2.60	2.00	2.00	--
Vengalapudi	4.00	2.20	1.80	1.80	1.80	--
Guntupalle	4.00	2.00	2.00	1.80	1.80	--
Veerannapalem	4.00	2.40	1.60	1.60	1.60	--
OVERALL	**4.30**	**2.30**	**2.00**	**1.80**	**1.80**	--
TELANGANA						
Jookal	5.20	3.40	1.80	3.40	3.20	0.20
Raigir	5.00	2.80	2.20	3.00	2.40	0.60
Andhra Nagar	4.80	2.80	2.00	2.60	2.60	--
OVERALL	**5.00**	**3.00**	**2.00**	**2.67**	**2.40**	**0.27**
ANDHRA PRADESH	*4.65*	*2.65*	*2.00*	*2.24*	*2.10*	*0.14*

average number of earning adults, the State average was 2.10 persons, whereas in Telangana it was 2.40 persons. In case of Coastal Andhra, the regional average and village averages were similar to that of overall average number of earning members of the family. Average number of earning children was nil in Coastal Andhra villages and very marginal in Telangana villages.

Casual Labour

Table 3.10 explains the average size of family and number of earning members of casual labourers. As could be observed from the table, the difference among the State average and regional averages in respect of average number of family members was marginal. Piridi and Guntupalle of Coastal Andhra, Sanjeevapuram of Rayalaseema and Jookal and Andhra Nagar of Telangana recorded more than the State average and their respective regional averages. The average number of

Table 3.10 : Average Size of Family and Number of Earning Members of Each Casual Labour

REGION AND VILLAGE	Average Size of Family	Average no. of Adults	Average no. of Children	Average no. of earning members in the Family	Average no. of earning Adults	Average no. of earning Children
COASTAL ANDHRA						
Piridi	4.72	3.06	1.66	2.89	2.43	0.46
Vengalapudi	3.97	2.20	1.77	2.34	2.17	0.17
Guntupalle	4.97	2.74	2.23	2.28	2.08	0.20
Veerannapalem	4.00	2.37	1.63	1.86	1.69	0.17
OVERALL	**4.42**	**2.60**	**1.82**	**2.34**	**2.09**	**0.25**
RAYALASEEMA						
Brahmanapalle	4.35	2.66	1.69	1.89	1.80	0.09
Sanjeevapuram	5.11	2.40	2.71	1.86	1.80	0.06
OVERALL	**4.73**	**2.53**	**2.20**	**1.88**	**1.80**	**0.08**
TELANGANA						
Jookal	4.57	2.43	2.14	2.32	2.29	0.03
Raigir	4.28	2.57	1.71	2.20	2.03	0.17
Andhra Nagar	4.69	2.86	1.83	2.63	2.60	0.03
OVERALL	**4.51**	**2.62**	**1.89**	**2.39**	**2.31**	**0.08**
ANDHRA PRADESH	***4.55***	***2.58***	***1.97***	***2.21***	***2.07***	***0.14***

adults at the State level was 2.58 persons and it was more in Andhra and Telangana. Piridi and Guntupalle of Coastal Andhra, Brahmanapalle of Rayalaseema and Andhra Nagar of Telangana recorded more than the State average and their regional averages. Rayalaseema recorded highest average number of children with 2.20 children which was more than State average of 1.97.

Regarding earning members, Piridi with 2.89 earning members stood first among all the nine villages followed by Andhra Nagar with 2.63 and Vangalapudi with 2.34 persons, which were more than the State average i.e., 2.21 persons. Coastal Andhra and Telangana regions recorded more than the State averages. The average number of earning adults at the State level was 2.07 persons, while the average of Telangana and Coastal Andhra were more than the State average. At village level, Andhra Nagar of Telangana was highest with 2.60 persons, followed by Piridi of Coastal Andhra with 2.43 persons which was more than the State and regional averages.

The lowest average was observed in Veerannapalem of Coastal Andhra with 1.69 persons. The average number of earning children was more in Piridi of Coastal Andhra compared to that of all other villages. In Jookal and Andhra Nagar of Telangana less number of earning children was found.

Economic Position

Distribution of Land Holding

The magnitude of agricultural activity and the number of labourers to be employed depend to a large extent on the size of land holding of each farmer. Further, the size of land holding decisively affects the cost of production, gross income and net income from agriculture. In addition, the application of improved technology, the extent of manual operations and the farmer's capacity to pay are all influenced by the size of holding.

The holding refered to above, may be either ownership holding or operational holding. While the size of ownership holding determines directly the farmer's economic status, the operational holding influences his earning capacity. It is needless to mention that operational holding includes area owned together with the area leased in less area leased out. While the distribution of ownership holdings gives an idea as to economic concentration on the basis of ownership, the distribution of operational holdings gives an idea as to sources of earning available to farmers. The study of distribution of holdings is also important from the point of view of concentration of economic power.

In view of the above, it is thought appropriate to study the distribution of farmers by the size of ownership holding and operational holding.

The same classification of size groups as has been adopted by the Directorate of Economics and Statistics, Government of Andhra Pradesh is followed. As per this classification, five groups-Marginal with less than one hectare; 'small' with 1 to 2 hectares; 'semi medium' with 4.94 to 9.88 hectares; 'medium' with 4 to 10 hectares and large with more than 10 hectares.

The land has also been classified into wet, dry and overall consisting of both wet and dry. This classification is justified on the ground that the cropping pattern, requirement of labour, methods of farming, degree of mechanisation, gross income available to the farmer and his paying capacity which vary significantly depending upon the land cultivated is wet or dry.

a. Distribution of Ownership Land Holdings

Very high proportion of farmers were having wet land of less than two hectares in many selected villages-Piridi with 65.72 per cent, Vangalapudi with 71.43 per cent, Brahmanapalle with 97.14 per cent Sanjeevapuram with 97.14 per cent, Jookal with cent per cent and Raigir with 80 per cent of Telangana. The position in other villages is comparatively better where land holdings with more than two hectares were held by more than 50 per cent of farmers in each village. With regard to percentage of area covered by these land holdings, 33.60 per cent of area was possessed by 65.72 per cent of farmers in Piridi village. In Vangalapudi slightly above 40 per cent of area was owned by nearly 72 per cent of farmers. In Guntupalle 45 per cent of the area was held by 77 percent of farmers. In Brahmanapalle and Sanjeevapuram villages all most all the respondent farmers with the exception of one did not possess wet land. In Jookal cent percent of the wet land area was distributed between marginal and small farmers. In Raigir village, nearly 52 per cent of total wet land area was covered by marginal and small farms and the remaining area was covered by semi-medium and medium farms. In Andhra Nagar, where most of the farmers were migrated from the coastal districts, more than 57 per cent of the total wet land area was in medium and large farms.

In respect of dry land, nearly 60 per cent of the area was covered by marginal and small farms in Piridi village. In Vangalapudi, this percentage was still higher with more than. As against this, the dry land distribution in Guntupalle and Vangalapudi villages was significantly in a better position. In Guntupalle, more than 67 per cent area was in semi-medium and medium farms. In Veerannapalem, nearly 80 per cent of the dry land area was distributed in medium and large sizes. The land distribution in the two Rayalaseema villages was also comparatively in a better position with more than 76 per cent of the area in medium and large farms in Brahmanapalle village. In Sanjeevapuram, this percentage was still higher with 76 per cent. The dry land holdings of Jookal and Raigir were comparatively of large sized compared to Andhra Nagar in Telangana.

The percentage distribution of farmers by size of ownership holding consisting of both wet and dry land is also studied and the figures are shown in Table 3.11. Nearly 43 per cent of the land in Piridi was owned by only 14 per cent of farmers. While this was so, the remaining 57 per cent of the area was owned by as many as 86 per cent of farmers. This shows unequal distribution of land in Piridi village. The average size of holding of 46 per cent of farmers was less than two hectares. The average size of holding of 14 per cent of farmers was around seven hectares. The distribution of land among farmers was slightly better in Vangalapudi village. In Guntupalle village, nearly 62 per cent of the land was owned by 29 per cent of farmers belonging to medium and large groups. In Veerannapalem village, 93 per cent of the land was in the hands of 77 per cent of farmers, the average size of holding in Veerannapalem was higher than Guntupalle. In Brahmanapalle above 43 per cent of farmers were owning 77 per cent of land and the average size of the entire village was worked out at above four hectares. Similarly, Sanjeevapuram presents more or less the same characteristics. The average size of holding of the 48.57 per cent of farmers was around six hectares and this was followed by next group i.e., 34.29 per cent of farmers whose average size of holding was above two and half hectares.

In Jookal village, 40 per cent of farmers were owning about 46 per cent of area where the average size of holding was worked out at two and half hectares. In Raigir village 17.14 per cent of farmers belonging to marginal group had command over only 2.30 per cent of the area; another 17.04 per cent of farmers, at the other end belonging to the large group were having command over 47.15 per cent of area. In Andhra Nagar while 14.29 per cent of farmers belonging to marginal group had command over only 2.76 per cent of the area; only 5.71 per cent of the farmers belonging to large size had command over 17.17 per cent of the area.

Table 3.11 : Percentage Distribution of Farmers by Size of Ownership Holding

SIZE GROUPS (*In Hectares*)	PIRIDI			VANGALAPUDI			GUNTUPALLE		
	WET	DRY	OVER-ALL	WET	DRY	OVER-ALL	WET	DRY	OVER-ALL
MARGINAL (Less than 1)									
Percentage of Farmers	25.72	80.00	8.57	34.29	82.85	25.71	28.50	88.57	22.86
Percentage of Area	7.24	35.92	1.64	10.87	31.58	6.09	5.58	24.31	3.43
Average size of Holding	0.62	0.37	0.22	0.57	0.21	0.56	0.54	0.13	0.49
SMALL (1–2)									
Percentage of Farmers	45.00	14.29	37.15	37.14	11.43	22.86	17.14	2.85	20.00
Percentage of Area	26.36	23.68	17.46	29.26	32.63	13.71	8.42	8.68	8.30
Average size of Holding	1.44	1.38	1.43	1.41	1.57	1.40	1.36	1.42	1.34
SEMI-MEDIUM (2–4)									
Percentage of Farmers	22.86	2.86	40.00	17.14	2.86	31.43	31.43	5.71	28.57
Percentage of Area	26.78	6.97	38.01	26.21	14.74	34.65	31.00	37.23	26.81
Average size of Holding	2.58	2.02	2.88	2.73	2.83	2.58	2.73	3.04	3.04
MEDIUM(4–10)									
Percentage of Farmers	8.57	2.85	8.57	11.43	2.86	20.00	20.00	2.85	22.86
Percentage of Area	23.00	33.43	18.49	33.66	21.50	45.55	42.48	29.78	39.31
Average size of Holding	6.14	9.72	6.54	5.26	4.05	5.32	10.51	4.86	5.57
LARGE (More than 10)									
Percentage of Farmers	2.85	--	5.71	--	--	--	2.85	--	5.71
Percentage of Area	15.74	--	24.40	--	--	--	12.52	--	22.15
Average size of Holding	12.15	--	12.96	--	--	--	12.15	--	12.55
TOTAL									
Percentage of Farmers	100.00	100.00	100.00	100.00	100.00	100.00	100.00	100.00	100.00
Percentage of Area	100.00	100.00	100.00	100.00	100.00	100.00	100.00	100.00	100.00
Average size of Holding	2.20	0.83	3.03	1.79	0.55	2.34	2.77	0.47	3.23

(Contd.)

Table 3.11 : (Contd..)

SIZE GROUPS (*In Hectares*)	VEERANNAPALEM			COASTAL ANDHRA			BRAHMANAPALLE		
	WET	DRY	OVER-ALL	WET	DRY	OVER-ALL	WET	DRY	OVER-ALL
MARGINAL (Less than 1)									
Percentage of Farmers	5.71	17.15	8.57	23.57	67.14	16.43	97.14	17.14	17.14
Percentage of Area	7.31	2.56	1.00	7.47	11.13	2.57	--	3.36	3.31
Average size of Holding	0.43	0.66	0.78	0.71	0.26	0.60	--	0.78	0.78
SMALL (1–2)									
Percentage of Farmers	14.29	2.85	2.86	27.14	7.86	20.71	--	17.14	17.14
Percentage of Area	9.06	1.04	0.70	17.11	7.38	7.48	--	6.23	6.14
Average size of Holding	1.42	1.62	1.62	1.42	1.47	1.38	--	1.45	1.45
SEMI-MEDIUM (2–4)									
Percentage of Farmers	60.00	28.58	11.43	32.85	10.00	27.86	2.86	22.87	22.86
Percentage of Area	35.58	16.98	5.38	30.90	16.96	20.89	100.00	14.05	13.85
Average size of Holding	2.74	2.63	3.14	2.11	2.66	2.86	2.02	2.45	2.67
MEDIUM(4–10)									
Percentage of Farmers	20.00	45.71	62.86	15.00	13.57	28.57	--	37.14	37.15
Percentage of Area	45.05	59.83	62.01	36.81	50.70	46.03	--	51.73	50.99
Average size of Holding	5.03	5.80	6.57	5.52	5.86	6.15	--	5.56	5.56
LARGE (More than 10)									
Percentage of Farmers	--	5.71	14.28	1.43	1.43	6.43	--	5.71	5.71
Percentage of Area	--	19.59	30.91	7.71	13.83	23.03	--	24.63	25.71
Average size of Holding	--	15.18	14.41	12.15	15.18	13.68	--	17.21	18.22
TOTAL									
Percentage of Farmers	100.00	100.00	100.00	100.00	100.00	100.00	100.00	100.00	100.00
Percentage of Area	100.00	100.00	100.00	100.00	100.00	100.00	100.00	100.00	100.00
Average size of Holding	2.24	4.43	6.66	2.45	1.57	3.81	0.06	3.99	4.05

(Contd.)

Table 3.11 : (Contd..)

SIZE GROUPS (*In Hectares*)	SANJEEVAPURAM			RAYALASEEMA			JOOKAL		
	WET	DRY	OVER-ALL	WET	DRY	OVER-ALL	WET	DRY	OVER-ALL
MARGINAL (Less than 1)									
Percentage of Farmers	97.14	2.86	2.86	97.14	10.00	10.00	77.14	37.14	20.00
Percentage of Area	--	0.51	0.51	--	1.86	1.83	54.55	12.46	6.77
Average size of Holding	--	0.81	0.81	--	0.79	0.79	0.44	0.53	0.75
SMALL (1–2)									
Percentage of Farmers	--	8.57	8.57	--	12.86	12.86	22.86	34.57	28.57
Percentage of Area	--	2.87	2.83	--	4.45	4.39	45.45	32.10	19.26
Average size of Holding	--	1.50	1.55	--	1.47	1.47	1.24	1.49	1.49
SEMI-MEDIUM (2–4)									
Percentage of Farmers	22.86	34.29	34.29	2.86	28.57	28.57	--	22.86	40.00
Percentage of Area	100.00	20.79	20.53	--	17.63	17.38	--	37.68	45.83
Average size of Holding	2.02	2.73	2.73	2.02	2.62	2.62	--	2.63	2.54
MEDIUM(4–10)									
Percentage of Farmers	--	48.57	48.57	--	42.86	42.86	--	5.71	11.43
Percentage of Area	--	59.09	59.61	--	55.62	55.55	--	17.76	28.14
Average size of Holding	--	5.47	5.00	--	5.51	5.58	--	4.96	5.47
LARGE (More than 10)									
Percentage of Farmers	--	5.71	5.71	--	5.71	5.71	--	--	--
Percentage of Area	--	16.74	16.52	--	20.45	20.85	--	--	--
Average size of Holding	--	13.16	13.16	--	15.18	15.69	--	--	--
TOTAL									
Percentage of Farmers	100.00	100.00	100.00	100.00	100.00	100.00	100.00	100.00	100.00
Percentage of Area	100.00	100.00	100.00	100.00	100.00	100.00	100.00	100.00	100.00
Average size of Holding	0.16	4.49	4.45	0.06	4.24	4.30	0.62	1.60	2.22

(Contd.)

Table 3.11 : (Contd..)

SIZE GROUPS (*In Hectares*)	RAIGIR			ANDHRA NAGAR		
	WET	DRY	OVER-ALL	WET	DRY	OVER-ALL
MARGINAL (Less than 1)						
Percentage of Farmers	48.57	40.00	17.14	14.28	88.57	14.29
Percentage of Area	54.55	12.46	6.77	18.34	3.07	2.30
Average size of Holding	0.50	0.30	0.77	0.61	0.30	0.73
SMALL (1–2)						
Percentage of Farmers	31.43	8.56	20.00	22.86	5.71	14.29
Percentage of Area	33.63	3.21	5.81	10.35	17.03	5.86
Average size of Holding	1.42	1.49	1.53	1.49	1.42	1.55
SEMI-MEDIUM (2–4)						
Percentage of Farmers	11.43	14.29	20.00	34.29	5.71	34.28
Percentage of Area	19.21	10.00	9.87	29.82	24.33	25.45
Average size of Holding	2.23	3.00	3.04	2.87	2.02	2.80
MEDIUM(4–10)						
Percentage of Farmers	8.57	22.86	25.72	22.71	--	31.43
Percentage of Area	8.82	36.79	34.87	47.20	--	48.76
Average size of Holding	4.45	6.38	6.44	6.03	--	5.86
LARGE (More than 10)						
Percentage of Farmers	--	14.29	17.14	10.18	--	17.17
Percentage of Area	--	46.13	47.15	29.00	--	28.00
Average size of Holding	--	12.79	13.71	11.74	--	11.34
TOTAL						
Percentage of Farmers	100.00	100.00	100.00	100.00	100.00	100.00
Percentage of Area	100.00	100.00	100.00	100.00	100.00	100.00
Average size of Holding	1.32	3.96	5.28	3.30	0.47	3.77

(Contd.)

Table 3.11 : (Contd..)

SIZE GROUPS (*In Hectares*)	TELANGANA			ANDHRA PRADESH		
	WET	DRY	OVER-ALL	WET	DRY	OVER-ALL
MARGINAL (Less than 1)						
Percentage of Farmers	46.67	55.24	17.14	47.62	50.48	15.24
Percentage of Area	2.63	58.64	2.76	9.35	7.00	2.67
Average size of Holding	0.48	0.36	0.75	0.31	0.32	0.68
SMALL (1–2)						
Percentage of Farmers	25.71	16.19	20.95	20.63	11.75	19.05
Percentage of Area	20.40	11.94	8.47	18.17	7.51	7.04
Average size of Holding	1.39	1.48	1.52	1.41	1.48	1.45
SEMI-MEDIUM (2–4)						
Percentage of Farmers	15.24	14.29	32.38	20.32	15.15	29.52
Percentage of Area	23.60	18.98	22.87	28.79	17.81	20.67
Average size of Holding	2.71	2.67	2.66	2.26	2.65	2.78
MEDIUM(4–10)						
Percentage of Farmers	11.43	9.52	21.91	10.48	18.73	29.52
Percentage of Area	36.83	28.86	37.44	36.52	40.37	45.60
Average size of Holding	5.64	6.09	6.43	5.56	5.72	5.97
LARGE (More than 10)						
Percentage of Farmers	26.40	30.29	27.97	0.95	3.45	6.67
Percentage of Area	29.00	31.60	33.86	7.17	21.31	24.02
Average size of Holding	11.74	12.79	13.71	12.01	14.10	14.07
TOTAL						
Percentage of Farmers	100.00	100.00	100.00	100.00	100.00	100.00
Percentage of Area	100.00	100.00	100.00	100.00	100.00	100.00
Average size of Holding	1.75	2.01	3.76	1.60	2.31	3.90

The above analysis gives the following overall observations.

i. In Coastal Andhra the distribution of land (Wet+Dry) was more uneven in Piridi village. This was followed by Guntupalle, Vangalapudi, Veerannapalem.

ii. In Rayalaseema, the inequality in the distribution of land was higher in Bhrahmanapalle than in Sanjeevapuram.

iii. In Telangana region, Raigir stood first in unequal distribution followed by Andhra Nagar and Jookal.

b. Distribution of Operational Holdings

Table 3.12 shows the percentage distribution of farmers by size of operational holdings in all the nine villages selected for the study. It can be seen from this Table that in Piridi village, nearly 46 per cent of farmers belonging to marginal and small groups of land holdings had command over slightly more than 17 per cent of the operational wet area. While this was so, nearly 23 per cent of farmers belonging to medium and large groups of land holdings had command over nearly 54 per cent of the operational wet area. In respect of dryland, its distribution among farmers was found to be much uneven compared to wet land. Seventeen per cent of farmers did not have any dry land in this village. In addition to this, nearly three fourths of farmers belonging to marginal i.e. less than one hectare size group of land holdings had command over nearly 50 per cent of the dry operational land. On the other hand nearly three per cent of farmers were controlling nearly 32 per cent of dry operational area. In Vangalapudi village nearly 37 per cent of farmers were holding 63 per cent operational wet area. Fifty seven percent of farmers were not having any dry operational area. Fourteen per cent of farmers in this village were holding 62 per cent dry operational area. Forty three per cent of farmers had command over 63 per cent of operational area.

In Guntupalle village, nearly two thirds of farmers belonged to medium and large groups of wet operational area. The percentage of area under their operation was slightly above 91 per cent. However, in this village, nearly 89 per cent of farmers were not having dry operational area. Among the rest three per cent of farmers were commanding 57 per cent of dry operational area. The overall position shows that two thirds of farmers in this village, were controlling more than 91 per cent of the total operational area.

In Veerannapalem more than 51 per cent of farmers were having control over only 19 per cent of wet operational area. The remaining 49

Table 3.12 : Percentage Distribution of Farmers by Size of Operational Holding

SIZE GROUPS (*In Hectares*)	PIRIDI			VANGALAPUDI		
	WET	DRY	OVER-ALL	WET	DRY	OVER-ALL
MARGINAL (Less than 1)						
Percentage of Farmers	17.15	91.43	5.71	2.86	77.14	--
Percentage of Area	2.76	49.79	1.33	0.63	16.81	--
Average size of Holding	0.64	0.39	0.81	0.81	0.14	--
SMALL (1–2)						
Percentage of Farmers	28.56	--	31.43	22.86	8.57	14.29
Percentage of Area	14.56	--	12.77	8.73	21.24	4.98
Average size of Holding	1.40	--	1.41	1.39	1.62	1.50
SEMI-MEDIUM (2–4)						
Percentage of Farmers	31.43	5.71	34.29	37.14	11.43	42.86
Percentage of Area	29.14	18.33	26.26	26.98	44.25	29.07
Average size of Holding	2.52	2.33	2.66	2.65	2.67	2.92
MEDIUM(4–10)						
Percentage of Farmers	20.00	2.86	22.86	34.28	2.86	34.28
Percentage of Area	40.69	31.88	39.36	54.13	17.70	43.07
Average size of Holding	5.53	8.10	5.99	5.75	4.05	5.40
LARGE (More than 10)						
Percentage of Farmers	2.86	--	5.71	2.86	--	8.57
Percentage of Area	12.86	--	20.28	9.53	--	22.88
Average size of Holding	12.15	--	12.35	12.15	--	11.47
TOTAL						
Percentage of Farmers	100.00	100.00	100.00	100.00	100.00	100.00
Percentage of Area	100.00	100.00	100.00	100.00	100.00	100.00
Average size of Holding	2.75	0.73	3.48	3.64	0.65	4.30

(Contd.)

Table 3.12 : (Contd..)

SIZE GROUPS (*In Hectares*)	GUNTUPALLE			VEERANNAPALEM		
	WET	DRY	OVER-ALL	WET	DRY	OVER-ALL
MARGINAL (Less than 1)						
Percentage of Farmers	5.71	91.43	5.71	34.29	14.28	8.57
Percentage of Area	0.47	9.52	0.46	7.74	1.33	0.59
Average size of Holding	0.63	0.02	0.63	0.47	0.45	0.47
SMALL (1–2)						
Percentage of Farmers	11.43	5.71	11.43	17.14	2.86	2.86
Percentage of Area	2.08	33.33	2.01	11.26	0.96	0.67
Average size of Holding	1.37	1.42	1.37	1.38	1.62	1.62
SEMI-MEDIUM (2–4)						
Percentage of Farmers	17.14	--	17.14	28.57	20.00	2.86
Percentage of Area	6.31	--	6.12	37.07	12.10	1.01
Average size of Holding	2.79	--	2.79	2.75	2.89	2.43
MEDIUM(4–10)						
Percentage of Farmers	40.00	2.86	40.00	20.00	57.15	74.29
Percentage of Area	36.01	57.15	35.63	43.93	67.46	72.37
Average size of Holding	6.81	4.86	6.95	4.62	5.64	6.70
LARGE (More than 10)						
Percentage of Farmers	25.72	--	25.72	--	5.71	11.43
Percentage of Area	55.13	--	55.78	--	18.15	25.36
Average size of Holding	16.20	--	16.92	--	15.18	15.28
TOTAL						
Percentage of Farmers	100.00	100.00	100.00	100.00	100.00	100.00
Percentage of Area	100.00	100.00	100.00	100.00	100.00	100.00
Average size of Holding	7.56	0.24	7.80	2.11	4.78	6.88

(Contd.)

Table 3.12 : (Contd..)

SIZE GROUPS (In Hectares)	OVERALL			BRAHMANPALLE			SANJEEVAPURAM		
	WET	DRY	OVER-ALL	WET	DRY	OVER-ALL	WET	DRY	OVER-ALL
MARGINAL (Less than 1)									
Percentage of Farmers	15.00	68.57	5.00	97.14	54.29	54.29	100.00	5.71	5.71
Percentage of Area	2.07	8.71	0.55	--	18.99	18.41	100.00	0.99	0.98
Average size of Holding	0.15	0.20	0.61	--	0.64	0.64	0.41	0.61	0.61
SMALL (1–2)									
Percentage of Farmers	20.00	4.28	15.00	--	17.14	17.14	--	25.71	25.71
Percentage of Area	6.91	4.15	3.84	--	12.34	11.96	--	11.01	10.98
Average size of Holding	1.39	1.55	1.44	--	1.32	1.32	--	1.51	1.51
SEMI-MEDIUM (2–4)									
Percentage of Farmers	28.57	9.29	24.28	2.86	17.14	17.14	--	25.71	25.71
Percentage of Area	18.89	15.63	15.15	100.00	25.32	24.54	--	19.18	19.12
Average size of Holding	2.66	2.69	3.50	2.02	2.70	2.70	--	2.62	2.62
MEDIUM(4–10)									
Percentage of Farmers	28.57	16.43	42.86	--	8.57	8.57	--	42.86	42.86
Percentage of Area	41.87	57.96	48.89	--	26.27	25.46	--	68.82	68.92
Average size of Holding	5.79	5.65	6.14	--	5.60	5.60	--	5.64	5.67
LARGE (More than 10)									
Percentage of Farmers	7.86	1.43	12.86	--	2.86	2.86	--	--	--
Percentage of Area	30.26	13.15	31.57	--	17.08	19.63	--	--	--
Average size of Holding	15.47	15.18	13.79	--	10.93	12.96	--	--	--
TOTAL									
Percentage of Farmers	100.00	100.00	100.00	100.00	100.00	100.00	100.00	100.00	100.00
Percentage of Area	100.00	100.00	100.00	100.00	100.00	100.00	100.00	100.00	100.00
Average size of Holding	4.02	1.60	5.62	0.06	1.83	1.88	0.01	3.51	3.53

(Contd.)

Table 3.12 : (Contd..)

SIZE GROUPS (*In Hectares*)	OVERALL			JOOKAL			RAIGIR		
	WET	DRY	OVER-ALL	WET	DRY	OVER-ALL	WET	DRY	OVER-ALL
MARGINAL (Less than 1)									
Percentage of Farmers	98.57	30.00	30.00	82.80	31.43	25.71	54.29	31.43	5.71
Percentage of Area	16.67	7.15	7.06	54.51	6.47	9.24	11.87	2.67	1.08
Average size of Holding	0.00	0.64	0.64	0.33	0.30	0.71	0.28	0.17	0.61
SMALL (1–2)									
Percentage of Farmers	--	21.43	21.43	17.14	42.86	25.71	25.71	28.57	45.71
Percentage of Area	--	11.45	11.32	45.09	44.99	19.71	30.14	22.26	21.40
Average size of Holding	--	1.43	1.43	1.32	1.54	1.51	1.49	1.52	1.51
SEMI-MEDIUM (2–4)									
Percentage of Farmers	1.43	21.43	21.43	--	22.86	45.72	11.43	20.00	28.58
Percentage of Area	83.33	21.29	21.00	--	39.07	62.52	22.37	23.73	25.00
Average size of Holding	2.02	2.65	2.65	--	2.51	2.69	2.48	2.31	2.81
MEDIUM(4–10)									
Percentage of Farmers	--	25.71	25.71	--	2.86	2.86	8.57	20.00	14.29
Percentage of Area	--	54.26	53.78	--	9.47	8.53	35.62	51.34	32.38
Average size of Holding	--	5.64	5.66	--	4.86	5.87	5.26	5.00	7.29
LARGE (More than 10)									
Percentage of Farmers	--	1.43	1.43	--	--	--	--	--	5.71
Percentage of Area	--	5.85	6.84	--	--	--	--	--	20.14
Average size of Holding	--	10.93	12.96	--	--	--	--	--	11.34
TOTAL									
Percentage of Farmers	100.00	100.00	100.00	100.00	100.00	100.00	100.00	100.00	100.00
Percentage of Area	100.00	100.00	100.00	100.00	100.00	100.00	100.00	100.00	100.00
Average size of Holding	0.04	2.67	2.71	0.50	1.47	1.97	1.27	1.95	3.22

(Contd.)

Table 3.12 : (Contd..)

SIZE GROUPS (*In Hectares*)	ANDHRA NAGAR			OVERALL			ANDHRA PRADESH		
	WET	DRY	OVER-ALL	WET	DRY	OVER-ALL	WET	DRY	OVER-ALL
MARGINAL (Less than 1)									
Percentage of Farmers	8.57	82.86	8.57	48.57	48.57	13.33	44.76	53.33	13.33
Percentage of Area	0.60	38.18	1.08	6.88	8.81	2.60	3.51	8.21	2.03
Average size of Holding	0.34	0.24	0.68	0.31	0.24	0.68	0.20	0.27	0.65
SMALL (1–2)									
Percentage of Farmers	20.00	14.28	11.43	20.96	28.57	27.62	15.88	16.19	20.64
Percentage of Area	6.46	39.74	3.50	13.93	33.04	11.99	8.93	13.89	7.12
Average size of Holding	1.56	1.46	1.64	1.46	1.52	1.53	1.42	1.49	1.47
SEMI-MEDIUM (2–4)									
Percentage of Farmers	28.57	--	31.43	13.33	14.29	35.24	17.46	13.65	27.30
Percentage of Area	17.46	--	16.32	17.08	26.28	27.58	18.56	20.23	19.39
Average size of Holding	3.00	--	2.78	2.82	2.42	2.75	2.68	2.58	3.03
MEDIUM(4–10)									
Percentage of Farmers	31.43	2.86	34.29	13.33	8.57	17.14	17.14	15.88	30.48
Percentage of Area	36.72	22.08	34.64	33.73	31.87	29.08	29.38	50.15	44.15
Average size of Holding	5.65	4.05	5.42	5.55	4.88	5.96	5.80	5.51	6.18
LARGE (More than 10)									
Percentage of Farmers	11.43	--	14.28	3.81	--	6.67	4.76	0.95	8.25
Percentage of Area	38.76	--	44.46	28.38	--	28.75	29.62	7.52	27.31
Average size of Holding	16.40	--	16.68	1.64	--	15.15	15.71	13.77	14.13
TOTAL									
Percentage of Farmers	100.00	100.00	100.00	100.00	100.00	100.00	100.00	100.00	100.00
Percentage of Area	100.00	100.00	100.00	100.00	100.00	100.00	100.00	100.00	100.00
Average size of Holding	4.64	0.52	5.36	2.20	1.31	3.51	2.53	1.74	4.27

per cent of farmers were having command over 81 per cent of the wet operational area. In respect of dry land 63 per cent of farmers belong to medium and large size groups with 86 per cent of the dry operational area. It is heartening to note the 86 per cent of farmers in this village belonged to medium and large size groups.

In Brahmnapalle village 97 per cent of farmers were not having wet operational area but 71 per cent of farmers in this village were having dry operational area of below two hectares. Slightly more than 11 per cent of farmers were cultivating 43 per cent of the dry operational area. The overall operational area represents the same characteristic features as that of dry land.

In Sanjeevapuram, 97 per cent of farmers did not have wet operational area. Sixty nine per cent of farmers in this village were having command over 88 per cent of total dry operational area.

In Jookal, more than one-third of the farmers did not have wet operational area. In respect of the remaining farmers, the average size of wet operational holding was less than one and half hectares. Fourteen per cent of farmers were not having dry operational area. Two thirds of farmers in this village belonged to either small or semi-medium groups. With regard to the overall operational area, more than half of the farmers in this village were having command over only 29 per cent of the operational area.

In Raigir village, 26 per cent of the farmers were not having wet operational area. Most of the remaining farmers were having wet operational area of less than two hectares. Twenty three per cent of farmers did not have dry operational area. The remaining farmers were distributed more or less equally among the three groups-small, semi-medium and medium. But the percentage of dry operational area held by the last group i.e., medium was very high with more than 51 per cent. In respect of overall operation area, 46 per cent of farmers were controlling 21 per cent of the area in small size group. On the other hand 6 per cent of farmers were having control over 20 per cent of total operational area.

In Andhra Nagar, 43 per cent of farmers were cultivating 76 per cent of the wet operational area. The average size of wet operational holding was more than two hectares in most of the cases. Forty three per cent of farmers did not have dry operational area. Even the remaining farmers mostly belonged to marginal and small size groups. Regarding overall operational area, 79 per cent of the area was held by 49 per cent of the farmers belonging to medium and large size groups.

c. Ratio Between Ownership and Operational Land Holdings

Tables 3.11 and 3.12 provide information relating to average size of ownership holding and operational holding following the classification of wet, dry and overall. In Coastal Andhra, Guntupalle stood first with the average size of 2.71 hectares of wet ownership holding followed by Veerannapalem with 2.24 hectares and Piridi with 5.44 hectares. In respect of dry land, Veerannapalem stood first with 40.43 hectares and all other villages were far behind from this village. With regard to ownership holding of wet and dry land combined, Veerannapalem stood first with 6.66 hectares followed by Guntupalle with 7.99 hectares and Piridi with 3.03 hectares. In respect of wet operational holding, the average size was very high in Guntupalle with 7.65 hectares, followed by Vangalapudi with 3.64 hectares. As in the case of ownership holding, Veerannapalem ranked number one in having highest average size of dry land holding with 4.78 hectares. In respect of overall operational holding Guntupalle recorded highest average with 7.80 hectares followed by Veerannapalem with 6.88 hectares and Vangalapudi with 4.30 hectares. Thus, the average size of operational holding significantly differed from that of ownership holding in respect of all the four villages with the exception of dry land of Piridi and Guntupalle, thus the average size of operational holding was more than ownership holding. The ratio between ownership holding and the operational holding given in Table 3.13 clearly indicates this situation. The practice of taking lands on lease must have influenced the average size of operational holding to be more than that of ownership holding. Migration of some of the farmers to the nearby towns and displeasure arising due to problems constantly faced in agriculture might have strengthened the practice of leasing out the agricultural lands. This trend was more perceptable in respect of wet lands of Guntupalle where the ratio was 1 : 2.73 followed by Vangalapudi with 1 : 2.04.

In Rayalaseema region, the dry land was dominant and wet land was insignificant. Consequently, the average size of dry land ownership holding was highest in Sanjeevapuram with 4.49 hectares followed by Brahmanapalle with 3.99 hectares. But, the average size of operational dry land holding was very much less than that of the ownership holding. Consequently, the ratio between these two (ownership holding and operational holding) was 1 : 0.78 in Sanjeevapuram and 1:0.46 in Brahmannapalle. The reason for less operational holding might have been due to uncultivable land. This is common in Rayalaseema region due to the nature of soil and its terrain. This also shows that it is not the

Table 3.13 : Village-wise Per Farmer Ownership and Operational Land Holding Ratio

(In hectares)

REGION AND VILLAGE	OWNERSHIP HOLDING			OPERATIONAL HOLDING			RATIO (between owenership and operational holding)		
	WET	DRY	OVER-ALL	WET	DRY	OVER-ALL	WET	DRY	OVER-ALL
COASTAL ANDHRA									
Piridi	2.20	0.83	3.03	2.75	0.73	3.48	1:1.25	1:0.87	1:1.15
Vangalapudi	1.79	0.55	2.34	3.64	0.65	4.30	1:2.04	1:1.18	1:1.18
Guntupalle	2.77	0.47	3.23	7.56	0.24	7.80	1:2.73	1:0.52	1:1.03
Veerannapalem	2.24	4.43	6.66	2.11	4.78	6.88	1:0.94	1:1.08	1:1.03
OVERALL	**2.45**	**1.57**	**3.81**	**4.02**	**1.60**	**5.62**	**1:1.79**	**1:1.02**	**1:1.40**
RAYALASEEMA									
Brahmanapalle	0.06	3.99	4.05	0.06	1.83	1.88	1:1.00	1:0.46	1:0.47
Sanjeevapuram	0.06	4.49	4.55	0.01	3.57	3.53	1:0.21	1:0.78	1:0.77
OVERALL	**0.06**	**4.24**	**4.30**	**0.04**	**2.67**	**2.71**	**1:0.64**	**1:0.63**	**1:0.63**
TELANGANA									
Jookal	0.62	1.60	2.22	0.50	1.47	1.97	1:0.00	1:0.92	1:0.89
Raigir	1.32	3.96	5.28	1.27	1.95	3.22	1:0.96	1:0.49	1:0.61
Andhra Nagar	3.30	0.47	3.77	4.64	0.52	5.36	1:1.47	1:1.40	1:1.42
OVERALL	**1.75**	**2.01**	**3.76**	**2.20**	**1.31**	**3.51**	**1:1.26**	**1:0.65**	**1:0.93**
ANDHRA PRADESH	***1.60***	***2.01***	***3.90***	***2.53***	***1.74***	***4.27***	***1:1.58***	***1:0.75***	***1:1.09***

ownership holding which determines the economic status but it is operational holding which influences the magnitude of agricultural activity, the farmers' economic status, requirement of labour and ultimately the paying capacity of farmer.

In Telangana region, while Jookal and Raigir were known for dry land, Andhra Nagar was famous for wet land due to the availability of irrigation facilities. In between Jookal and Raigir, the average size of ownership holding was very high in Raigir with 5.28 hectares followed by Jookal with only 2.22 hectares. The average size of ownership holding in Andhra Nagar was 3.77 hectares which lies in between the above two villages. Coming to operational holding, its average size was less than that of ownership holding in Jookal and Raigir villages. In Andhra nagar the average size of operational holding was very much high compared to that of ownership holding. The ratio between ownership holding and the operational holding was the lowest in Raigir with 1 : 0.61 followed by Jookal with 1 : 0.89 and Andhra Nagar with 1 : 1.42. The same reasons as mentioned above in respect of Rayalaseema must have influenced the situation in Jookal and Raigir villages. The reasons explained in respect of Coastal Andhra region area are applicable to Andhra Nagar village where the irrigation facilities, the skills of farmers, techniques of agriculture applied and fertility of the soil are more or less of the same variety.

Cropping Pattern

The cropping pattern, depicting as it does with regard to the percentage of area devoted to principal crops and the percentage of farmers involved in the cultivation of these crops is of great significance in revealing the demand pattern to which it responds as also to many other economic and social factors that have been in the operation over time. In general, the cropping pattern in India, is determined mainly by natural factors like rainfall, climate and soil conditions, by economic factors like demand for the crop, its market prices, expected surplus etc., and social factors like tendency to follow the neighbour, food habits etc. The above factors varies from region to region and within the same region, from district to district. The variations in croping pattern influence naturally the quantum and quality of labour required, capacity to pay of farmers, mode of recruitment and mode of payment of wages of agriculture labourers.

In Table 3.14, the cropping pattern in nine selected villages has been shown with reference to percentage of acreage under principal crops and the percentage of farmers cultivating these principal crops. The table explains that, paddy was the main crop in almost all the villages except in Sanjeevapuram of Rayalaseema region. This may be due to lack of irrigation facilities in that village. In respect of second major crop it varies from village to village, sugarcane in Piridi, mustard and tobacco in Vangalapudi, Bengal gram in Guntupalle and cotton in Veerannapalem of Coastal Andhra, Banana in Rayalaseema, cotton in Jookal, jower in Raigir and groundnut in Andhra Nagar of Telangana. It shows clearly that the regional variations influenced the second principal crop.

As could be observed from the trend of three years under the study, the percentage of hectares under paddy had no significant variation in the three years. In respect of the farmers' involvement in the principal crops,

Table 3.14 : Cropping

(In hectares)

VILLAGE	1988–'89		1989–'90		1990–'91		AVERAGE	
	A	FI	A	FI	A	FI	A	FI
PIRIDI								
Paddy	55.15	97.14	65.98	100.00	58.22	100.00	64.60	99.04
Sugarcane	15.39	82.86	17.53	80.00	17.90	85.71	18.37	82.85
Jute	11.86	48.57	14.79	54.28	15.89	68.57	15.22	57.14
VANGALAPUDI								
Paddy	54.98	100.00	55.38	100.00	52.68	100.00	54.31	100.00
Mustard	11.00	31.43	13.06	37.14	11.66	40.00	11.91	36.19
Tobacco	16.05	25.71	14.78	22.86	14.81	22.86	15.20	23.81
GUNTUPALLE								
Paddy	50.80	94.28	55.61	94.29	51.29	100.00	52.53	196.19
Bengal Gram	45.82	88.57	44.07	85.71	46.08	97.14	45.33	90.47
VEERANNAPALEM								
Paddy	29.55	82.86	29.71	82.86	29.86	88.57	29.71	84.76
Cotton	70.45	88.57	70.29	91.43	70.14	94.28	70.29	91.42
BRAHMANAPALLE								
Paddy	45.28	77.14	40.12	80.00	37.91	71.43	41.15	76.19
Banana	19.29	51.43	18.25	54.28	20.39	57.14	19.28	54.28
SANEEVAPURAM								
Groundnut	97.35	94.28	97.96	94.28	91.46	97.14	95.75	95.23
JOOKAL								
Paddy	23.32	37.14	34.18	60.00	25.47	62.86	27.66	53.33
Cotton	29.89	62.86	20.13	65.71	33.97	88.57	28.00	72.38
Groundnut	27.90	51.43	30.81	60.00	21.84	51.43	26.58	54.28
Chillies	14.35	34.29	13.18	34.29	13.41	22.86	13.88	38.48
RAIGIR								
Paddy	40.04	77.14	45.34	77.14	37.02	74.25	40.60	76.17
Jowar	22.74	57.14	29.11	65.71	22.97	71.43	24.80	64.76
Castor Seeds	15.23	34.29	15.88	34.29	11.48	37.14	14.08	35.24
ANDHRA NAGAR								
Paddy	65.58	97.14	66.74	97.14	64.98	97.14	65.77	97.14
Groundnut	12.98	34.29	14.31	22.86	14.92	34.29	14.07	30.48

Note : A—Percentage of hectares under each principal crop.
FI—Percentage of farmers involved in each principal crop.

the trend is that, their involvement in paddy cultivation had increased in all the Coastal Andhra villages. But in Brahmanapalle of Rayalaseema, the farmers' involvement in paddy had decreased from second year (1989-90) to third year (1990-91) and it had increased in banana cultivation. Whereas in Jookal, farmers' involvement in paddy and cotton cultivation had increased but in case of chillies decreased. In Raigir farmers' involvement in paddy cultivation decreased from 77.14 per cent in 1989-90 to 74.25 in 1990-91. In respect of jowar cultivation, it increased from 57.14 in 1988-89 to 71.43 in 1990-91. In Andhra Nagar the farmers' involvement in paddy and groundnut cultivation i.e., 97.14 per cent and 34.29 remained almost constant in all the three years.

Average Yield Per Hectare

The economic position of the farmer mostly depends on the average yield per hectare and its market value. The farmer's paying capacity and extending other benefits to labourer is influenced by the yield and its value. Yield per hectare of major crops relating to three years is given in Table 3.15. The productivity of the major crops, during the study period (1988-'89 to 1990-'91) had steadily increased. In respect of cotton in Veerannapalem of Coastal Andhra, cotton and groundnut of Jookal and jowar of Raigir of Telangana, it was fluctuating marginally.

Taking into account the three year average yield of paddy per hectare of nine villages, Vangalapudi of coastal Andhra recorded highest yield of 74.15 bags of paddy and the lowest was recorded in Jookal of Telangana with 45.47 bags of paddy. In coastal Andhra, next to Vangalapudi, Guntupalle, Piridi and Veerannapalem recorded 68.91, 61.87 and 52.54 bags of paddy respectively. Whereas, in Rayalaseema, paddy was not the main crop. In Telangana, Andhra Nagar recorded 68.52 bags, Raigiri 53.90 bags and Jookal recorded only 45.47 bags. In respect of dry crops, cotton, jute, tobacco, banana, groundnut, orange, bengal gram and jowar were the main crops. The average yield of groundnut recorded highest in Brahmanapalle of Rayalaseema. Next to Brahmanapalle, Andhra Nagar recorded 28.50 bags. The lowest yield per hectare 17.46 bags was recorded in Jookal of Telangana.

Financial Performance of Farmers

a. Return on Investment (ROI)

More and more farmers have come to treat agriculture not as a way of living but as a business proposition. This attitude is getting strengthened with the application of latest techniques of farming, with high degree

Table 3.15 : Average Yield per Hectare

(In hectares)

VILLAGE AND CROPS		Qunatity	1988–'89	1989–'90	1990–'91	AVERAGE
PIRIDI						
Wet	–Paddy	Bags	50.64	52.29	54.71	52.54
	–Sugarcane	Tonnes	51.35	51.87	54.22	52.49
Dry	–Jute	Tonnes	18.55	18.53	20.30	19.17
VANGALAPUDI						
Wet	–Paddy	Bags	70.30	70.99	81.16	74.15
	–Mustard	Bags	8.18	7.51	8.82	8.15
Dry	–Tobbacco	Quintals	14.82	17.29	17.29	16.48
GUNTUPALLE						
Wet	–Paddy	Bags	68.79	68.79	69.16	68.91
	–Bengal Grams	Bags	6.79	7.41	7.41	7.21
VEERANNAPALEM						
Wet	–Paddy	Bags	61.92	55.75	67.97	61.87
Dry	–Cotton	Quintals	22.85	20.38	17.29	20.18
BRAHMANAPALLE						
Dry	–Groundnut	Quintals	30.88	32.11	32.11	31.69
	–Banana	Galas	2,024.02	2,038.39	2,124.82	2,062.40
SANJEEVAPURAM						
Dry	–Groundnut	Quintals	15.64	18.03	21.56	18.40
	–Orrange Fruits	No. in Thousands	74.10	76.57	80.28	76.99
JOOKAL						
Wet	–Paddy	Bags	41.05	45.74	49.65	45.47
Dry	–Cotton	Qunitals	24.90	19.96	19.59	21.49
	–Chillis	Quintals	18.11	16.67	18.23	17.66
	–Groundnut	Quintals	24.43	15.51	12.47	17.46
RAIGIR						
Wet	–Paddy	Bags	51.62	52.24	57.80	53.90
Dry	–Jowar	Bags	7.78	6.92	6.79	7.16
	–Castor Seeds	Quintals	6.79	6.60	5.31	6.22
ANDHRA NAGAR						
Wet	–Paddy	Bags	62.59	67.43	75.36	68.52
	–Groundnut	Quintals	21.00	30.55	33.96	28.50

of machanisation, improved varieties of seeds, chemical fertilisers, irrigation facilities etc. This environment is reinforced by the availability of marketing facilities and strong urge on the part of the farmer to maximise the surplus from agriculture.

An absolute measure of net income from agriculture can be calculated by deducting agricultural expenditure from agricultural gross income. But, the return on investment (ROI) is considered to be not only as a relative measure of net income from agriculture but also as an important yardstick of the performance of agricultural activity[1].

Table 3.16 shows Return on Investment in agriculture for the three years 1988-89, 89-90 and 90-91 and also its average for the three year period. It may be noted here that the Return on Investment is calculated based on the market value of land prevailing during 1983-84 which is considered to be as standard year. It is surprising to note that the Return on Investment was highest in Brahmanapalle with 26.94 per cent followed by Veerannapalem with 16.81 per cent Andhra Nagar with 13.94 per cent and Guntupalle with 12.76 per cent. This shows that the Return on Investment in almost all the villages with exception of Brahmanapalle was less than the bank rate of interest. It was only in Andhra Nagar, the Return of Investment was found to be increasing continuously and also significantly. Region wise Coastal Andhra stood first with 13.24 per cent followed by Telangana with 8.6 per cent and Rayalaseema with 8.14 per cent.

The above analysis of Return of Investment indicates unmistakably that the Return on Investment earned by the farmers in all the villages (exception being Brahmanapalle) was low and hence not satisfactory. This low return on Investment naturally restricts the paying capacity of the farmers in relation to the wages of agricultural labour. This situation naturally leads to shift of farmers from agricultural to non-agricultural pursits. The solution to this lies partly in improving the yield per acre and partly in obtaining the remunarative price for agricultural produce.

b. Surplus/Deficit

The financial position of farmers is shown in Table 3.17 for the three years 1988-89, 89-90 and 90-91.

The annual average net income from agriculture per farmer was found to be highest in Veerannapalem with Rs.50,465/- followed by

1. Return on investment is percentage of net income to investment i.e., market value of land as it prevails during 1983-'84.

Table 3.16 : Return on Investment from Agriculture

(In hectares)

REGION AND VILLAGE	1988–'89	1989–'90	1990–'91	AVERAGE
COASTAL ANDHRA				
Piridi	7.86	9.75	11.64	9.75
Vengalapudi	13.20	11.13	11.35	11.90
Guntupalle	11.35	10.46	16.47	12.76
Veerannapalem	21.08	19.25	10.11	16.81
OVERALL	**14.14**	**13.05**	**12.54**	**13.23**
RAYALASEEMA				
Brahmanapalle	29.17	27.01	24.62	26.94
Sanjeevapuram	3.91	–1.13	–11.80	–3.01
OVERALL	**13.32**	**9.35**	**1.74**	**8.14**
TELANGANA				
Jookal	12.43	2.99	5.63	7.02
Raigir	2.96	4.92	–3.29	1.53
Andhra Nagar	6.48	10.41	24.93	13.94
OVERALL	**6.25**	**7.35**	**12.24**	**8.61**
ANDHRA PRADESH	***11.54***	***10.70***	***10.82***	***11.02***

Note : ROI—ANIAPF/AMVLPF
ANIAPF—Annual Net Income from Agriculture Per Farmer
AMVLPF—Average Market Value of Land Per Farmer

Guntupalle with Rs.39,534/- and Vangalapudi with Rs.34,843/- and Andhra Nagar with Rs.32,294/-. Thus the average net income from agriculture per farmer for the three year period was found to be very high in Coastal Andhra with Rs.34,861/- followed by Telangana with Rs.13,330/- and Rayalaseema with Rs.6,065/-. It may be further noted that the annual average net income was negative in Sanjeevapuram indicating thereby the expenditure on agricultural activity was more than the gross income.

Some of the farmers had income from other sources also which is shown in the table 3.17. The annual average net income for the three year period refered above from other sources was found to be the highest in Raigir with Rs.6,969/- followed by Guntupalle with Rs.5,359/- Vangalapudi with Rs.2,543/- and Andhra Nagar with Rs.1,929/- and Veerannapalem with Rs.1,835/-.

Table 3.17 : Financial Performance of Farmers

(In ruppees)

REGION AND VILLAGE	Net Income from Agriculture	Net Income from other Sources	Total net Income	Family expenditure	Surplus or Deficit
PIRIDI					
1988–'89	11,767	815	12,582	19,923	–7,341
1989–'90	14,608	765	15,373	21,227	–5,854
1990–'91	17,430	1,730	19,160	23,758	–4,598
AVERAGE	**14,602**	**1,103**	**15,705**	**21,636**	**–5,931**
VANGALAPUDI					
1988–'89	38,680	2,212	40,892	28,539	12,253
1989–'90	32,590	2,731	35,321	30,651	4,670
1990–'91	33,260	2,686	35,946	31,779	4,167
AVERAGE	**39,534**	**2,543**	**37,386**	**30,323**	**7,063**
GUNTUPALLE					
1988–'89	35,168	5,341	40,509	37,421	3,088
1989–'90	32,424	5,357	37,781	39,136	–1,355
1990–'91	51,011	5,380	56,391	39,806	16,585
AVERAGE	**39,534**	**5,359**	**44,893**	**38,788**	**6,106**
VEERANNAPALEM					
1988–'89	63,232	1,987	65,219	36,447	28,772
1989–'90	57,817	1,566	59,383	37,672	21,711
1990–'91	30,344	1,951	32,295	44,072	–11,777
AVERAGE	**50,464**	**1,835**	**52,299**	**39,397**	**12,902**
COASTAL ANDHRA					
1988–'89	37,212	2,589	39,801	30,583	9,218
1989–'90	34,360	2,605	36,965	32,171	4,794
1990–'91	33,011	2,937	35,948	34,884	1,094
AVERAGE	**34,861**	**2,710**	**37,571**	**32,536**	**5,035**
BRAHMANAPALLE					
1988–'89	16,177	1,959	18,136	27,249	–9,113
1989–'90	14,982	1,210	16,192	28,994	–12,802
1990–'91	13,656	1,904	15,560	28,840	–13,289
AVERAGE	**14,938**	**1,691**	**16,629**	**28,364**	**–11,735**

(Contd..)

Table 3.17 : (Contd..)

(In ruppees)

REGION AND VILLAGE	Net Income from Agriculture	Net Income from other Sources	Total net Income	Family expenditure	Surplus or Deficit
SANJEEVAPURM					
1988–'89	3,650	654	4,304	23,119	–18,815
1989–'90	–1,057	635	–422	23,124	–23,546
1990–'91	–11,016	688	-10,328	25,896	–36,224
AVERAGE	**–2,808**	**659**	**–2,149**	**24,046**	**-26,195**
RAYALASEEMA					
1988–'89	9,913	1,306	11,219	25,184	–13,964
1989–'90	6,962	922	7,884	26,059	–18,174
1990–'91	1,320	1,296	2,616	27,372	–24,756
AVERAGE	**6,065**	**1,175**	**7,240**	**26,205**	**–18,965**
JOOKAL					
1988–'89	9,374	1,248	10,622	13,673	–3,051
1989–'90	2,251	1,253	3,504	13,900	–10,396
1990–'91	4,247	1,327	5,574	14,227	–8,653
AVERAGE	**5,291**	**1,276**	**6,567**	**13,600**	**–7,367**
RAIGIR					
1988–'89	4,560	6,622	11,272	22,984	–11,712
1989–'90	7,743	7,080	14,823	23,786	–8,963
1990–'91	–5,177	7,205	2,028	23,949	–21,921
AVERAGE	**2,405**	**6,969**	**9,374**	**23,573**	**–14,199**
ANDHRA NAGAR					
1988–'89	15,006	1,831	16,837	35,231	–18,394
1989–'90	24,124	1,921	26,046	37,112	–11,066
1990–'91	57,752	2,035	59,787	37,914	21,873
AVERAGE	**32,294**	**1,929**	**34,223**	**36,752**	**–2,513**
TELANGANA					
1988–'89	9,677	3,234	12,911	23,963	-11,052
1989–'90	11,373	3,418	14,791	24,933	-10,142
1990–'91	18,941	3,522	22,463	25,363	–2,900
AVERAGE	**13,330**	**3,391**	**16,721**	**24,753**	**–8,031**
ANDHRA PRADESH					
1988–'89	18,934	2,376	21,310	26,577	–5,267
1989–'90	17,565	2,315	19,880	27,721	–7,841
1990–'91	17,751	2,585	20,342	29,196	–8,854
AVERAGE	**18,085**	**2,425**	**20,510**	**27,831**	**–7,321**

The average annual net income from all sources is also given in the table 3.17. Veerannapalem, Guntupalle, Vangalapudi and Andhra Nagar occupied the first four places in that order.

The above average net income is available for family expenditure. The average annual expenditure per farmer and the ultimate surplus/deficit are also shown in the above table. The average annual family expenditure per farmer was found to be very high in relation to the average annual net income from all sources, in both the villages of Rayalaseema which resulted in heavy deficit to the farmers for all the three years. Further the deficit is found continuously in all the three villages of Telangana (the exception being Andhra Nagar for 1990-91). In Coastal Andhra the farmers of Piridi were suffering from deficit for all the three years under study. Guntupalle and Veerannapalem also experienced deficit atleast in one year of the study. Thus, the solitary exception was Vangalapudi which earned surplus although with the declining trend for all the three years under study.

The above analysis shows that the financial position of the farmers was not encouraging in all most all the villages with the exception of Vangalapudi. Incurring of continuous deficit would only make the farmers indebted more and more. This situation naturally discourages the farmers from taking more interest in agriculture. This inevitably restricts the paying capacity of the farmers in respect of wages to labourers. The solution to this situation lies partly in curtailing the family expenditure and partly in taking steps to increase the net income primarly from agriculture and secondarily from other sources.

Income of Labour:

Attached Labourers

The annual income of attached labourers is the determining factor of the standard of living of the attached labourers. The income may be obtained through different sources Viz., self employment, spouse employment and from other assets like land, house and livestock etc. An enquiry has been made into the sources of the income of attached labourers and particulars are shown in Table 3.18. The sources are broadly divided into three: *i)* self emloyment; *ii)* spouse employment and *iii)* all other sources.

The total annual income of attached labourers was Rs.3,515.42/- out of which, nearly 69 per cent of income was from the self employment and 25 per cent from the spouse employment and 6 per cent of income was

Table 3.18 : Average Annual Income of Each Attached Labour

REGION AND VILLAGE	SELF EMPLOYMENT			SPOUSE EMPLOYMENT			OTHER SOURCES			TOTAL	
	A(%)	B (Rs.)	C (%)	A(%)	B(Rs.)	C(%)	A(%)	B(Rs.)	C(%)	B(Rs.)	C(%)
COASTAL ANDHRA											
Piridi	100.00	2,120	67.31	100.00	1,030	32.69	--	--	--	3,150	100.00
Vangalapudi	100.00	2,360	76.13	80.00	740	23.87	--	--	--	3,100	100.00
Guntupalle	100.00	2,120	67.95	80.00	800	25.64	40	200	6.41	3,120	100.00
Veerannapalem	100.00	4,600	88.47	60.00	600	11.53	--	--	--	5,200	100.00
OVERALL	**100.00**	**2,800**	**76.87**	**80.00**	**792**	**21.76**	**10**	**50**	**1.37**	**3,642**	**100.00**
TELANGANA											
Jookal	100.00	2,280	62.99	80.00	640	17.67	80	700	19.34	3,620	100.00
Raigir	100.00	2,600	65.53	100.00	1,120	28.14	80	260	6.53	3,980	100.00
Andhra Nagar	100.00	3,340	72.30	100	1,160	25.11	20	120	2.59	4,620	100.00
OVERALL	**100.00**	**2,055**	**60.65**	**93.33**	**973**	**28.73**	**60**	**360**	**10.62**	**3,388**	**100.00**
ANDHRA PRADESH	***100.00***	***2,427***	***69.06***	***86.67***	***883***	***25.11***	***35***	***205***	***5.83***	***3,515***	***100.00***

Note : i. A—Percentage of Attached Labourers having income from this Source.
B—Average Annual Income from this Source
C—Percentage of Annual Income from this Source to the Total Annual Income from all Sources
ii. No Attached Labourers in Rayalaseema Villages.

from other sources (Table 3.18). Hence, it may pointed out that, most of the income was either from self employment or spouse employment. In Coastal Andhra, the income of attached labourers was more than the State average i.e., Rs.3,642.50/- whereas in Telangana, the attached labourer's income was only Rs.3,388.33/-. In Veerannapalem of Coastal Andhra, Jookal, Raigir and Andhra Nagar of Telangana, attached labourers were getting income more than that of State average and regional average. In Piridi of Coastal Andhra and Raigir and Andhra Nagar of Telangana, spouses of all attached labourers were employed. There were no other sources of income in Piridi, Vanagalapudi and Verannapalem of Coastal Andhra, while Jookal of Telangana recorded highest percentage of income from other sources.

Casual Labour

The average annual income of casual labourers was Rs.2,591.17; out of which, 59.81 per cent of income was from self employment 26.31 per cent of income was from spouse employment and 13.88 per cent from other sources (Table 3.19). In all, 68.40 per cent of the casual labourers' spouses were employed and only 24.40 per cent of casual labourers had other sources of income. The average annual income of casual labourers in Rayalaseema was less than that of the other two regions. Spouses of 41.43 percent of casual labour in Rayalaseema were employed, whereas in Coastal Andhra it was 80 per cent; and in Telangana it was 83.81 per cent. The highest average annual income was Rs.4,002.85 in Vangalapudi followed by Piridi with Rs.3,455.71 and Guntupalle with Rs.3,337.15 which were more than that of State average. The income of casual labourers from self employment was lowest in Rayalaseema compared to that of the two other regions and also State average. The highest income from the self employment of the casual labourers was Rs.2,362 in Vangalapudi followed by Guntupalle with Rs.2,173; Andhra Nagar with Rs.2,111.43 and Piridi with Rs.2,030 which were more than the State average as well as their respective regional averages. The average annual income from spouse employment was highest in Vangalapudi with Rs.1,497.14 followed by Guntupalle with Rs.1,035.43 Andhra Nagar of Telangana with Rs.928.57 which was highest than the of State average. It is worth mentioning that even though the percentage of spouse employment was same in Jookal and Andhra Nagar of Telangana and Vangalapudi and Guntupalle of Coastal Andhra, the income was more in Coastal Andhra villages probably due to variations in wage rates. Nearly 41 per cent of casual labourers in Telangana had other sources of income.

Table 3.19 : Average Annual Income of Each Casual Labour

REGION AND VILLAGE	SOURCES OF INCOME										
	SELF EMPLOYMENT			SPOUSE EMPLOYMENT			OTHER SOURCES			TOTAL	
	A(%)	B (Rs.)	C (%)	A(%)	B(Rs.)	C(%)	A(%)	B(Rs.)	C(%)	B(Rs.)	C(%)
COASTAL ANDHRA											
Piridi	100.00	2,030	58.76	82.86	744	21.53	42.85	681	19.71	3,456	100.00
Vangalapudi	100.00	2,363	59.03	91.43	1,497	37.41	5.79	143	3.56	4,003	100.00
Guntupalle	100.00	2,173	65.12	74.29	1,035	31.03	5.87	129	3.85	3,337	100.00
Veerannapalem	94.29	1,414	65.83	71.43	528	24.59	5.79	206	9.58	2,148	100.00
OVERALL	**98.57**	**1,995**	**61.66**	**80.00**	**951**	**29.39**	**15.07**	**290**	**8.95**	**3,235**	**100.00**
RAYALASEEMA											
Brahmanapalle	100.00	1,285	83.55	31.43	253	16.45	--	--	--	1,538	100.00
Sanjeevapuram	100.00	1,301	53.11	51.43	378	15.42	34.37	771	31.47	2,451	100.00
OVERALL	**100.00**	**1,293**	**64.85**	**41.43**	**316**	**15.82**	**17.18**	**386**	**19.33**	**1,995**	**100.00**
TELANGANA											
Jookal	100.00	1,809	59.44	91.43	709	23.29	34.29	526	17.27	3,043	100.00
Raigir	100.00	1,661	59.97	65.71	699	25.22	54.28	410	14.81	2,769	100.00
Andhra Nagar	100.00	2,111	63.66	94.29	929	27.99	34.36	277	8.35	3,317	100.00
OVERALL	**100.00**	**1,860**	**61.13**	**83.81**	**779**	**25.59**	**40.97**	**404**	**13.28**	**3,043**	**100.00**
ANDHRA PRADESH	***99.52***	***1,550***	***59.81***	***68.41***	***682***	***26.31***	***24.40***	***360***	***13.88***	***2,591***	***100.00***

Note : A—Percentage of Casual Labourers having income from this source.

B—Average Annual Income from this source

C—Percentage of annual Income from this source to the total annual income from all sources

The percentage of other sources' income was highest with 19.33 per cent in Telangana out of the three regions. It is interesting to note that the average annual income of casual labour in Coastal Andhra was highest probably due to continuous employment opportunity and also due to higher wage rates. This was followed by Telengana and Rayalaseema region.

Average Per Capita Income

Having considered average size of the family and its average annual income independently, it is now appropriate to study the average per capita income, which indicates directly the economic status of farmers, attached labourers and casual labourers (Table 3.20).

Table 3.20 : Average Per Capita Income of Farmers, Attached Labour and Casual Labour

REGION AND VILLAGE	Farmers Rs.	Attached Labour Rs.	Casual Labour Rs.
COASTAL ANDHRA			
Piridi	2,562	606	732
Vangalapudi	7,161	775	1,008
Guntupalle	10,501	780	671
Veerannapalem	6,116	1,300	537
OVERALL	**5,962**	**847**	**732**
RAYALASEEMA			
Brahmanapalle	1,835	--	354
Sanjeevapuram	–1,528	--	480
OVERALL	**343**	--	**422**
TELANGANA			
Jookal	1,206	696	666
Raigir	279	796	647
Andhra Nagar	10,695	963	707
OVERALL	**4,254**	**678**	**675**
ANDHRA PRADESH	***3,165***	***756***	***569***

Note : No Attached Labourers in Rayalaseema Villages

Farmers

The per capita income of farmers was highest in Andhra Nagar with Rs.10,695 followed by Guntupalle, Vangalapudi and Veerannapalem with Rs.10,501, Rs.7,161 and Rs.6,116 respectively.

In respect of casual labourers Vangalapudi stood first with Rs.1,008 followed by Piridi and Andhra Nagar with Rs.732 and Rs.707 respectively.

Thus, the analysis shows that the per capita income was highest in Coastal Andhra in respect of all the three groups—farmers, attached labourers and casual labourers. This was followed by Telangana and Rayalaseema.

Asset-Debt Ratio

The asset-debt ratio is a good indicator of the financial position. This ratio indicates the number of times each rupee of debt is covered by the assets of the respondent. Higher the ratio, larger the number of times each rupee of debt is covered by assets. The agriculture labourers who are economically poor generally live in an environment of very few assets in the form of a small piece of land, a small thatched house and one buffalo. But, they struggle with increasing amount of indebtedness.

Attached Labourers

The asset-debt ratio of attached labour is given in Table 3.21. It

Table 3.21 : Asset-Debt Ratio of Attached Labour

REGION AND VILLAGE	Average Value of Assets per Attached Labour Rs.	Average Amount of Debt per Attached Labour Rs.	Surplus Rs.	Asset Debt Ratio Rs.
COASTAL ANDHRA				
Piridi	720	60	660	12.00
Vangalapudi	320	22	298	14.54
Guntupalle	7,520	1,260	6,658	6.48
Veerannapalem	1,440	1,100	340	1.30
OVERALL	**2,500**	**586**	**1,989**	**4.26**
TELANGANA				
Jookal	18,840	480	18,360	39.25
Raigir	6,840	840	6,000	8.14
Andhra Nagar	2,560	560	2,000	4.57
OVERALL	**9,413**	**627**	**8,787**	**15.02**
ANDHRA PRADESH	***5,957***	***607***	***5,388***	***9.82***

Note : No Attached Labourers in Rayalaseema Villages

$$\text{Asset - Debt Ratio} = \frac{\text{Average value of Assets per AL}}{\text{Average amount of debt per AL}}$$

could be observed from this table that very surprisingly the ratio was highest in Jookal with 39.25 followed by Vangalapudi with 14.54 and Piridi with 12.00. The financial position of attached labourers in Telangana villages seems to be better comparable to that of Coastal Andhra villages.

Casual Labourers

The casual labourers of Vangalapudi were definitely in a much better financial position (Table 3.22) compared to casual labourers of all other villages. Each rupee of debt in this villages was covered by assets worth Rs.143.95/-, Piridi had an asset-debt ratio of 31.21 followed by Raigir with 21.47 and Jookal with 21.27. In all other villages, the asset-debt ratio was in single digit. Region wise, Coastal Andhra was in a better position with the ratio 26.21 followed by Telangana with 11.31 and Rayalaseema with 2.09.

Table 3.22 : Asset-Debt Ratio of Casual Labour

REGION AND VILLAGE	Average Value of Assets per Casual Labour Rs.	Average Amount of Debt per Casual Labour Rs.	Surplus Rs.	Asset Debt Ratio Rs.
COASTAL ANDHRA				
Piridi	7,151	229	6,921	31.21
Vangalapudi	16,820	117	16,694	143.95
Guntupalle	1,093	258	836	4.24
Veerannapalem	2,187	435	1,752	5.02
OVERALL	**3,406**	**260**	**6,551**	**26.51**
RAYALASEEMA				
Brahmanapalle	6,123	1,292	4,830	4.73
Sanjeevapuram	3,701	3,391	310	1.09
OVERALL	4,912	2,342	2,570	2.09
TELANGANA				
Jookal	6,559	308	6,251	21.27
Raigir	7,733	360	7,733	21.47
Andhra Nagar	2,616	825	1,791	3.16
OVERALL	**5,636**	**408**	**5,138**	**11.31**
ANDHRA PRADESH	***4,651***	***1,003***	***4,753***	***5.60***

Note: $\text{Asset - Debt Ratio} = \frac{\text{Average value of Assets per Casual Labour}}{\text{Average amount of debt per Casual Labour}}$

4

Procurement and Utilization

In this chapter, an attempt is made to discuss the issues relating to recruitment, utilisation, leave and absenteeism of agricultural labour.

Recruitment and Selection

Recruitment constitutes the first operative function of human resource management. It is concerned with obtaining right quality and right number of personnel necessary to accomplish organisational goals. It deals specifically with such subjects as the determination human resource requirement and their recruitment, selection and placement.[1]

Significance of Recruitment and Selection

Recruitment is generally regarded as the first major function of human resource management. It includes human resource planning, recruitment and selection. Earlier, much attention had not been paid to these processes. But, with the growth of industrialisation and development of social sciences, the need to determine human resources both in terms of quantity and quality has been realised. The increasing competition in the product market have all emphasised the importance of recruitment function. The human resource is perhaps the last great cost that is relatively unmanaged.[2] This may be an over statement but it is true that human resource planning traditionally has not received the same

1. Edwin B. Flippo, *Personnel Management* (New York: McGraw Hill Book Company, 1987), p.6.
2. Charless F. Russ Jr., "Manpower Planning Systems:Part II," *Personnel Journal,* 61 (February, 1982),p.123.

attention as other components of business planning. Indeed, neglecting human resources in the planning process can be very disruptive if adequately trained people are not available when needed.[1]

Employee selection is perhaps the most significant task that manager performs. If a mediocre or poor performer is hired, a firm cannot be successful even of it has a perfect plan, a sound organisational structure and fine tuned control systems. Only when competent people are available, they only "make things happen".[2] It almost goes without saying that the calibre of the work force of an organisation largely determines its strength and its success as an enterprise.[3] If right people are selected, the remaining functions of human resource management become easier, the employee contribution and commitment will be at optimum level and employee and employer relations will be constructive, cooperative and congenial. If the right person is selected he is a valuable asset to the organisation and if faulty selection is made the employee will become a liability to the organisation.[4]

Employment in Agriculture

As already explained in chapter I, employment in agriculture has certain pecularities as compared to industry. For millions of persons born in rural areas there is no escape from an agricultural career. While other industries are selective and attract roughly that number of candidates who can find accommodation, agriculture starts with too many candidates; neither selection nor rejection is possible. Another outstanding feature of employment in agriculture is its seasonal character.

The quantum of agricultural employment and its pattern also depends upon many factors - the extent of land utilisation, cultivated area, single cropped and double cropped areas, irrigated area, crops grown, duration of crop seasons and size of land holdings.

While thus the demand for wage paid to agricultural labour is indeterminate, the supply side is generally one of over abundance. There

---

1. Douglas B. Gehrman, "Objective Based Human Resource Planning", *Personnel Journal,* 16 (December,1981), p.942.
2. R.Wayne Mondy, Robert M.No III, *Human Resource Management* (Boston: Allyn and Bacon, 1990), p.208.
3. Dale S.Beach,*Personnel : The Management of People at Work* (New York: Macmillan Publishing Co.,INC, 1975) p.224.
4. P. Subba Rao and V. S. P. Rao, *Personnel/Human Resource Management* (Delhi:Konark Publishers Pvt.,Ltd., 1990), p.181.

are at the same time local shortages and surpluses in different regions depending upon the agricultural labour market which has its own imperfections and there is a certain amount of unplanned mobility from surplus areas to areas of labour shortage during busy seasons. The availability of women and child labour for agricultural work is another factor which also influences the supply of labour.

Source of Recruitment

When the human resource planning indicates the need for employees, the firm may evaluate alternative ways to meet this demand. When other alternatives[1] are not appropriate, the recruitment process starts. Frequently, recruitment begins when a manager initiates an amployee requisition. The next step in the recruitment process is to determine whether qualified employees are available within the firm (the internal source) or must be recruited from external sources, such as colleges, universities and other organisations. Because of the high cost of recruiting, organisations need to utilise the most productive recruitment sources and methods available. Recruitment sources are where qualified individuals can be found. Recruitment methods are the specific means by which potential employees can be attracted to the firm. When the sources of potential employees have been identified, appropriate methods for either internal or external recruitment are used to accomplish recruitment objectives.[2]

a. Mode of Securing Labour

It is necessary to enquire into the mode of securing labourers both attached and casual- as it influences the quality, quantity and time of availability of labour. As shown in Table 4.1, at State level,while the most important mode of securing attached labourers was through other attached labourers, the most important mode of securing casual labour was through direct contact. The next important mode for securing both attached labourers and casual labourers was through casual labourers. 'Other farmers' constituted the third important mode of securing both attached labourers and casual labourers . At regional and village level, the same modes occupy first three places with minor differences. This shows that the use of services of professional middlemen in securing labour have not become prominent with the exception of Guntupalle and

1. Alternatives are Viz.,overtime, sub-contracting, Temporary employees, employee leasing etc.
2. R.Wayne Mondy, Robert M. Noe III, *Human Resource Management* (Boston : Allyn and Bacon, 1990), pp.174-175.

Veerannapalem where this mode occupied first place in securing casual labourers. In Piridi this mode is slowly becoming prominent with second rank in securing casual labourers and third rank in securing attached labourers.

Thus, this table shows that while attached labourers were secured mostly through other attached labourers and casual labourers; the casual labourers were secured either through direct contact or through other casual labourers.

Table 4.1 : Farmers' Ranking of Mode of Securing Attached and Casual Labour

REGION AND VILLAGE	Mode of Securing Attached Labour and Casual Labour									
	TDC		TAL		TCL		TOF		TPM	
	AL	CL	AL	CL	AL	CL	AL	CL	AL	CL
COASTAL ANDHRA										
Piridi	IV	I	I	III	II	IV	IV	V	III	II
Vangalapudi	III	I	II	III	I	II	II	V	IV	IV
Guntupalle	IV	II	I	V	II	III	III	IV	IV	I
Veerannapalem	IV	II	I	III	II	V	III	IV	--	I
OVERALL	**IV**	**I**	**I**	**III**	**II**	**IV**	**III**	**V**	**V**	**II**
RAYALASEEMA										
Brahmanapalle	--	I	--	--	--	II	--	III	--	IV
Sanjeevapuram	--	I	--	--	--	II	--	III	--	IV
OVERALL	**--**	**I**	**--**	**--**	**--**	**II**	**--**	**III**	**--**	**IV**
TELANGANA										
Jookal	V	I	III	III	I	II	II	IV	IV	--
Raigir	V	I	II	II	I	III	IV	IV	III	--
Andhra Nagar	V	II	I	III	II	I	III	IV	IV	V
OVERALL	**V**	**I**	**II**	**III**	**I**	**II**	**III**	**IV**	**IV**	**V**
ANDHRA PRADESH	***V***	***I***	***I***	***V***	***II***	***II***	***III***	***III***	***IV***	***IV***

Note i) Ranking of different modes is decided after applyjng weighted score to each item of response. Thus, first rank is given three marks; second-two; and the third is given one.

ii) No Attached Labour in Rayalaseema Villages.

iii) TDC—Through Direct Contact;
TAL—Through Attached Labour
TCL—Through Casual Labour
TOF—Through Other Farmers
TPM—Through Professional Middlemen.

iv) AL—Attached Labour; CL—Casual Labour

b. Problems of Procurement

An enquiry was made into the problems faced by the farmers in procuring labourers and the problems faced by the labourers in securing employment. As shown in Table 4.2 while 28 percent of farmers were facing problems in procuring attached labourers, 47 percent of farmers were facing problems in procuring casual labourers. This problem was of serious magnitude in recruting casual labourers particularly in villages like Vangalapudi and Guntupalle of Coastal Andhra; Brahmanapalle and Sajeevapuram of Rayalaseema and Andhra Nagar of Telangana. It may be noted in this context, that all these villages are located close to cities/towns and consequently farmers of theses villages must have been facing the problem of non-availability of adequate casual labourers at the right time due to the labourers demanding for higher wage rates taking the advantage of employment opportunities in nearby cities/towns.

Table 4.2 : Percentage of Farmers Facing Problems in Procuring Labour and Percentage of Labour Facing Problems in Securing Employment

REGION AND VILLAGE	Farmers' Facing Problems AL	Farmers' Facing Problems CL	Labourers Facing Problems AL	Labourers Facing Problems CL
COASTAL ANDHRA				
Piridi	14.29	8.57	40.00	80.00
Vangalapudi	27.27	57.14	20.00	60.00
Guntupalle	40.00	71.43	--	97.14
Veerannapalem	--	28.57	80.00	91.43
OVERALL	**21.28**	**41.43**	**35.00**	**82.14**
RAYALASEEMA				
Brahmanapalle	--	71.43	--	88.57
Sanjeevapuram	--	57.14	--	88.57
OVERALL	--	**64.28**	--	**88.57**
TELANGANA				
Jookal	33.33	25.71	41.00	97.14
Raigir	30.00	40.00	60.00	91.43
Andhra Nagar	46.67	65.71	--	77.14
OVERALL	**38.23**	**43.81**	**33.33**	**88.57**
ANDHRA PRADESH	***28.40***	***47.30***	***34.31***	***85.71***

Note i. No Attached Labourers in Rayalaseema

ii. AL–Attached Labour; CL–Casual Labour.

The labourers were also enquired into the problems faced by them in securing employment. Most of the casual labourers-about 86 percent expressed that they were facing problems in securing employment. Most of the attached labourers of Veerannapalem of Coastal Andhra and Raigir of Telangana also reported these problems.

The above analysis invariably emphasises that the present arrangement of securing attached labourers and casual labourers cannot serve the best interests of both farmers and labourers in the longrun. Setting up of an organised agency with which the labourers register their names seeking employment and to which the farmers send their requisitions for supplying labour may be considered to put the entire system of employment of agricultural labour on an organised basis. The details of the institutional frame work are given latter.

Basis of Selection/Joining

The number of labourers may certainly differ with respect to the size of landholdings under cultivation. Bigger cultivating families had their attached farm labour[1] and larger a farm higher is usually the proportion of hired labour in its total labour input.[2]

Cultivators and labourers assumed different roles. The process of coming together and the maintenance of these roles always indicate the quality of the mutual relations. Hence the recruitment pattern of labour by the cultivators bears significant position in agrarian structure which was different in various areas. By the very nature of agrarian character, it is quite natural that recruitment of labourers by the cultivators will be based on the ability and efficiency of service.[3] The hierarchies of caste and land relations set limits about who will serve whom in agricultural operations. Polluting castes are usually less preferable, but they are employed for supplementary labour in times of certain needs, Oommen[4] has observed in this respect that among landlords, small holders also employ labour due to caste prejudice. Very often it was found in our society that caste had its deep-rooted influence in the recruitment of labour.

---

1. T.C. Varghese, *Agrarian Change and Economic Consequences* (Bombay : Allied Publishers, 1970).
2. Biplab Dasgupta, *The New Agrarian Technology and India*, (Bombay : McMillon Company, 1977).
3. A. Lukose, *Labour Movements and Agrarian Relations* (Jaipur : Rawat Publications, 1991), p.42.
4. M.A. Oommen, *Land Reforms and Agrarian Change in Kerala Economy Since Independence* (New Delhi: Oxford and IBH Publishing Company).

a. Basis of Selection

It is interesting to enquire into farmers' basis of selection of labourers- both attached labourers and casual labourers. Table 4.3 provides the information relating to this enquiry. "Trust worthiness" and "Skill and Capacity to work" were the two major bases on which most of the attched labourers were selected in all the villages. It is needless to mention that the nature and place of work of attached labour naturally demand the fulfilment of the criteria of "trust worthiness". Consequently this was given first priority by the farmers in selecting attached labourers in most of the villages. The skill and capacity to work of attached labourers was found to be next important consideration. In respect of casual labourers, where "trust worthiness" was not the main consideration, `their availability' followed by `skill and capacity to work' were taken into consideration in most of the villages.

Table 4.3 : Basis of Selection of Labour-Farmers' Ranking

REGION AND	WB		TW		SCW		A		FBG		AD	
VILLAGE	AL	CL	AL	CL	AL	CL	AL	CL	AL	CL	AL	CL
COASTAL ANDHRA												
Piridi	IV	III	I	IV	II	II	IV	I	III	V	V	VI
Vangalapudi	III	IV	II	III	I	II	I	I	IV	V	--	--
Guntupalle	IV	IV	I	I	II	III	III	II	IV	V	--	VI
Veerannapalem	IV	IV	I	I	II	III	III	II	--	V	--	--
OVERALL	**IV**	**IV**	**I**	**II**	**II**	**III**	**III**	**I**	**V**	**V**	**VI**	**VI**
RAYALASEEMA												
Brahmanapalle	--	IV	--	III	--	II	--	I	--	V	--	--
Sanjeevapuram	--	IV	--	II	--	I	--	III	--	--	--	--
OVERALL	--	**IV**	--	**III**	--	**II**	--	**I**	--	**V**	--	--
TELANGANA												
Jookal	V	V	III	III	I	II	II	I	IV	IV	V	--
Raigir	V	IV	II	I	I	II	IV	III	III	V	--	VI
Andhra Nagar	V	IV	II	III	II	II	III	I	IV	V	--	VI
OVERALL	**V**	**IV**	**II**	**III**	**I**	**II**	**III**	**I**	**IV**	**V**	**VI**	**VI**
ANDHRA PRADESH	***V***	***VI***	***I***	***III***	***II***	***II***	***III***	***I***	***IV***	***V***	***VI***	***VI***

Note i) No Attached Labour in Rayalaseema Villages.

ii) WB—Wage and Benefits; TW—Trust Worthiness; SCW—Skill and capacity to Work; A—Availability; FBG—Family Back Ground; AD—Amicable Disposition.

iii) AL—Attached Labour; CL—Casual Labour.

b. Reasons for joining Employment

The labourers must have their own reasons for joining employment under particular farmer. As could be observed from Table 4.4 most of the attached labourers were found to be guided by the consideration of the farmers readiness to help in times of need. The next important consideration for them was the farmers treatment. The casual labourers too followed the same consideration in seeking employment with different farmers. Their economic indebtedness inevitably makes them to get themselves tied to particular farmers who extend credit as and when required. While this situation is tolerable in the short run, it cannot be in the long run as it restricts the freedom of employment and opportunities of improving his economic status. Setting up of an independent agency with the support of farmers and labourers is likely to break these bonds and make the labourers to act independently.

Table 4.4 : Reasons for Joining Employment Under this Farmer-Labour Opinion

REGION AND	R		SES		RT		T		ECF		VWI	
VILLAGE	AL	CL	AL	CL	AL	CL	AL	CL	AL	CL	AL	CL
<u>**COASTAL ANDHRA**</u>												
Piridi	III	II	II	V	I	I	I	III	IV	IV	--	VI
Vangalapudi	IV	II	IV	VI	I	III	II	I	III	IV	VI	V
Guntupalle	--	IV	--	I	I	III	II	IV	III	II	IV	--
Veerannapalem	III	II	IV	VI	I	I	II	III	--	IV	--	V
OVERALL	**V**	**II**	**IV**	**IV**	**I**	**I**	**II**	**III**	**III**	**VI**	**VI**	**VI**
<u>**RAYALASEEMA**</u>												
Brahmanapalle	--	III	--	IV	--	I	--	II	--	V	--	--
Sanjeevapuram	--	II	--	V	--	I	--	III	--	IV	--	--
OVERALL	--	**III**	--	**IV**	--	**I**	--	**II**	--	**V**	--	--
<u>**TELANGANA**</u>												
Jookal	V	VI	II	V	I	I	II	II	IV	IV	V	III
Raigir	III	V	IV	IV	I	I	IV	II	II	III	--	VI
Andhra Nagar	IV	IV	I	VI	II	I	II	II	IV	III	--	V
OVERALL	**V**	**IV**	**II**	**V**	**I**	**I**	**III**	**II**	**IV**	**III**	**VI**	**VI**
ANDHRA PRADESH	***V***	***III***	***III***	***V***	***I***	***I***	***II***	***II***	***IV***	***IV***	***VI***	***VI***

Note i) No Attached Labour in Rayalaseema Villages.

ii) R—Remuneration; SES—Social and Economic Status;
RT—Readiness to Help in Times of Need; T—Treatment;
ECF—Earlier Contact and Familiarity; VWI—Volume of work Involved

iii) AL—Attached Labour; CL—Casual Labour.

Utilization

Nature of Employment

While industrial labour is relatively characterised by continuity of employment, agricultural labour has its peak and slack seasons. While peak seasons may offer optimum level of employment to agricultural labour, in other seasons, the position is just the reverse. Holdings of small size, with population pressure increasing in its incidence, hardly provide adequate employment to all working members, either of the land holders or of agriculture labour families. They need to be continuously in search of other avenues of employment, wage paid or otherwise which being scare, reduce them to surplus working force exposed to under-employment and unemployment.

Attached Labourers are employed for a longer period, the duration of employment contract varying usually from three months to one year. Land holdings who have the need and capacity to employ them are limited in number. Unless there is routine work to be attended daily, land owners need not appoint them. This routine work ranges from tending cattle, cleaning the pen, preparing cattle feed, milking cattle,making dung cakes, doing some work in the field like levelling and embanking. Generally speaking, it is only land holders who have atleast a medium size holding, and have milk cattle and draught animals, find it economical to employ attached labourer. There is continuity of employment for these labourers. Only men are generally employed as attached labourers. In certain cases, children are also employed for grazing cattle/doing domestic work.

Casual Labourers are free to engage themselves in different types of wage employment while attached workers are not. The casual labourers are engaged in ploughing and preparation of land; transplantation, weeding and harvesting operations. The number of days engaged in a season/year varies. Further, the working day of the agricultural labourer also shows considerable variations. During the peak seasons of agricultural activity, the working days are longer, while they are shorter during weeding or preparatory operations. The hours of work of women labourers particularly are shorter in operations (weeding, transplanting, etc.) in which they are usually employed.

a. Nature Of Work Rendered By Attached Labourers

The nature of work entrusted to attached labourers generally consisted of household duties, work on agricultural fields; supervision over routine agricultural activities and livestock maintenance etc. An enquiry into the nature of work entrusted to attached labourers showed that work on agricultural fields, followed by livestock maintenance and supervision over routine agricultural activities were the major activities of work as indicated by Table 4.5.

Table 4.5 : Ranking of Nature of Work Entrusted to Attached Labour

REGION AND	Farmers' Response				Labourers' Response				
VILLAGE	HHD	WA	SAA	LM	HHD	WA	SAA	LM	Others
COASTAL ANDHRA									
Piridi	III	I	III	II	--	I	III	II	III
Vangalapudi	III	I	IV	II	II	I	III	I	--
Guntupalle	I	II	III	II	I	I	I	--	--
Veerannapalem	II	I	--	--	--	I	--	--	--
OVERALL	**III**	**I**	**IV**	**II**	**II**	**I**	**II**	**III**	**IV**
TELANGANA									
Jookal	I	--	II	I	III	I	III	II	--
Raigir	IV	--	III	II	--	I	II	III	--
Andhra Nagar	III	I	IV	II	I	I	II	III	--
OVERALL	**III**	**I**	**IV**	**II**	**IV**	**I**	**II**	**III**	--
ANDHRA PRADESH	***III***	***I***	***IV***	***II***	***IV***	***I***	***II***	***III***	***V***

Note i) No Attached Labour in Rayalaseema Villages.
ii) HHD—House Hold Duties; WA—Work on Agricultural Fields
SAA—Supervision Over Routine Agricultural Activities; LM—Live Stock Maintenance

b. Operational Land Holdings vs Employment of Attached Labour

It is generally believed that the size of operational land holding influence the employment of attached labourers. Larger the size of operational land holding more the requirement of the services of attached labourers. It is with this view the relationship between operational land holding and employment of attached labourers is assessed and the information is presented in Table 4.6.

It could be observed from the table that positive relationship between operational land holdings and the employment of attached labourers may be found in the study. As the size of operational holding increases, the percentage of farmers engaging attached labourers also increases. Thus, the percentage of farmers engaging attached labourers at State level increased from 10 per cent under 'marginal' group to 80 per

Table 4.6 : Operational Land Holding *vs.* Employment of Attached Labour

REGION AND VILLAGE	Marginal <1	Small 1–2	Semi-Medium 2–4	Medium 4–10	Large >10
COASTAL ANDHRA					
Piridi	50.00	45.45	66.67	75.00	50.00
Vangalapudi	--	--	26.67	33.33	100.00
Guntupalle	--	25.00	16.67	14.29	66.67
Veerannapalem	--	--	--	7.69	75.00
OVERALL	**16.67**	**28.57**	**38.24**	**23.33**	**72.22**
TELANGANA					
Jookal	--	33.33	37.50	--	--
Raigir	50.00	12.50	20.00	60.00	100.00
Andhra Nagar	--	--	36.36	50.00	100.00
OVERALL	**7.14**	**17.24**	**32.43**	**50.00**	**100.00**
ANDHRA PRADESH	***10.00***	***22.00***	***35.21***	***29.49***	***80.00***

Note: i. No Attached Labour in Rayalaseema Villages.
ii. Land Holding Size Groups in Hectares.

cent under 'large' group. The same trend is applicable in respect of Coastal Andhra and Telangana regions and in Vangalapudi, Veerannapalem, Raigir and Andhra Nagar villages.

Mode of Employment

The mode of employment influences to some extent the employment security and the relations between the farmers and labourers. The two important modes of employment are *i*) employment on contract basis and *ii*) employment on daily wage basis. The employment on contract basis provides secured employment for the period of contract and develops long term relationships between the two parties. The employment on daily wage basis provides neither employment security nor develops attachment between the two parties. As shown in Table 4.7, 70 per cent of casual labourers were on daily wage and the remaining were on both contractual and daily wage basis. The practice of employing casual labourers on contract basis was largely prevalent in Piridi, Vangalapudi and Guntupalle of Coastal Andhra and Andhra Nagar of Telangana. In all other villages, the casual labourers were employed mostly on daily wage basis.

Table 4.7 : Mode of Employment of Casual Labour

REGION AND VILLAGE	On Contract Basis %	Daily Wages Basis %	Both %	Total %
COASTAL ANDHRA				
Piridi	2.86	31.43	65.71	100.00
Vangalapudi	--	--	100.00	100.00
Guntupalle	--	60.00	40.00	100.00
Veerannapalem	--	94.29	5.71	100.00
OVERALL	**0.71**	**46.43**	**52.86**	**100.00**
RAYALASEEMA				
Brahmanapalle	--	100.00	--	100.00
Sanjeevapuram	--	97.14	2.86	100.00
OVERALL	--	98.57	1.43	100.00
TELANGANA				
Jookal	--	100.00	--	100.00
Raigir	--	100.00	--	100.00
Andhra Nagar	--	51.43	48.57	100.00
OVERALL	--	**83.81**	**16.19**	**100.00**
ANDHRA PRADESH	***0.32***	***70.48***	***29.21***	***100.00***

Duration of Employment

a. Annual Employment

The average number of days of employment of casual labour at State level was worked out at 172 days in the year (Table 4.8). While Piridi and Vangalapudi of Coastal Andhra; Brahmanapalle of Rayalaseema and Andhra Nagar of Telangana were above the State average, all other five villages were below the State average in providing employment to their casual labourers. Further, Brahamanapalle stood first in providing maximum number of days of employment with 225 days for all the seasons followed by Vangalapudi with 221 days and Andhra Nagar with 208 days. Availability of assured inigation facilities and practice of multiple cropping might have been responsible for providing employment to casual labourers for large number of days in these villages.

However, the casual labourers may not get employment to that extent. Hence, it has been enquired into as to the percentage distribution of casual labourers, by days of emplyoment. It could be observed from

Table 4.8 that slightly more than one third of casual labourers could get employment between 50 and 150 days. Half of the casual labourers had managed to secure employment between 150 and 250 days. Only ten percent of casual labourers were fortunate enough to secure employment for more than 250 days. Village wise, Brahmanapalle of Rayalaseema and Andhra Nagar of Telangana stood first in providing employment between 150-250 days in a year to 80 per cent of their casual labourers followed by Jookal of Telangana and Piridi of Coastal Andhra which provided employment in the same bracket to 74 per cent and 63 per cent of their casual labourers respectively. As already observed, Veerannapalem was at the lowest rung of the ladder in providing employment to casual labourers as all of them could secure employment for less than 150 days. Majority of casual labourers were in the employment bracket of less than 150 days in Gunutupalle, Sanjeevapuram and Raigir.

Table 4.8 : Percentage Distribution of Casual Labour by Days of Employment

REGION AND VILLAGE	Av. No. of worked per Labourer	Number of days worked per Year			
		50–150 %	150–250 %	250–350 %	Total %
COASTAL ANDHRA					
Piridi	190.29	20.00	62.86	17.14	100.00
Vangalapudi	221.43	--	54.29	45.71	100.00
Guntupalle	149.29	51.43	48.57	--	100.00
Veerannapalem	103.29	100.00	--	--	100.00
OVERALL	**166.08**	**42.86**	**41.43**	**15.71**	**100.00**
RAYALASEEMA					
Brahmanapalle	224.57	2.86	80.00	17.14	100.00
Sanjeevapuram	138.71	54.29	42.86	2.86	100.00
OVERALL	**181.64**	**28.57**	**61.43**	**10.00**	**100.00**
TELANGANA					
Jookal	163.43	25.71	74.29	--	100.00
Raigir	133.00	68.57	31.43	--	100.00
Andhra Nagar	208.00	11.43	80.00	8.57	100.00
OVERALL	**168.14**	**35.24**	**61.90**	**2.86**	**100.00**
ANDHRA PRADESH	***171.95***	***37.14***	***52.70***	***10.16***	***100.00***

b. Seasonal Employment

The agricultural activity is largely seasonal and consequently the duration of employment of casual labourers varies from season to season. It is interesting to enquire into the percentage of casual labourers having employment available in each season. It may be mentioned in this context, that the seasonal employment influences wage rate, total earnings and thereby standard of living. Table 4.9 shows average number of days of employment in different seasons and the percentage of casual labourers having employment in each season. It could be observed from this table that cent per cent of casual labourers have got employment in rainy and winter seasons-the two main seasons of agricultural activity. In summer, with the exception of very few casual labourers in Piridi, Guntupalle and Veerannapalem of Coastal Andhra and Sanjeevapuram of Rayalaseema all others were having employment in summer season also. But the employment is not provided to casual labourers throughout each season. The number of days employed in each season is given in this table. On an average, at State level, the casual labourers were employed for 63 days in rainy season, 59 days in winter season, 50 days in summer season and for 172 days in all seasons. Thus the casual labourers were unemployed for nearly half of the year. Village wise Vangalapudi stood first in providing maximum number of days of employment (83 days) followed by Andhra Nagar with 77 days and Brahmanapalle with 76 days in rainy season. Brahmanapalle stood first in providing maximum number of days of employment with 74 days followed by Vangalapudi with 73 days and Andhra Nagar with 70 days in winter season. In respect of summer season Brahmanapalle again stood first with 74 days followed by Vangalapudi with 66 days and Piridi with 62 days. The lowest number days of employment for all the seasons was found in Veerannapalem with 44 days, 42 days and 17 days for rainy, winter and summer seasons respectively.

Leave and Absenteeism

Meaning, Significance and Control

Leave refers to authorised absence. It is meant to enable the worker to attend to personal work. It is also meant to remain absent during such contingences as sickness or accident which are often beyond the control of the worker. It is a common practice with all organisations to grant leave for the worker for some specific period and often such leave becomes a part of conditions of employment and becomes a right of the employee to enjoy the same.

Table 4.9 : Average Seasonal Employment of Casual Labour

REGION AND VILLAGE	Average Number of Days of Employment											
	Rainy Season (123 days)			*Winter Season* (120 days)			*Summer Season* (122 days)			*All Seasons* (365 days)		
	PCN	AND	PDTS	PCN	AND	PDTS	PCN	AND	PDTS	PCN	AND	PDTS
COASTAL ANDHRA												
Piridi	100	66.58	54.57	100	61.42	51.18	97.14	62.29	51.06	99.04	190.29	52.28
Vangalapudi	100	83.15	68.16	100	72.57	60.48	100.00	65.71	53.86	100.00	221.43	60.83
Guntupalle	100	55.72	45.67	100	54.71	45.59	97.14	38.86	31.85	99.04	149.29	41.01
Veerannapalem	100	44.29	36.30	100	41.72	34.77	34.28	17.28	14.16	78.09	103.29	28.37
OVERALL	**100**	**62.43**	**51.17**	**100**	**57.60**	**48.00**	**82.14**	**46.03**	**37.73**	**94.04**	**166.08**	**45.62**
RAYALASEEMA												
Brahmanapalle	100	76.00	62.29	100	74.28	61.90	100.00	74.29	60.89	100.00	224.57	61.69
Sanjeevapuram	100	48.58	39.82	100	45.71	38.09	97.14	44.42	36.41	99.04	138.71	38.11
OVERALL	**100**	**62.29**	**51.06**	**100**	**59.99**	**49.99**	**98.57**	**59.35**	**48.65**	**99.52**	**181.64**	**49.90**
TELANGANA												
Jookal	100	64.58	52.93	100	61.71	51.42	100.00	37.14	30.44	100.00	163.43	44.90
Raigir	100	50.00	40.98	100	47.28	39.40	100.00	35.72	29.28	100.00	133.00	36.54
Andhra Nagar	100	77.43	63.47	100	69.71	50.09	100.00	60.86	50.72	100.00	208.00	57.14
OVERALL	**100**	**64.00**	**52.46**	**100**	**59.56**	**49.63**	**100.00**	**44.57**	**36.53**	**100.00**	**168.14**	**46.19**
ANDHRA PRADESH	***100***	***62.90***	***51.56***	***100***	***59.05***	***49.21***	***93.57***	***49.98***	***40.97***	***97.85***	***171.95***	***47.24***

Note : PCN—Percentage of Casual Labourers having Employment,
AND—Average Number of Days.
PDTS–Percentage of Days Employed in the total days of this season.

Absenteeism is a condition that exists when a person fails to come to work, when he is scheduled to work.[1] According to Labour Bureau, Simla "Absenteeism is the total manshifts lost because of absence as a percentage of the total number of manshifts scheduled to work.[2] It signifies the absence of an employee from work when he is scheduled to be at work; it is unauthorised, unexplained, avoidable and willful absence from work.

The tendency to absent on the part of the worker can be an obstacle in the smooth running of the organisation. The incidence of absenteeism affects adversely not only the organisation but also the worker who remains absent. It is believed that when workers stay away in an unpredictable manner, employers find it impossible to plan production. Absenteeism hinders proper manpower planning and thereby affects the quality of industrial relations. Thus a business organisation looks at absenteeism as a pathological feature which interferes with its smooth functioning.[3] The worker does not remain unaffected by this problem. If he shows unpredictable behaviour in absenting himself, it is a reflection on his commitment to the job. The periods of absence beyond the authorised limits, will result in loss of earnings which effects his standard living as well as his morale.

A number of factors are attributed for the incidence of absenteeism. The general causes are viz., maladjustment with organisation, sickness, industrial fatigue, social and religious ceremonies, unhealthy working conditions, indebtedness, alcohalism, unsatisfactory housing conditions. inadequate leave facilities, etc.

Steps to Control

The problem of absenteeism needs a multi-pronged attack, if it is to be effectively controlled. Infact all the factors which lead to absenteeism have to be counteracted. Labour Investigation Committee, 1946 refering to the measures to be adopted in this regard, was of the opinion that "proper.conditions of work, adequate wages, protection from accidents and sickness and facilities for obtaining leave for rest and recreation constitute the most effective means of reducing absenteeism".[4] To deal

---

1. Flippo B Edwin, *Personnel Management* (New York : McGraw-Hill Book Company, 1987), p.533.
2. *Indian Labour Statistics* (Simla : Bureau of Labour, 1962),p.16.
3. Baldev R. Sharma, "Absenteeism: A search for correlates", *Indian Journal of Industrial Relations,* Vol.5, No.3, (January 1970), p.267.
4. Report of the Labour Investigation Committee, p.101.

with this problem, both negative disciplinary action and positive reinforcement programmes based on organisational behaviour modification have been used with success[1] in industry.

Leave and Absenteeism in Agriculture Sector

The farmer is concerned with the problem of absenteeism particularly in busy agricultural operations like tilling, sowing, transplanting, harvesting and thrashing.

But the problem of leave and absenteeism is not associated with casual agricultural labourers as much as the attached labourers. Since the employment of casual labour is on daily basis, the question of leave and absenteeism does not arise.

In case of attached labourers, the amount of leave is not as extensive and varied as in the case of industrial workers. The incidence of absenteeism is of a less serious nature when compared to his industrial counterpart. Usually the custom and loyalty dictate the extent of leave facility rather than any formal or statutory arrangement. The attached labourer is normally allowed to remain absent for some fixed number of days in a year and it may vary from place to place. Beyond this period, if he remains absent when he is scheduled to work, that period will be treated as absenteeism and wages are deducted.

An attempt is made to enquire into the leave facility and absenteeism of agriculture labour in selected villages and the results are given in the following few pages.

Leave Facility

a. Agreements with Provision for Leave

Whether the agreement entered into between the farmers and attached labourers contain the provision for leave is enquired into by eliciting the opinions of both the farmers and attached labourers. As shown in Table 4.10, 31 per cent of farmers and 34 per cent of attached labourers at State level had expressed that the agreements entered between them contained leave facility. At regional level, 17 per cent of farmers and 10 per cent of attached labourers of Coastal Andhra, 50 per cent farmers and 67 per cent of attached labourers of Telangana had accepted that the agreements contained the provision for leave facility.

1. Loretta M Schmitz and Herbert G Heneman III, "Do positive Reinforcement Programs Reduce Employee Absenteeism?" *The Personnel Administrator,* Vol.25, No.9, (September 1980), pp.87-93.

Table 4.10 : Percentage of Attached Labour Agreement with Provision for Leave

REGION AND VILLAGE	Farmers' Response			Attached Labour Response		
	Yes	*No*	*Total*	*Yes*	*No*	*Total*
COASTAL ANDHRA						
Piridi	--	100.00	100.00	20.00	80.00	100.00
Vangalapudi	36.36	63.64	100.00	--	100.00	100.00
Guntupalle	40.00	60.00	100.00	20.00	80.00	100.00
Veerannapalem	--	100.00	100.00	--	100.00	100.00
OVERALL	**17.02**	**82.98**	**100.00**	**10.00**	**90.00**	**100.00**
TELANGANA						
Jookal	22.22	77.78	100.00	100.00	--	100.00
Raigir	20.00	80.00	100.00	--	100.00	100.00
Andhra Nagar	86.57	13.33	100.00	100.00	--	100.00
OVERALL	**50.00**	**50.00**	**100.00**	**66.67**	**33.33**	**100.00**
ANDHRA PRADESH	***30.86***	***69.14***	***100.00***	***34.29***	***65.71***	***100.00***

Note : No Attached Labour in Rayalaseema Villages.

This reveals that while most of the agreements in Coastal Andhra did not provide for leave facility, nearly half of the agreements in Telangana provided this facility. Cent per cent of farmers of Piridi and Veerannapalem, cent per cent of attached labourers of Vangalapudi and Veerannapalem and Raigir had expressed that no leave facility was provided for in the agreements.

b. Adequacy of Leave Facility

The opinions of farmers and attached labourers on the adequacy of leave facility was also elicited and presented in Table 4.11. Nearly 70 per cent of farmers and 57 per cent of attached labourers were satisfied with the quantum of leave facility. This percentage of satisfied farmers was slightly higher in the case of Coastal Andhra than in Telangana. Further one fourth of farmers in Coastal Andhra as well as Telangana region were of the opinion that attached labourers were enjoying leave facility more than what was required. This percentage of attached labourers was only five in Coastal Andhra and zero in Telangana.

c. Availing of Leave Facility

Irrespective of the provision for leave facility in the agreement, it may be availed with or without the prior of permission of the farmer. An enquiry has been made as to the availing of leave facility by the attached

Table 4.11 : Percentage Distribution of Farmers and Attached Labour as per their Opinion on Adequacy of Leave Facility

REGION AND VILLAGE	Farmers' Response				Attached Labour Response			
	MR	*JS*	*IA*	*TOTAL*	*MR*	*JS*	*IA*	*TOTAL*
COASTAL ANDHRA								
Piridi	14.29	19.05	66.67	100.00	20.00	80.00	--	100.00
Vangalapudi	36.36	27.28	36.36	100.00	--	20.00	80.00	100.00
Guntupalle	50.00	50.00	--	100.00	--	20.00	80.00	100.00
Veerannapalem	--	100.00	--	100.00	--	100.00	--	100.00
OVERALL	**25.53**	**36.17**	**38.30**	**100.00**	**5.00**	**55.00**	**40.00**	**100.00**
TELANGANA								
Jookal	33.33	55.56	11.11	100.00	--	40.00	60.00	100.00
Raigir	50.00	10.00	40.00	100.00	--	60.00	40.00	100.00
Andhra Nagar	20.00	66.67	13.33	100.00	--	60.00	40.00	100.00
OVERALL	**32.36**	**47.06**	**20.59**	**100.00**	--	**53.33**	**46.67**	**100.00**
ANDHRA PRADESH	***28.40***	***40.74***	***30.86***	***100.00***	***2.86***	***54.29***	***42.85***	***100.00***

Note : i) No Attached Labour in Rayalaseema Villages.
ii) MR–More than Required
JS–Just Sufficient
IA–Inadequate

labourers with or without prior permission of the farmer. It is needless to mention that availing of leave without the prior permission disturbs the work schedule and it is an indicator of strained relations between the two parties. Table 4.12 provides the information relating to availing of leave facility with or without prior permission. The responses of both the farmers and attached labourers had been elicited; tabulated and shown in this Table . Fifty two per cent of farmers and 49 per cent of attached labourers were of the opinion that leave facility was being availed both with and without prior permission. While this was so, 36 per cent of farmers and 43 per cent of attached labourers had expressed that leave facility was being availed only with the prior permission. The same trend could be observed at the regional level. But at village level, certain deviations are noticed. Availing of leave facility without prior permission was expressed by large percentage of farmers and attached labourers of Piridi village. In Veerannaplem, cent per cent of farmers and attached labourers had reported that leave facility was made use of only with prior permission.

Table 4.12 : Availing of Leave Facility

REGION AND VILLAGE	Farmers' Response				Attached Labourers' Response			
	WPP %	*WOP* %	*BOTH* %	*TOTAL* %	*WPP* %	*WOP* %	*BOTH* %	*TOTAL* %
COASTAL ANDHRA								
Piridi	28.57	42.86	28.57	100.00	20.00	60.00	20.00	100.00
Vangalapudi	18.17	9.10	72.73	100.00	20.00	--	80.00	100.00
Guntupalle	30.00	--	70.00	100.00	60.00	--	40.00	100.00
Veerannapalem	100.00	--	--	100.00	100.00	--	--	100.00
OVERALL	**34.04**	**21.28**	**44.68**	**100.00**	**50.00**	**15.00**	**35.00**	**100.00**
TELANGANA								
Jookal	--	--	100.00	100.00	20.00	--	80.00	100.00
Raigir	40.00	--	60.00	100.00	20.00	--	80.00	100.00
Andhra Nagar	60.00	--	40.00	100.00	60.00	--	40.00	100.00
OVERALL	**38.24**	--	**61.74**	**100.00**	**33.33**	--	**66.67**	**100.00**
ANDHRA PRADESH	***35.80***	***12.35***	***51.85***	***100.00***	***42.86***	***8.57***	***48.51***	***100.00***

Note : i) No Attached Labour in Rayalaseema Villages.

ii) WPP—With Prior Permission
WOP—Without Prior Permission.

Absenteeism

a. Regularity Among Attached Labour

Regular attendence at the work spot is an important item influencing work discipline and productivity. This indicates the positive side of harmonious relations between farmers and labourers. An attempt has been made to enquire into the percentage of attached labourers with regular attendance. Table 4.13 shows this information as opined by farmers and attached labourers. While only one fourth of farmers had expressed that attached labourers were regular in their attendence; nearly two thirds of attached labourers had been emphatic in saying that they were regular in attending to their duty. At regional level, the same trend could be observed. At village level, cent per cent of farmers of Guntupalle and Jookal were of the oipinion that the attached labourers were not regular in their attendance. Similarly cent per cent of attached labourers of Veerannapalem had expressed that they were regular to their duties.

b. Rate of Absenteeism Among Attached Labourers

The average rate of absenteeism determines the mandays actually worked and thereby the quantum of production. Lower the rate of absenteeism, higher the quantum of the production and both undoubtedly

Table 4.13 : Percentage of Attached Labour with Regular Attendance—A Contrast of Opinion

REGION AND VILLAGE	Farmers' Response			Attached Labourers' Response		
	Yes	*No*	*Total*	*Yes*	*No*	*Total*
COASTAL ANDHRA						
Piridi	28.57	71.43	100.00	40.00	60.00	100.00
Vangalapudi	27.27	72.73	100.00	40.00	60.00	100.00
Guntupalle	--	100.00	100.00	80.00	20.00	100.00
Veerannapalem	40.00	60.00	100.00	100.00	--	100.00
OVERALL	**23.40**	**76.60**	**100.00**	**65.00**	**35.00**	**100.00**
TELANGANA						
Jookal	--	100.00	100.00	60.00	40.00	100.00
Raigir	20.00	80.00	100.00	80.00	20.00	100.00
Andhra Nagar	46.67	53.33	100.00	40.00	60.00	100.00
OVERALL	**26.47**	**73.53**	**100.00**	**60.00**	**40.00**	**100.00**
ANDHRA PRADESH	***24.69***	***75.31***	***100.00***	***62.86***	***37.14***	***100.00***

Note : No Attached Labour in Rayalaseema Villages.

reflect the results of good practice of human resources management. An attempt has been made in this study to measure the average rate of absenteeism among attached labourers in different villages. As shown in Table 4.14 at State level, the average is worked out at 14.42, in Coastal Andhra 16.05 and in Telangana it was 11.31. Piridi stood first with 15.58 and Vangalapudi with 11.3. The lowest rate of absenteeism was recorded in Jookal with 7.55.

Table 4.14 : Average Rate of Absenteeism among Attached Labour

REGION AND VILLAGE	Average Rate of Absenteeism per Attached Labourer
COASTAL ANDHRA	
Piridi	22.70
Vangalapudi	11.30
Guntupalle	8.63
Veerannapalem	7.76
OVERALL	**16.05**
TELANGANA	
Jookal	7.55
Raigir	15.58
Andhra Nagar	10.18
OVERALL	**11.31**
ANDHRA PRADESH	***14.42***

Note : No Attached Labour in Rayalaseema Villages.

Commitment in Employment

a. Duration of employment of attached labourers under the same farmer

It is needless to mention that the commitment of attached labourers is very much essential to improve the quality of work and the relations between the farmer and attached labourer. It is with this view that an enquiry into the commitment of attached labourer as reflected by the duration of employment under the same farmer for the last five years is made and the responses are tabulated and presented in Table 4.15. Highest percentage of attached labourers, thirty per cent, had worked for one year; twenty nine per cent of attached labourers for two years; fifteen per cent of attached labourers for three years and eleven per cent of attached labourers for five years. The same trend could be observed in the villages of Coastal Andhra and Telangana. The average duration of employment was 2.25 years in Coastal Andhra and it was only 1.94 years in Telangana. It is evident from this that the period of continuous employment with the same farmer was neither large nor small.

Table 4.15 : Commitment of Attached Labour

REGION AND VILLAGE	Percentage Distribution of Attached Labourers by Duration of Employment under the same Farmer for the Last Five Years						Average Duration of Employment *(in Years)*
	LT 1	1 Year	2 Years	3 Years	4 Years	5Years	
COASTAL ANDHRA							
Piridi	13.21	30.19	30.19	20.75	--	5.66	1.88
Vangalapudi	5.55	16.66	27.78	16.67	5.56	27.78	2.88
Guntupalle	--	29.17	29.17	8.33	8.33	25.00	2.70
Veerannapalem	--	63.64	9.09	--	9.09	18.18	2.09
OVERALL	**7.55**	**31.33**	**27.36**	**15.09**	**3.78**	**15.09**	**2.25**
TELANGANA							
Jookal	25.00	25.00	29.14	16.67	4.16	--	1.62
Raigir	11.11	29.63	33.33	18.52	--	7.41	1.96
Andhra Nagar	10.26	30.77	28.20	12.82	7.69	10.26	2.12
OVERALL	**14.45**	**28.90**	**30.00**	**15.55**	**4.44**	**6.66**	**1.94**
ANDHRA PRADESH	***10.71***	***30.11***	***28.58***	***15.30***	***4.08***	***11.22***	***2.11***

Note : No Attached Labour in Rayalaseema Villages.
LT 1—Less Tan 1 year.

b. Reasons for Continuation of Employment

Having enquired into the period of continuous employment under the same farmer, it is necessary to assertain the reasons for this continued employment. Both the farmers and attached labourers have been contacted for this purpose. The farmers had expressed 'cordiality' coupled with 'trust worthiness' and 'resposibility felt by attached labourers' were mainly responsible for this continuation (Table 4.16). The attached labourers were by and large unanimous in revealing that the farmers' help in times of need was the dominant factor which induced them to continue their employment with the same farmer. Thus other factors like 'attractive remuneration' and 'indebtedness' occupied second priority in their decision making.

Table 4.16 : Reasons for Continuation of Attached Labour

REGION AND VILLAGE	Farmers' Reasons for Continuing the same Attached Labour				Labourers' Reasons for continuing under the same Farmer		
	TWCP	CT	R	WAAA	AR	HN	I
COASTAL ANDHRA							
Piridi	II	I	III	--	II	I	--
Vangalapudi	III	II	I	--	--	I	II
Guntupalle	--	I	II	--	--	I	--
Veerannapalem	I	--	--	--	--	I	--
OVERALL	**III**	**I**	**II**	--	**II**	**I**	**II**
TELANGANA							
Jookal	--	II	I	II	--	I	II
Raigir	III	I	II	--	--	I	--
Andhra Nagar	II	III	I	--	--	I	--
OVERALL	**III**	**II**	**I**	**IV**	--	**I**	**II**
ANDHRA PRADESH	***III***	***II***	***I***	***IV***	***II***	***I***	***II***

Note : i) No Attached Labour in Rayalaseema Villages.

ii) RWCP—Remuneration within the capacity to pay;
CT—Cordially and Trust Worthiness
R—Responsibility;
WAAA—Willingness and Ability to carryout any work assigned.
HN—Help in Times of Need
I—Indebtness

c. Reasons for Leaving Employment

An enquiry is also made as to the reasons which prompted both the farmers as well as attached labourers in severing their employment relationship. Both the farmers and attached labourers have expressed that personal problems of attached labourers were mainly responsible for the break of employment relationship (Table 4.17). Other reasons from the side of farmers were, attached labourers' demands beyond the farmers' capacity to pay; irresponsible behaviour; lack of trust worthiness and frequent failure to carry out the assigned work. Other reasons mentioned by some of the attached labourers were low remuneration; heavy work; ill treatment and unhelpful attitude of farmers.

Table 4.17 : Reasons for Leaving Employment by Attached Labour

REGION AND VILLAGE	Farmers' Reasons for Discontinuing the Attached Labourer					Labourers' Reasons for leaving the Farmer				
	DBCP	IB	LTW	FFCW	PPLT	LR	HW	IT	UA	PP
COASTAL ANDHRA										
Piridi	II	III	II	--	I	II	--	--	I	--
Vangalapudi	--	--	--	--	I	--	--	--	--	I
Guntupalle	II	--	--	--	I	--	--	II	--	I
Veerannapalem	I	--	--	--	I	--	--	--	--	--
OVERALL	**II**	**IV**	**III**	--	**I**	**III**	--	**III**	**II**	**I**
TELANGANA										
Jookal	--	--	II	III	I	--	II	--	--	I
Raigir	--	II	II	--	I	--	--	--	--	I
Andhra Nagar	II	--	--	--	I	--	--	--	--	I
OVERALL	**II**	**III**	**II**	**III**	**I**	--	**II**	--	--	**I**
ANDHRA PRADESH	***II***	***IV***	***III***	***V***	***I***	***III***	***III***	***III***	***II***	***I***

Note : i) No Attached Labour in Rayalaseema Villages.

ii) DBCP—Demands Beyond the Capacity to Pay;
IB—Irresponsible Behaviour
LTW—Lack of Trust Worthiness;
FFCW—Frequent Failure to Carryout the Work
PPLT—Personal Problems of Labourers' themselves
LR—Low Remuneration
HW—Heavy Work;
IT—Ill Treatment;
UA—Unhelpful Attitude
PP—Personal Problems

5

Employee Compensation and Inducements

This chapter is planned to deal with four important aspects-wages, incentives, fringe benefits and indebtedness-relating to Employee-Compensation and Inducements. The meaning and significance of wages; determinants and features of agrarian wage structure; mode of wage payment; wage levels and perceptions and statutory minimum wages are delt with in the section on Wages. The meaning and significance of incentives; their applicability in agriculture and in selected villages are explained in the section dealing with Incentives. The significance of fringe benefits; their existence in agriculture sector with special reference to selected villages are presented in the section on Fringe Benefits. An account of indebtedness of both attached and casual laboures in the selected villages is given towards the end of the Chapter.

Wages

Meaning and Significance

Compensation refers to every type of reward that individuals receive in return for their labour[1].

One of the most difficult functions of human resource management is that of determining rates of monetary compensation. Not only it is one of the most complexties, but it is also one of the most significant to both the organisation and the employees. The money paid to employees in return for their service is probably the largest expenditure for an employer

1. R. Wayne Mondy and Robert M. Noe III "*Human Resource Management*" (Boston: Allyn and Bacon,1990) p,432.

while to the employee, it is usually the main source of income. Therefore, proper administration of compensation programme can have a profound effect on both employer and employees. It can save an organisation from costs involved with high turnover, while attracting, retaining and motivating capable and productive employees.[1]

Employees are compensatead with two-fold objectives: as a reward for past services to the organisation and as a stimulus to improved performance in the future.[2] There are several other purposes performed by compensation, including attracting better employees for performing work they otherwise would not do. A keen element an organisation's compensation programme is the employee's assessment of fairness and equitableness of the internal wage structure. He is interested in and affected by relationship of his salary with that of fellow employees. In fact, pay inequalities within a firm, whether real or imagined, adversely affect an employee's morale and job performance.[3]

Determinants and Features of Agrarian Wage Structure

The determinants of levels wage in agriculture can be broadly divided into economic and social factors. Economic factors, like the extent of population pressure, land utilisation, size of holdings, the pull of urban and industrial production centres on the proximate rural regions, the nature of crops grown and other connected causes influence wage levels in agriculture. Sociological factors such, as social strata from which labourers are drawn, custom and tradition, which manifest themselves in many ways, also influence the fixation of wages.

Further, the wage rates for different agricultural operations differ. These differences may, to some extent, are based on the nature of work, strain involved, seasonal importance of the operation, conditions under which work has to be done and the degree of dexterity or skill required. There are operations which adult male labourers alone can do and there are certain items of work for which women are better suited. While wage determination for agricultural operations for men and women labourers takes place on a purely empirical basis, still consideration of strain, dexterity, etc., have their influence to some extent.

---

1. W.A. Groenekamp, "Essentials of a Sound Wage and Salary Programme" in *Handbook of Modern Personnel Administration*, ed. by J.J. Faumlaro (Toronto : Mc Graw-Hill Book Company,1972), p.27.3.
2. Groenekamp, op.cit., p.27.
3. Leon C. Megginson, "*Personnel and Human Resources Administration*" (Homewood, Illinois : Richard D. Irwin, Inc., 1977), p.380.

More than these intrinsic factors that are basically relevant to wage determination, there are many other factors that influence wage rates in pushing them up or pulling them down. These considerations relate to agricultural prosperity of the region, availability of labour force, its caste and sex composition, awareness of labourers about prevailing wage levels in neighbouring areas, composition of agricultural classes and prevalence of big land holders in a region etc. In the early period, the wage rates were mainly determined by the cultivators or land owners as they were the monopolies in the agrarian system and no organised demand for fair wage existed. Thus in the early period, not only the wages, but the general position of the agricultural labourers has been one of extreme exploitation[1].

Attached Labour

The attached worker is more or less in continuous employment throughout the year. Even within a village, there is no uniformity in the conditions of work of different attached workers. Each worker enters into a contract with an employer. It lays down his tenure and terms of employment which take into account his skill, his economic position and his personal relations with the employer.

The conditions of work and wages of attached workers cannot be directly compared with those of casual labourers. Unlike the casual workers, the wages of attached workers are fixed for a definite period and are not generally subject to variation according to the seasonal type of work or the seasonal demand for labour. Secondly, the attached worker has not the same extent of insecurity of employment as his casual counterpart. For this security, he might accept a lower daily wage than that obtained by a casual worker.

Main Features of Agrarian Wage Structure

Wage structure[2] in agriculture is a complex one. Wage differentials as among different agricultural operations obtaining in different regions for men, women and children are often determined by forces that may defy economic analysis.[3]

1. J.P. Mencher, *Agriculture and Social Structure in Tamilnadu* (New Delhi: Allied Publishers, 1978), p.351.
2. The term "*wage structure*" has been defined by the International Labour Organisation as comprising, on the one hand, the pattern of wage differentials among occupations, types of wage earner, firms, industries and regions and on the other hand, various components of wage earnings.
3. I.L.O, Wage policy in Asian Countries, 1956, p.122.

Wage structure in agriculture has its unique features as compared with that of industry. The main difference lies in the fact that industrial wages are more or less completely monetised while agricultural wages are not. The degree of monetisation again varies as among different kinds of crops grown. In so far as cash and commercial crops are concerned the process of monetisation is generally at a quick pace since wages are paid mostly in cash. But it is not the case in respect of food crops.

Another feature of agrarian wages is their irregularity of payment. In industry, wages though daily rated may be paid daily, weekly, fortnightly or monthly. The wage period does not, however, go beyond one calendar month. In agriculture, casual workers, who form the bulk of agricultural labourers, are paid wages daily in return for their day's work. This is evidently on account of their intermittent employment. Attached workers who have continuity of employment for a period ranging from 3 to 12 months, or even longer are generallyl paid wages once in a quarter, half year or year as the case may be. Usually, payment of advance precedes their actual employment.

Wage differentials in agriculture as among different regions and as between men, women and children are not easily apparent in as far as payments in kind are concerned since the nature of kind payments as well as quants of wages vary widely and imputation value too differs on account of regional and commodity-wise differences in price levels. But in so far as cash wages are concerned, disparity in wage differentials is strikingly obvious and generally differentials between wages of men and women workers are more than what they are among industrial workers.

While wage payments in industry are related to a normal working day constituting statutorily specified number of hours of work, over and above which up to a limit over time remuneration is paid, in agriculture the length of the working day is not so rigidly observed even though the rules framed under the Minimum Wage Act, 1948 by the Government of India, which inter alia apply to agricultural employments, fix nine hours a day and 48 hours a week for adults with specific rates at which over time work has to be remunerated.

Payment by piece rate is not uncommon in agriculture. Enbanking and levelling operations are paid for, in certain cases by measurements at a specified piece rate. Harvesting and threshing are also paid for at times by pieces, the unit of work being in terms of bundles. Attached labourers are also paid wages on a crop-sharing basis at a stipulated rate.

Wages of labourers may vary under several conditions. Regional differences are important in this context. As Thorner remarked, terms of employment, duration of work, amount and form of payment may vary from district to district.[1]

Wages in agriculture lag behind those of industry. It is evidently due to low earning power of agriculture. By comparison with industry, agriculture is far behind in its productive capacity because it is far less well equipped, financed and organised; by comparison with the output of the industrial worker, the agricultural workers' output is modest. In fact, agriculture is not a carefully thought out business proposition launched at a propitious moment and continues just as long as market conditions hold.[2] In under-developed countries agricultural wage situation is likely to be more depressed in view of population pressure on land and impaired efficiency of agricultural enterprise. As a result of the general lag in industrial development, even industrial wages compare unfavourably with wage levels obtaining in industrially advanced countries for identical occupations.

However, the wage differentials between agriculture and industry are to be considered against are receipt by some farm labourers of other benefits (housing, fire wood, cattle fodder, or other perquisites) in addition to cash wages, and a lower cost of living in rural areas. Industrial workers, in turn, usually obtain or have access to more and better services and facilities (hospitals, schools, libraries and other educational facilities, recreation facilities and transportation).[3] The continuous employment enjoyed by the industrial as compared with the intermittent employment of agricultural labour has also to be borne in mind while attempting this comparison.

Wages of Women Workers

Women are employed mostly as casual workers. They employed generally in transplantation, weeding and harvesting. The wage rates of female workers are lower as compared to those of male workers. This

1. Danial Thorner and Alice Thorner, "*Land and Labour in India*" (Bombay : Asia Publishing House, 1962), p.21.
2. L.E. Howard "Labour in Agriculture", quoted in *Agriculture Labour Enquiry,* 1950-'51 (New Delhi : Ministry of Labour, 1954), I-All India.
3. L.J. Ducoff "Wages of Agricultural Labour in the United States", quoted in *Agriculture Labour in India,* Report on The Second Agricultural Labour Enquiry, 1956-'57 (New Delhi : Labour Bureau, Ministry of Labour and Employment, 1960), I - All India.

fact is corroborated by several studies conducted in different parts of India over different periods of time. The reasons for lower wage rates for female workers are: lack of continuity in employment due to their domestic preoccupations, lesser number of hours of work per day in some cases and nature of farm operations.

Mode of Wage Payment

Wages are paid either in cash or in kind or partly in cash and partly in kind. It may be noted here that wage payments are influenced by factors like crops grown, custom and tradition; availability of cash resources and the general level of agricultural prices.

The respondent farmers have been asked as to the mode of payment of wages to attached labour and casual labourer. Table 5.1 shows the responses given by farmers in this regard. It could be observed from this table that nearly 47 per cent of attached labourers at State level were paid wages in cash; 22 per cent of them in kind; 31 per cent of them in cash as well as in kind. In between the regions payment of wages to attached labourers in cash was widely prevalent in Telangana villages where nearly three fourths of them were paid in cash. This percentage was slightly above one fourth in Coastal Andhra. Most of the attached labourers in Coastal Andhra were paid their wages partly in cash and partly in kind.

Table 5.1 : Mode of Payment of Wages to Labour—Farmers' Response

REGION AND VILLAGE	Mode of Payment							
	By Cash		By Kind		By Cash & Kind		Total	
	AL%	CL%	AL%	CL%	AL%	CL%	AL%	CL%
COASTAL ANDHRA								
Piridi	27.66	98.57	29.79	1.43	42.55	--		
Vangalapudi	4.76	94.29	66.67	5.71	28.57	--		
Guntupalle	18.18	100.00	--	--	81.82	--		
Veerannapalem	50.00	100.00	--	--	50.00	--		
OVERALL	**100.00**	**100.00**	--	--	--	--		
RAYALASEEMA								
Brahmanapalle	--	48.57	--	--	--	51.43		
Sanjeevapuram	--	45.71	--	--	--	54.29		
OVERALL	--	**51.43**	--	--		**48.57**		
TELANGANA								
Jookal	73.53	85.72	11.76	0.95	14.71	13.33		
Raigir	66.67	100.00	--	--	33.33	--		
Andhra Nagar	60.00	57.14	40.00	2.86	--	40.00		
OVERALL	**86.67**	**100.00**	--	--	**13.33**	--		
ANDHRA PRADESH	***46.92***	***83.17***	***22.22***	***0.95***	***30.86***	***15.88***		

In respect of casual labourers, 99 per cent of them in Coastal Andhra; 49 per cent Rayalaseema and nearly 86 per cent in Telangana were paid in cash. It was only in Rayalaseema, majority of casual labourers (51 per cent) were paid partly in cash and partly in kind. There may be one inherent weakness in the system of payment of wages in kind. It may leave room for exploitation of workers by the farmers in the form of short measurement, payment through of inferior grain, etc.

Wage Levels and Perceptions

a. Money Wages

Attached Labour

The annual money wages of attached labourers, their index with base year 1983-'84; their growth rates and coefficient of variation for the period 1983-'84 to 1990-'91 are shown in table 5.2. it could be seen from this table that the annual money wage of attached labourers was highest in Andhra Nagar with Rs.5,690 followed by Guntupalle with Rs.4,768 and Veerannapalem with Rs.4,000 in 1983-'84. The lowest annual money wage was found in Piridi with Rs.2,200/- in the same year. However, the index of annual money wages of attached labourers had gone up to the maximum extent in Piridi with 204.55 by 1990-'91. This was followed by Veerannapalem with 150.00; Raigir with 148.91 and Vangalapudi with 144.40. By 1990-'91 Andhra Nagar stood first again with highest annual wage of Rs.6,500/- followed by Veerannapalem with Rs.6,000/- and Vangalapudi with Rs.5,500/-. The coefficient of variation of annual wages of attached labourers for individual villages for all the eight years is also shown in this table. It could be seen from these figures that coefficient of variation was highest in Piridi with 58.80685 followed by Raigir with 54.05721. The lowest coefficient of variation is found in Guntupalle with 51.78067. Thus the annual money wage of attached labourers was relatively more stable in Guntupalle and its stability was very low in Piridi.

Casual Labourers

It is needless to mention that the annual earnings of male and female casual labourers fluctuate from year to year depending upon the number of working days available in each year. But in the absence of these figures only the daily wage rates payable to them during the period under study 1983-'84 to 1990-'91 could be analysed to examine. Wage differentials in between villages; in between male and female casual labourers and the growth in wage rates over the period of eight years.

Table 5.2 : Annual Money Wages of Attached Labour

(In Rs.)

YEAR	P	VP	GP	VPM	CA	J	R	AN	TE	AP
1983–'84	2,200 (100)	3,809 (100)	4,768 (100)	4,000 (100)	3,694.25 (100)	3,922 (100)	3,022 (100)	5,690 (100)	4,194.67 (100)	3,944.46 (100)
1984–'85	2,300 (104.55)	3,577 (93.91)	4,789 (100.44)	4,200 (105.00)	3,716.50 (100.60)	3,867 (98.60)	3,078 (101.85)	5,727 (101.54)	4,244.00 (100.99)	3,970.25 (100.65)
1985–'86	2,400 (109.09)	4,055 (106.46)	4,789 (100.44)	4,350 (108.75)	3,898.50 (105.53)	3,944 (100.56)	2,958 (97.89)	5,907 (104.73)	4,269.67 (101.79)	4,084.09 (103.54)
1986–'87	2,600 (118.18)	4,500 (118.14)	4,790 (100.46)	4,450 (111.25)	4,085.00 (110.58)	4,100 (104.54)	3,200 (105.89)	5,950 (105.50)	4,416.67 (105.29)	4,250.84 (107.77)
1987–'88	3,000 (136.36)	4,800 (126.02)	4,8800 (100.67)	4,500 (112.50)	4,275.00 (115.72)	4,150 (105.81)	3,400 (112.51)	6,000 (106.38)	4,516.67 (107.68)	4,395.84 (111.44)
1988–'89	3,500 (159.09)	5,000 (131.27)	4,850 (101.72)	4,700 (117.50)	4,512.50 (122.15)	4,600 (117.29)	3,600 (119.13)	6,000 (106.38)	4,800.00 (114.43)	4,656.00 (118.04)
1989–'90	4,000 (181.82)	5,200 (136.52)	4,900 (102.77)	5,500 (137.50)	4,900.00 (132.64)	4,800 (122.39)	4,000 (132.36)	6,200 (109.93)	5,000.00 (119.20)	4,950.00 (125.49)
1990–'91	4,500 (204.55)	5,500 (144.40)	5,000 (104.87)	6,000 (150.00)	5,250.00 (142.11)	5,000 (127.49)	4,500 (148.91)	6,500 (115.25)	5,333.33 (127.15)	5,291.67 (134.16)
CV	***58.80685***	***53.92640***	***51.78067***	***53.76292***	***53.39449***	***52.75363***	***54.05721***	***51.93563***	***52.52907***	***52.90464***

Note : i) Figures within parantheses indicate index numbers with 1983–84 as base year.

ii) P–Piridi; VP–Vangalapudi; GP–Guntupalle; VPM–Veerannapalem; CA–Coastal Andhra; J–Jookal; R–Raigir; AN–Andhra Nagar; TE–Telangana; AP–Andhra Pradesh

iii) CV–Coefficient of Variation.

The money wage rates and their indices and their coefficient of variation with base year 1983-'84 of male and female casual labourers are shown for the period 1983-'84 to 1990-'91 in Table 5.3. It could be seen from this table that the money wage rates of male casual labourers had gone up from Rs.11 in 1983-'84 to Rs.25 in 1990-'91—a growth of 127.27 per cent in Piridi village. The daily wage rate of female casual labourer, during the same period had increased from Rs.5 in 1983-'84 to Rs.15 in 1990-'91 - a growth of 200 per cent. It may be noted that Piridi village recorded highest growth rate in respect of daily wage rates of both male and female casual labourers in Coastal Andhra region. The lowest growth rate was found in Veerannapalem village where the wage rate of male casual labourers had gone up by 66.67 and that of female casual labourers by 50 per cent. In Rayalaseema region, the daily wage rates of male casual labourers, in both the villages had increased from Rs.10 in 1983-'84 to Rs.25 in 1990-'91 - a growth of 150 per cent. But the wage rates of female casual labourers having increaed from Rs.6 in Brahmanapalle village to Rs.16 and from Rs.5 to Rs.20 in Sanjeevapuram village - had shown much more higher growth rate than that of male casual labourers. Further, both the Rayalaseema villages had registered highest growth rate of 150 per cent during the period under study in respect of wage rate of male casual labourers in the entire State. Added to this, Sanjeevapuram registered highest growth rate in respect of wage rate of female casual labourers - 300 per cent in the entire State.

Among Telangana villages, Jookal stood first in respect of growth rate of both male and female casual labourers followed by Raigir and Andhra Nagar.

It is also to be noted that the highest daily wage rate for 1983-'84 in respect of both male and female casual labourers was found in Guntupalle village for the entire State. Similarly for the latest year 1990-'91 also highest daily wage rates of both male and female casual labourers are found in the same village. The reason for this might be attributed to its close proximity to Vijayawada city. While this being so, the lowest wage rates of both male and female casual labourers for 1983-'84 were found in Sanjeevapuram village of Rayalaseema. In 1990-'91 the lowest wage rates of both male and female casual labourers were found in Raigir of Telangana.

This table also shows variations in the daily wage rates between male and female casual labourers. For 1983-'84 while the highest variation of Rs.7/- in daily wage rate was found in Guntupalle in Coastal

Table 5.3 : Money Wages of Casual Labour (Male and Female)

(In Rs.)

YEAR	PIRIDI		VANGALAPUDI		GUNTUPALLE		VEERANNAPALEM		OVERALL	
	M	F	M	F	M	F	M	F	M	F
1983–'84	11.00 (100.00)	5.00 (100.00)	13.00 (100.00)	11.00 (100.00)	19.00 (100.00)	12.00 (100.00)	15.00 (100.00)	10.00 (100.00)	14.50 (100.00)	9.50 (100.00)
1984–'85	11.00 (100.00)	5.00 (100.00)	14.00 (107.69)	12.00 (109.09)	20.00 (105.26)	12.00 (100.00)	15.00 (100.00)	10.00 (100.00)	15.00 (103.45)	9.75 (102.63)
1985–'86	11.00 (100.00)	6.00 (120.00)	16.00 (123.08)	13.00 (118.18)	20.00 (105.26)	12.00 (100.00)	15.00 (100.00)	10.00 (100.00)	15.50 (106.90)	10.25 (107.90)
1986–'87	12.00 (109.09)	6.00 (120.00)	17.00 (130.77)	13.00 (118.18)	22.00 (115.79)	12.00 (100.00)	15.00 (100.00)	10.00 (100.00)	16.50 (113.79)	10.25 (107.90)
1987–'88	13.00 (118.18)	7.00 (140.00)	18.00 (138.46)	14.00 (127.27)	25.00 (131.58)	15.00 (125.00)	15.00 (100.00)	10.00 (100.00)	17.75 (122.41)	11.50 (121.05)
1988–'89	15.00 (136.36)	8.00 (160.00)	19.00 (146.15)	14.00 (127.27)	30.00 (157.90)	20.00 (166.67)	15.00 (100.00)	10.00 (100.00)	19.75 (136.21)	13.00 (136.84)
1989–'90	20.00 (181.82)	10.00 (200 .00)	20.00 (153.85)	15.00 (136.36)	30.00 (157.90)	20.00 (166.67)	20.00 (133.33)	12.00 (120.00)	12.50 (155.17)	14.25 (150.00)
1990–'91	25.00 (227.27)	15.00 (300.00)	25.00 (192.31)	20.00 (181.82)	35.00 (184.21)	25.00 (208.33)	25.00 (166.67)	15.00 (150.00)	27.50 (189.66)	18.75 (197.37)
CV	***62.42285***	***67.59781***	***55.94400***	***55.29536***	***56.85711***	***60.59600***	***56.25440***	***54.35890***	***57.06271***	***57.85106***

Note : i) M–Male; F–Female.

ii) CV–Coefficient of Variation.

(Contd...)

Table 5.3 : (Contd...)

(In Rs.)

YEAR	Brahmanapalle		Sanjeevapuram		Overall		Jookal	
	M	F	M	F	M	F	M	F
1983–'84	10.00	6.00	10.00	5.00	10.00	5.50	11.00	6.00
	(100.00)	(100.00)	(100.00)	(100.00)	(100.00)	(100.00)	(100.00)	(100.00)
1984–'85	10.00	6.00	10.00	6.00	10.00	6.00	11.00	6.00
	(100.00)	(100.00)	((100.00)	(120.00)	(100.00)	(109.09)	(100.00)	(100.00)
1985–'86	11.00	6.00	10.00	6.00	10.50	6.00	11.00	6.00
	(110.00)	(100.00)	(100.00)	(120.00)	(105.00)	(109.09)	(100.00)	(100.00))
1986–'87	12.00	7.00	12.00	7.00	12.00	7.00	15.00	8.00
	(120.00)	(116.67)	(120.00)	(140.00)	(120.00)	(127.27)	(136.36)	(133.33)
1987–'88	15.00	10.00	15.00	10.00	15.00	10.00	20.00	10.00
	(150.00)	(116.67)	(150.00)	(200.00)	(150.00)	(181.82)	(181.82)	(166.67)
1988–'89	18.00	12.00	20.00	12.00	19.00	12.00	20.00	10.00
	(180.00)	(200.00)	(200.00)	(240.00)	(190.00)	(218.18)	(181.82)	(166.67)
1989–'90	20.00	15.00	25.00	15.00	22.50	15.00	25.00	15.00
	(200.00)	(250.00)	(250.00)	(300.00)	(225.00)	(272.73)	(227.27)	(250.00)
1990–'91	25.00	16.00	25.00	20.00	25.00	18.00	25.00	15.00
	(250.00)	(266.67)	(250.00)	(400.00)	(250.00)	(327.27)	(227.27)	(250.00)
CV	***63.11048***	***67.11507***	***62.12674***	***69.70272***	***60.21987***	***66.13454***	***58.12997***	***61.03905***

Note : i) M–Male; F–Female.

ii) CV–Coefficient of Variation.

(Contd...)

Table 5.3 : (Contd...)

(In Rs.)

YEAR	Raigir		Andhra Nagar		Overall		Andhra Pradesh	
	M	F	M	F	M	F	M	F
1983–'84	13.00	6.00	17.00	13.00	13.67	8.33	12.72	7.78
	(100.00)	(100.00)	(100.00)	(100.00)	(100.00)	(100.00)	(100.00)	(100.00)
1984–'85	13.00	6.00	17.00	13.00	14.00	8.33	13.00	8.03
	(100.00)	(100.00)	(105.88)	(100.00)	(102.00)	(100.00)	(102.20)	(103.21)
1985–'86	14.00	6.00	18.00	13.00	14.33	8.33	13.44	8.19
	(107.69)	(100.00)	(105.88)	(100.00)	(104.83)	(100.00)	(105.66)	(105.27)
1986–'87	15.00	7.00	19.00	13.00	16.33	9.33	14.94	8.86
	(115.39)	(116.67)	(111.76)	(100.00)	(119.46)	(112.00)	(117.45)	(113.88)
1987–'88	16.00	8.00	20.00	12.00	18.67	10.00	17.14	10.50
	(123.08)	(133.33)	(117.65)	(92.31)	(136.58)	(120.00)	(134.75)	(134.96)
1988–'89	18.00	9.00	25.00	15.00	19.33	11.33	19.36	12.11
	(138.46)	(150.00)	(117.65)	(115.39)	(141.40)	(136.01)	(152.20)	(155.66)
1989–'90	20.00	10.00	25.00	20.00	23.33	15.00	22.78	14.75
	(153.85)	(166.67)	(147.06)	(153.85)	(170.67)	(180.00)	(179.09)	(189.59)
1990–'91	22.00	12.00	30.00	25.00	25.67	17.33	26.06	18.03
	(169.23)	(200.00)	(176.47)	(192.31)	(187.78)	(208.04)	(204.87)	(231.75)
CV	***50.57423***	***53.86825***	***51.34676***	***54.98084***	***52.43983***	***55.71157***	***54.27871***	***57.23470***

Note : i) M–Male; F–Female.

ii) CV–Coefficient of Variation.

Andhra and Raigir of Telangana; the lowest variation of Rs.2 was found in Vangalapudi of Coastal Andhra. In respect of 1990-'91 the maximum variation of Rs.10 was found in Piridi, Guntupalle and Veerannapalem of Coastal Andhra; Jookal and Raigir of Telangana. The lowest variation of Rs.5 was found in Veerannapalem of Coastal Andhra; Sanjeevapuram of Rayalaseema and Andhra Nagar of Telangana. It may be noted here that the minimum wage committees had been very emphatic in their recommendations that no discrimination should be made on the basis of sex while fixing the daily wage rates. However, wage differentials based on sex still persist in villages of Andhra Pradesh.

The coefficient of variation of wage rates of male and female casual labourers over the period of eight years of 1983-'84 to 1990-'91 is also calculated and shown in this table. In respect of male casual labourers while the highest coefficient of variation was found in Brahmanapalle village with 63.11048; the lowest coefficient of variation was found in Raigir with 50.57423. In respect of female casual labourers, the highest coefficient of variation i.e., 69.70272 was found in Sanjeevapuram; the lowest coefficient of variation of 53.86825 was found in Raigir.

b. Per Unit Output Price

Having considered the annual money wages of attached labourers, it is appropriate to examine the trends in market price of the most important produce of farmers which decides their paying capacity. The market price of Paddy in the respective years is taken for this purpose in respect of all the villages of Coastal Andhra and Telangana. Regarding Rayalaseema, the market price of groundnut in Brahmanapalle and Sanjeevapuram are taken for this purpose.

It can be seen from Table 5.4 that per unit output price has gone up by 152.10 per cent in Veerannapalem followed by 150.00 in Sanjeevapuram, 122.22 per cent in Piridi and 121.31 in Guntupalle. Thus the increase in output price was found to be higher than the increase in annual money wages of attached labourers of all the selected villages. The growth in money wage rates of casual labourers can also be compared with the growth in per unit output price as shown in table 5.4. It could be observed from this table that, unlike in the case of annual money wages of attached labourers the money wage rates of casual labourers had increased more than that of per unit output price during the period under study at least in some villages like Piridi of Coastal Andhra; Brahmanapalle and Sanjeevapuram of Rayalaseema and Jookal of Telangana. In all the remaining five villages the growth in per unit output price was higher than

Table 5.4 : Annual Money Wages of Attached Labour

(In Rs.)

YEAR	P	VP	GP	VPM	CA	BP	SP	RS	J	R	AN	TE	AP
1983–'84	108	119	122	119	117.00	173	160	166.50	128	126	137	133.33	132.44
	(100)	(100)	(100)	(100)	(100)	(100)	(100)	(100)	(100)	(100)	(100)	(100)	(100)
1984–'85	109	121	124	119	118.25	166	135.00	150.50	127	127	136	130.00	129.33
	(100.93)	(101.68)	(101.64)	(100.00)	(101.07)	(95.95)	(84.38)	(90.39)	(99.22)	(100.79)	(99.27)	(99.75)	(100.37)
1985–'86	110	125	130	125	122.50	177	145	161.00	133	136	136	135.00	135.22
	(101.85)	(105.04)	(106.56)	(105.04)	(104.70)	(102.31)	(90.63)	(96.70)	(103.91)	(107.94)	(99.27)	(103.58)	(104.11)
1986–'87	140	150	150	150	147.50	170	180	175.00	150	155	150	151.67	155.00
	(129.63)	(126.05)	(122.95)	(126.05)	(126.07)	(98.27)	(112.50)	(105.11)	(117.19)	(123.02)	(109.49)	(116.37)	(120.96)
1987–'88	160	175	195	180	177.50	170	190	180.00	175	170	180	175.00	177.22
	(148.15)	(147.06)	(159.84)	(151.26)	(151.71)	(98.27)	(118.75)	(108.11)	(136.72)	(134.92)	(131.39)	(134.28)	(142.52)
1988–'89	180	200	200	225	201.25	200	200	200.00	200	200	200	200.00	200.55
	(166.67)	(168.07)	(163.93)	(189.08)	(172.81)	(115.61)	(125.00)	(120.12)	(156.25)	(158.73)	(145.99)	(153.46)	(162.23)
1989–'90	210	230	225	240	226.25	270	250	260.00	220	225	225	223.33	232.78
	(194.44)	(193.28)	(184.43)	(201.68)	(193.38)	(156.07)	(156.25)	(156.16)	(171.88)	(178.57)	(164.23)	(171.36)	(181.77)
1990–'91	240	250	270	300	265.00	400	400	400.00	270	270	275	271.67	297.22
	(222.22)	(210.08)	(221.31)	(252.10)	(226.50)	(231.21)	(250.00)	(240.24)	(210.94)	(214.29)	(200.73)	(208.45)	(216.98)

Note : i) Figures within parantheses indicate index numbers with 1983–84 as base year.

ii) P–Piridi; VP–Vangalapudi; GP–Guntupalle; VPM–Veerannapalem; CA–Coastal Andhra; BP—Brahmanaplle; SP—Sanjeevapuram RS--Rayalaseema; J–Jookal; R–Raigir; AN–Andhra Nagar; TE–Telangana; AP–Andhra Pradesh

the growth in money wage rates of both male and female casual labourers during the period under the study.

c. Real Wages

The labourers, invariably make a comparison of increase in their money wages with that of cost of living index. In other words, their interest is more in purchasing capacity of their money wages which, however varies depending upon increase or decrease in cost of living. Hence, it is necessary to enquire into the trends in annual real wages of attached labourers during the period under study. This information is shown in Table 5.5. It could be observed from this table that the annual real wages of attached labourers had gone up by nearly 38 per cent over the period of eight years in Piridi village. But it has remained more or less constant in Veerannapalem and Raigir villages. In all other villages, the annual real wages of attached labourers had declined and the largest decline was in Guntupalle followed by Andhra Nagar. This indicates that the annual money wages of attached labourers had, no doubt, increased; but this increase was more than neutralised by increase in cost of living. The purchasing capacity of attached labourers had gone down by nearly 30 per cent in Guntupalle and by 22 per cent in Andhra Nagar because of the inadequate increase in money wages coupled with very steep increase in cost of living during the same period.

The coefficient of variation of annual real wages of attached labourers is also calculated for the eight years period and is shown in this table. This coefficient of variation was more or less the same in different villages and it was highest in Piridi and lowest in Raigir.

The real wages of casual labourers have been calculated by deflating the money wage rates with the help of cost of living index applicable to agricultural labour and are shown in Table 5.6. The real wages of male casual labourers were found to be the highest in Guntupalle village with Rs.19.04 and lowest in both the Rayalaseema villages with Rs.9.52. In respect of female casual labourers, the highest rate was found in Andhra Nagar with Rs.12.38 and lowest was found in Piridi with Rs.4.76 in 1984-'85. In respect of 1990-'91 the highest male wage rate was found in Guntupalle with Rs.23.59 and lowest wage rate was found in Raigir with Rs.14.83. Regarding female casual labourers the highest real wage rate could be seen in Guntupalle as well as Andhra Nagar with Rs.16.85 each. The lowest wage rate was found in Raigir with Rs.8.09.

Table 5.5 : Annual Real Wages of Attached Labour

(In Rs.)

YEAR	P	VP	GP	VPM	CA	J	R	AN	TE	AP
1983–'84	2,200 (100)	3,809 (100)	4,768 (100)	4,000 (100)	3,694.25 (100)	3,922 (100)	3,022 (100)	5,690 (100)	4,194.67 (100)	3,944.46 (100)
1984–'85	2,190 (99.53)	3,405 (89.40)	4,559 (95.62)	3,998 (99.96)	3,539.52 (95.77)	3,681 (93.87)	2,930 (96.96)	5,452 (96.67)	4,021.32 (95.87)	3,779.75 (95.82)
1985–'86	2,215 (100.67)	3,742 (98.25)	4,420 (92.69)	4,014 (100.36)	3,592.72 (97.39)	3,640 (92.80)	2,730 (90.34)	5,451 (96.65)	3,940.26 (93.94)	3,769.00 (95.55)
1986–'87	2,333 (106.04)	4,038 (106.00)	4,298 (90.14)	3,993 (99.82)	3,665.32 (99.22)	3,679 (93.80)	2,871 (95.01)	5,339 (94.66)	3,962.91 (94.47)	3,814.12 (96.70)
1987–'88	2,553 (116.02)	4,084 (107.22)	4,084 (85.66)	3,829 (95.72)	3,632.36 (98.46)	3,551 (90.03)	2,893 (95.73)	5,105 (90.51)	3,842.99 (91.62)	3,740.18 (94.82)
1988–'89	2,534 (115.17)	3,619 (95.03)	3,511 (73.64)	3,402 (85.06)	3,266.61 (88.43)	3,330 (84.91)	2,606 (86.24)	4,343 (77.01)	3,474.73 (82.84)	3,370.49 (85.45)
1989–'90	2,737 (124.40)	3,558 (93.40)	3,352 (70.31)	3,763 (94.08)	3,352.49 (90.75)	3,284 (83.74)	2,737 (90.56)	4,242 (75.21)	3,420.90 (81.56)	3,386.69 (85.86)
1990–'91	3,031 (137.79)	3,705 (97.27)	3,368 (70.64)	4,042 (101.04)	3,536.54 (95.73)	3,368 (85.88)	3,031 (100.31)	4,378 (77.64)	3,592.67 (85.65)	3,564.61 (90.37)
CV	***53.16065***	***52.12059***	***53.59219***	***52.05662***	***51.93192***	***52.11603***	***52.02170***	***53.06484***	***52.27152***	***52.06523***

Note :
i) Figures within parantheses indicate index numbers with 1983–84 as base year.
ii) P–Piridi; VP–Vangalapudi; GP–Guntupalle; VPM–Veerannapalem; CA–Coastal Andhra; J–Jookal; R–Raigir; AN–Andhra Nagar; TE–Telangana; AP–Andhra Pradesh
iii) CV–Coefficient of Variation.

Table 5.6 : Real Wages of Casual Labour (Male and Female)

(In Rs.)

YEAR	PIRIDI		VANGALAPUDI		GUNTUPALLE		VEERANNAPALEM		OVERALL	
	M	F	M	F	M	F	M	F	M	F
1983–'84	11.00 (100.00)	5.00 (100.00)	13.00 (100.00)	11.00 (100.00)	19.00 (100.00)	12.00 (100.00)	15.00 (100.00)	10.00 (100.00)	14.50	9.50
1984–'85	10.47 (95.20)	4.76 (105.04)	13.32 (102.52)	11.42 (103.86)	19.04 (100.21)	11.42 (95.20)	14.28 (95.20)	9.52 (95.20)	14.28 (98.49)	9.28 (97.71)
1985–'86	10.15 (92.29)	5,53 (130.03)	14.75 (113.58)	11.99 (109.06)	18.44 (97.14)	11.06 (92.29)	13.83 (92.29)	9.22 (92.29)	14.29 (98.65)	9.45 (99.58)
1986–'87	10.77 (97.88)	5.38 (122.60)	15.25 (117.34)	11.66 (106.04)	19.73 (103.89)	10.76 (89.73)	13.45 (89.73)	8.97 (89.73)	14.80 (102.10)	9.19 (96.82)
1987–'88	10.06 (100.55)	5.96 (139.23)	15.31 (117.81)	11.91 (108.29)	21.27 (111.95)	12.76 (106.36)	12.77 (85.09)	8.51 (85.09)	15.10 (104.15)	9.78 (103.00)
1988–'89	1086 (98.71)	5.79 (162.09)	13.76 (105.80)	10.14 (93.13)	21.72 (114.30)	14.48 (120.65)	10.81 (72.39)	7.24 (72.39)	14.29 (98.60)	9.41 (99.06)
1989–'90	13.68 (124.40)	6.84 (160.77)	13.68 (105.26)	10.27 (99.30)	20.52 (108.03)	13.68 (114.03)	13.68 (91.22)	8.21 (82.10)	15.39 (106.17)	9.75 (102.63)
1990–'91	16.84 (153.10)	10.10 (195.95)	16.85 (129.55)	13.48 (122.48)	23.59 (124.09)	16.85 (140.34)	16.85 (112.27)	10.11 (101.04)	18.53 (127.76)	12.64 (132.95)
CV	***55.22708***	***58.70972***	***52.51615***	***52.58247***	***52.43887***	***54.16988***	***53.25505***	***52.85874***	***52.60598***	***53.01709***

Note : i) M–Male; F–Female.

ii) CV–Coefficient of Variation.

(Contd...)

Table 5.6 : (Contd...)

(In Rs.)

YEAR	Brahmanapalle		Sanjeevapuram		Overall		Jookal	
	M	F	M	F	M	F	M	F
1983–'84	10.00	6.00	10.00	5.00	10.00	5.50	11.00	6.00
	(100.00)	(100.00)	(100.00)	(100.00)	(100.00)	(100.00)	(100.00)	(100.00)
1984–'85	9.52	5.71	9.52	5.71	9.52	5.71	10.42	5.71
	(95.20)	(95.20)	(95.20)	(114.24)	(95.20)	(103.86)	(106.53)	(106.53)
1985–'86	10.14	5.53	9.22	5.53	9.68	5.53	10.12	5.53
	(101.51)	(92.29)	(92.29)	(110.74)	(996.90)	(100.67)	(107.76)	(107.76)
1986–'87	10.76	6.28	10.76	6.28	10.78	6.28	13.45	7.18
	(107.67)	(104.68)	(107.67)	(125.62)	(107.67)	(114.20)	(145.37)	(142.14)
1987–'88	12.76	8.51	12.76	8.51	12.76	8.51	17.02	8.57
	(127.63)	(141.81)	(144.78)	(173.74)	(137.54)	(157.94)	(214.13)	(196.29)
1988–'89	13.03	8.67	14.42	8.69	13.76	8.69	14.48	7.24
	(130.03)	(144.78)	(144.78)	(173.74)	(137.54)	(157.94)	(214.13)	(196.29)
1989–'90	13.68	10.26	17.10	10.26	15.39	10.26	17.10	10.26
	(136.84)	(171.05)	(171.05)	(205.26)	(153.94)	(186.60)	(271.40)	(298.54)
1990–'91	16.85	10.78	16.85	13.48	16.85	12.13	16.85	10.11
	((168.41)	(179.64)	(168.41)	(237.52)	(168.41)	(220.46)	(264.64)	(291.10)
CV	***55.67112***	***58.54189***	***43.66253***	***50.92993***	***42.00519***	***47.51701***	***41.58587***	***43.28132***

Note : i) M–Male; F–Female.

ii) CV–Coefficient of Variation.

(Contd...)

Table 5.6 : (Contd...)

(In Rs.)

YEAR	Raigir		Andhra Nagar		Overall		Andhra Pradesh	
	M	F	M	F	M	F	M	F
1983–'84	13.00	6.00	17.00	13.00	13.67	8.33	12.72	7.78
	(100.00)	(100.00)	(100.00)	(100.00)	(100.00)	(100.00)	(100.00)	(100.00)
1984–'85	12.38	5.71	17.17	12.38	13.33	7.77	12.38	7.64
	(106.53)	(106.53)	(100.86)	(95.20)	(97.00)	(95.00)	(97.30)	(106.07)
1985–'86	12.91	5.53	16.60	11.99	13.21	7.68	12.38	7.55
	(116.05)	(107.76)	(97.71)	(92.29)	(96.74)	(92.00)	(97.51)	(107.96)
1986–'87	13.45	6.28	17.04	11.66	14.65	8.34	13.40	7.95
	(123.02)	(124.38)	(100.28)	(89.73)	(107.19)	(100.49)	(105.38)	(108.07)
1987–'88	13.62	6.81	17.02	10.21	15.89	8.51	14.59	8.94
	(136.71)	(148.10)	(100.10)	(78.54)	(116.21)	(102.00)	(114.65)	(114.83)
1988–'89	13.03	6.52	14.48	10.86	13.99	8.20	14.02	8.77
	(163.07)	(176.66)	(85.17)	(83.53)	(102.36)	(98.46)	(110.18)	(112.68)
1989–'90	13.68	6.84	17.10	13.68	15.96	10.26	15.58	10.09
	(183.72)	(199.03)	(100.62)	(105.62)	(116.71)	(123.00)	(122.53)	(129.71)
1990–'91	14.83	8.09	20.22	16.85	17.30	11.68	17.56	12.15
	(197.05)	(232.88)	(118.88)	(129.55)	(126.49)	(140.14)	(138.01)	(156.11)
CV	***35.77602***	***37.50690***	***36.50513***	***38.93209***	***36.75830***	***38.59670***	***37.59581***	***39.61665***

Note : i) M–Male; F–Female.

ii) CV–Coefficient of Variation.

The growth in real wage rates is also shown through index in this table. In respect of male casual labourers the highest growth rate was observed in Jookal with 164.64 per cent and the lowest was found in Veerannapalem with only 12.27 per cent. In fact there had been a decline in real wage rates in the intermittent years in all the villages with the exception of Jookal and Raigir of Rayalaseema. Thus the increase in cost of living index had exceeded the increase in money wage rates in all the villages of Coastal Andhra and Telangana in the intervening years of the period under study. It was only male casual labourers of Rayalaseema villages who were benefited consistently through continuous increase in real wage rates during the period under study.

In respect of female casual labourers, the highest growth rate of 191.10 per cent was found in Jookal of Telangana and the lowest growth rate of 1.04 per cent was found in Veerannapalem of Coastal Andhra. The real wage rates of female casual labourers had continuously increased in Piridi of Coastal Andhra and Jookal and Raigir of Telangana - indicating thereby the excess of growth rate in money wage rates over the growth rate of cost of living. In all other villages, the real wage rates of female casual labourers had declined for some intervening years during the period under the study.

d. Wage Levels

Attached Labourers

The annual wages payable to attached labourers can be compared with *i)* wages of casual labourers; *ii)* wages of labourers working in other unorganised sector; *iii)* statutory minimum wage; *iv)* farmers' ability to pay; *v)* attached labourers' contribution and *vi)* cost of living. The attached labourers as well as the farmers had expressed their opinions regarding this comparison. It may be noted here that their assessment of wage level in comparison with the above factors will influence their attitudes and behaviour. With this idea, their perceptions are elicited and shown in Table 5.7. As shown in this table, the responses are classified into four catagories viz., 'high', 'fair', 'low' and 'no idea'. It could be seen from this table that in comparison with the wages of casual labourers, while the attached labourers of Piridi, Guntupalle and Veerannapalem had felt that their wages were 'high'; the attached labourers of all other villages expressed that their wages were 'low'. On this issue, surprisingly, the farmers, by and large, agreed with the opinion expressed by attached labourers.

Table 5.7 : Wage Level of Attached Labour

REGION AND VILLAGE	Compared To											
	WCL		WWUS		SMW		FAP		ALC		CL	
	AL	F	AL	F	AL	F	AL	F	AL	F	AL	F
COASTAL ANDHRA												
Piridi	H	N	H	L	L	N	N	F	H	N	L	N
Vangalapudi	L	L	L	F	N	N	L	H	L	H	L	F
Guntupalle	H	H	F	H	N	N	F	F	L	H	F	F
Veerannapalem	H	H	H	F,L	N	N	F	H	F	F	L	F
OVERALL	**H**	**H**	**L**	**F,L**	**N**	**N**	**F**	**H**	**L**	**H**	**L**	**N**
TELANGANA												
Jookal	L	F,L	L	I	--	N	L	F	L	F	L	F
Raigir	L	H,L	L	F	N	N	L	H	L	L	L	F
Andhra Nagar	L	L	L	L	N	N	F	H	L	H	L	F
OVERALL	**L**	**L**	**L**	**L**	**N**	**N**	**L**	**H**	**L**	**L**	**L**	**F**
ANDHRA PRADESH	***L***	***H***	***L***	***L***	***N***	***N***	***L***	***H***	***L***	***H***	***L***	***F***

Note : i) No Attached Labour in Rayalaseema Villages.
ii) WCL—Wage of Casual Labour;
SMW—Statutory Minimum Wages; FAP—Farmers' Ability to Pay.
iii) H—High; L—Low; F—Fair, N—No Idea.

The wages of labourers working in other unorganised sector is next taken up for comparison. With the exception of attached labourers of Piridi and Veerannapalem, all other attached labourers felt that their wages were 'low' compared to this factor. The farmers of individual villages, with exception of Jookal and Andhra Nagar, differed from the opinion of attached labourers.

The government of Andhra Pradesh has taken steps in fixing as well as revising the minimum wages payable to attached labourers. It is interesting to elicit the opinions of both attached labourers and farmers as to the level of their actual wages in comparison with the minimum wages fixed by the government. It is unfortunate that both attached labourers and farmers had expressed their ignorance of the statutory minimum wages. This suggests that it is the responsibility of the government to educate both the attached labourers and farmers through intensive publicity. It is only then, the attached labourers will come to know of the statutory minimum wages and insist on their payment.

The farmers' ability to pay which is determined by yield per acre and the market value of produce, is also to be considered while fixing the wages payable to attached labourers. While the attached labourers of Guntupalle, Veerannapalem and Andhra Nagar had felt that their wages were 'fair' compared to the farmer's capacity to pay; the attached labourers of Guntupalle, Jookal and Raigir had termed their wages 'low'. On the other hand the farmers of almost all the villages expressed that the wages of attached labourers were 'high' compared to their capacity to pay.

The contribution of attached labourers to the farmers is also to be taken into consideration while assessing their wage level. While the attached labourers of most of the villages were of the view that their wages were 'low'; the farmers of most of the villages felt that they were 'high'.

The cost of living is another important factor which is to be considered against wages payable to attached labourers. The opinions of attached labourers and farmers differed on this aspect also. While the attached labourers of almost all the villages veiwed their wages as 'low'; the farmers of almost all the villages viewed them as 'fair' compared to cost of living.

Casual Labourers

The casual labourers and farmers are also asked about their opinion on wage level in comparison with i. wages of attached labourers; ii. wages of labourers working in other unorganised sector; iii. statutory mimimum wages; iv. farmers' ability to pay; v. casual labourers' contribution and vi. cost of living. The results are given in Table 5.8.

Since the attached labourers work along with casual labourers, it is but natural for casual labourers to make a comparison of their wages with that of attached labourers. The casual labourers of all villages with the exception of Vangalapudi, felt that their wages were 'low' compared to that of attached labourers. While this was so, the farmers of all the three villages of Telangana and Vangalapudi of Coastal Andhra felt that the wages of casual labourers were 'high' compared to that of attached labourers. The farmers of Piridi, Guntupalle and Veerannapalem agreed with the opinion of casual labourers and felt that their wages were 'low'.

The wages of labourers working in other unorganised sector is next taken up for comparison. The casual labourers of almost all the villages with exception of Andhra Nagar felt that their wages were 'low'. The farmers of most of the villages also agreed with this opinion of casual labourers.

Statutory minimum wages fixed by the government is another important comparable factor. As in the case of attached labourers, the casual labourers and farmers of all the villages had expressed that they

Table 5.8 : Wage Level of Casual Labour

REGION AND VILLAGE	Compared To											
	WAL		WUS		SMW		FAP		CLC		COL	
	CL	F	CL	F	CL	F	CL	F	CL	F	CL	F
COASTAL ANDHRA												
Piridi	L	L	L	L	N	N	L	H	L	H	L	F
Vangalapudi	H	H	L	F	N	N	L	H	L	H	L	F
Guntupalle	L	L	L	L	N	N	L	H	L	H	L	F
Veerannapalem	L	L	L	H	N	N	L	H	L	H	L	F
OVERALL	**L**	**L**	**L**	**L**	**N**	**N**	**L**	**H**	**L**	**H**	**L**	**F**
RAYALASEEMA												
Brahmanapalle	--	--	L	L	N	L	L	H	L	H	L	F
Sanjeevapuram	--	--	L	L	N	N	L	H	L	H	L	H
OVERALL	--	--	**L**	**L**	**N**	**N**	**L**	**H**	**L**	**H**	**L**	**H**
TELANGANA												
Jookal	L	H	L	L	N	N	L	F	L	F	L	H
Raigir	L	H	L	L	N	N	L	H	L	L	L	F
Andhra Nagar	L	H	H	L	N	N	F	H	L	L	L	F
OVERALL	**L**	**H**	**L**	**L**	**N**	**N**	**L**	**H**	**L**	**L**	**L**	**H**
ANDHRA PRADESH	***L***	***H***	***L***	***L***	***N***	***N***	***L***	***H***	***L***	***H***	***L***	***F***

Note i) H—High; L—Low; F—Fair; N—No Idea.
ii) WAL—Wages of Attached Labour;
SMW—Statutory Minimum Wages; FAP—Farmers' Ability to Pay.
COL—Cost of Living. F—Farmers;
WUS—Wages of Labour Working in Other Unorganized Sector;
CLC—Casual Labourers' Contribution;
CL—Casual Labour;

were not aware of the statutory minimum wage. This calls for an intensive campaign by the government about the statutory minimum wage which helps its implementation.

Compared to farmers' ability to pay, the casual labourers of all the villages, with the exception of Andhra Nagar, had felt that their wages were 'low'. The farmers of all the villages with the exception of Jookal had felt that the wages of casual labourers were 'high' in comparison with their own capacity to pay.

The wages of casual labourers are compared with their own contribution. The casual labourers of all the villages unanimously pointed out that their wages were 'low' compared to their contribution. While this was so, the farmers of Coastal Andhra and Rayalaseema had opined that the wages of casual labourers were 'high' compared to their contribution. The farmers of Telangana villages particularly of Raigir and Andhra Nagar agreed with the views of casual labourers in this regard.

In comparison with the cost of living, the casual labourers of all the villages were of the view that their wages were 'low'. As against this, the farmers of all villages with the exception of Sanjeevapuram and Jookal felt that the wages of casual labourers were 'fair' compared to that of cost of living.

e. Ranking of Villages by Money Wages and their Index

The absolute money wages paid to attached labourers and casual labourers in different villages and their growth index have been studied and the villages are ranked accordingly. Table 5.9 shows the ranking of villages as per the absolute money wages and their growth index applicable to attached labourers for two years namely 1984-'85 and 1990-'91. It is to be noted from this table that in respect of absolute money wages, while the first rank is retained by Andhra Nagar in both the years; there has been a change in the ranks of all other villages in between these two years. In respect of growth index, there has been a change in the ranks of the villages of Coastal Andhra. But the villages of Telangana retained the same rank in between the two years.

The villages have also been ranked in respect of wages paid to male and female casual labourers and are shown in Table 5.10. While Guntupalle stood first; Andhra Nagar second in respect of the absolute money wages paid to male agricultural labourers in both the years.

Table 5.9 : Ranking of Villages by Absolute Money Wages and by Growth Index Thereof— Attached Labourers' Opinion

VILLAGES	Absolute Money Wages		Growth Index of Money Wages	
	1984–85	1990–91	1984–85	1990–91
Piridi	VII	IV	II	I
Vanagalapudi	V	III	VII	IV
Guntupalle	II	IV	VI	VII
Veerannapalem	III	II	I	II
Jookal	IV	V	V	V
Raigir	VI	V	III	III
Andhra Nagar	I	I	IV	IV

Table 5.10 : Ranking of Villages by Absolute Money Wages and by Growth Index Thereof—Male and FemaleCasual Labourers' Opinion

VILLAGES	Absolute Money Wages				Growth Index of Money Wages			
	1984-85		1990-91		1984-85		1990-91	
	Male	Female	Male	Female	Male	Female	Male	Female
PIRIDI	VI	V	III	IV	IV	III	II	II
VANAGALAPUDI	IV	II	III	II	I	II	III	VIII
GUNTUPALLE	I	II	I	I	III	III	IV	V
VEERANNAPLEM	III	II	II	IV	IV	III	VII	IX
BRAHMANAPALLE	VII	IV	III	III	IV	III	I	III
SANJEEVAPURAM	VII	IV	III	II	IV	I	I	I
JOOKAL	VI	IV	III	IV	IV	III	II	IV
RAIGIR	V	IV	IV	V	IV	III	IV	Vi
ANDHRA NAGAR	II	I	II	I	II	III	V	VII

Similarly Andhra Nagar stood first; Vangalapudi stood second in respect of the absolute money wages paid to female casual labourers in both the years. In respect of growth index of money wages, there was no consistancy in case of male casual labourers and the ranks changed in between the two years. But in respect of female casual labourers, Sanjeevapuram stood first and Brahmanapalle stood third in both the years.

f. Satisfaction with Wages

Attached Labourers

The percentage distribution of attached labourers by their satisfaction with and percentage distribution of farmers by their perception of attached labourers' satisfaction with wages are shown in Table 5.11. It could be seen from this table that nearly three fourths of attached labourers were not satisfied with their wages. Further cent per cent of attached labourers of Guntupalle, Jookal and Raigir were dissatisfied with their wages. It is only in Piridi that 60 per cent of attached labourers were satisfied. As against this, 79 per cent of farmers were of the view that the attached labourers were satisfied with their wages. Thus this analysis shows the perceptual gap between the attached labourers and farmers. This continuance of gap is not desirable from the point of view of harmonious relation between the two groups. The farmers have to enquire into the dissatisfaction and take appropriate remedial steps so as to bridge the gulf between the two.

Table 5.11 : Satisfaction with Attached Labourers' Wages

REGION AND VILLAGE	Satisfied Completely		Satisfied to Some Extent		Not Satisfied		Total	
	AL	F	AL	F	AL	F	AL	F
COASTAL ANDHRA								
Piridi	60.00	71.43	40.00	23.81	--	4.76	100.00	100.00
Vanagalapudi	20.00	54.55	--	36.36	80.00	9.09	100.00	100.00
Guntupalle	--	80.00	--	20.00	100.00	--	100.00	100.00
Veerannapalem	--	80.00	20.00	40.00	80.00	20.00	100.00	100.00
OVERALL	**20.00**	**65.96**	**15.00**	**27.66**	**65.00**	**6.38**	**100.00**	**100.00**
TELANGANA								
Jookal	--	88.89	--	--	100.00	11.11	100.00	100.00
Raigir	--	100.00	--	--	100.00	--	100.00	100.00
Andhra Nagar	--	100.00	40.00	--	60.00	--	100.00	100.00
OVERALL	--	**97.06**	**13.33**	--	**86.6**	**2.94**	**100.00**	**100.00**
ANDHRA PRADESH	***11.42***	***79.01***	***14.29***	***16.05***	***74.29***	***4.94***	***100.00***	***100.00***

Note : i) No Attached Labour in Rayalaseema Villages.
ii) AL—Attached Labour.
F—Farmers.

Casual Labourers

The percentage distribution of casual labourers by their satisfaction with and the percentage distribution of farmers by their perception of casual labourers' satisfaction with wages are shown in Table 5.12. It could be observed from this table that while 86 per cent of casual labourers were not satisfied with their wages. As against this, 69 per cent of farmers were of the view that casual labourers were satisfied with their wages. Thus this table shows the perceptual gap between the casual labourers and attached labourers. As already suggested, this gap is to be eliminated by instituting appropriate remedial steps.

g. Percentage of Labour Cost in the Market Value of Produce

The wage rates payable to attached labourers and casual labourers have been increased from year to year during the period under study i.e., 1983-'84 to 1990-'91. The burden of this increase in wage rates can be assessed through the percentage of labour cost in the market value of produce. It may be noted that the market value of produce is influenced by yield per acre and the output price. The share of labour in the farmers'

Table 5.12 : Satisfaction with Casual Labourers' Wages

REGION AND VILLAGE	Satisfied Completely		Satisfied to Some Extent		Not Satisfied		Total	
	CL	F	CL	F	CL	F	CL	F
COASTAL ANDHRA								
Piridi	20.00	62.86	34.29	17.14	45.71	20.00	100.00	100.00
Vanagalapudi	--	74.29	2.86	14.28	97.14	11.43	100.00	100.00
Guntupalle	--	77.14	--	17.14	100.00	5.72	100.00	100.00
Veerannapalem	--	48.57	2.86	11.43	97.14	40.00	100.00	100.00
OVERALL	**5.00**	**65.71**	**10.00**	**15.00**	**85.00**	**19.29**	**100.00**	**100.00**
RAYALASEEMA								
Brahmanapalle	2.86	40.00	22.86	28.57	74.28	31.43	100.00	100.00
Sanjeevapuram	--	40.00	--	25.71	100.00	34.29	100.00	100.00
OVERALL	1.43	40.00	11.43	27.14	87.14	32.86	100.00	100.00
TELANGANA								
Jookal	--	80.00	--	2.86	100.00	17.14	100.00	100.00
Raigir	--	100.00	--	--	100.00	--	100.00	100.00
Andhra Nagar	--	100.00	31.14	--	68.57	--	100.00	100.00
OVERALL	--	**93.33**	**10.48**	**0.95**	**89.52**	**5.72**	**100.00**	**100.00**
ANDHRA PRADESH	***2.54***	***69.21***	***11.11***	***13.01***	***86.35***	***17.78***	***100.00***	***100.00***

Note : CL—Casual Labour.
F—Farmers.

revenue can be assessed through the information given in Table 5.13. It is interesting to note that the percentage of the labour costs in the market value of produce had declined in all the villages with the exception of Jookal and Raigir villages during the period 1983-'84 to 1990-'91. While the percentage of the labour cost in the market price of produce varied between 21.30 in Veerannapalem to 63.53 in Brahmanapalle in 1983-'84; it varied from 15.14 in Veerannapalem to 32.93 in Sanjeevapuram in 1990-'91. Thus the average percentage of labour cost in the market value of produce is worked out at 19.32 in Coastal Andhra; 27.61 in Rayalaseema and 24.38 in Telangana.

The decline in percentage of labour cost in the market value of produce should be attributed to the implementation of new agricultural strategy consisting of mechanisation of agricultural operations, use of high yielding varieties, and extension of irrigation facilities—resulting in

Table 5.13 : Percentage of Labour Cost in the Market Value of Produce

(In Rs.)

YEAR	COASTAL ANDHRA					RAYALASEEMA			TELANGANA				AP
	P	VP	GP	VPM	OA	BP	SP	OA	J	R	AN	OA	
1983–'84	26.08	27.51	34.85	21.30	27.92	63.58	47.39	55.58	23.60	22.41	27.02	24.85	30.68
1984–'85	25.20	27.26	34.27	23.34	28.07	37.86	71.28	47.38	24.09	22.96	29.25	26.06	30.62
1985–'86	25.76	23.20	33.72	23.73	26.80	40.11	63.53	48.36	24.40	23.31	30.51	26.67	30.71
1986–'87	22.03	21.16	29.88	19.84	23.49	41.71	61.11	48.81	33.33	23.16	27.78	27.55	29.50
1987–'88	25.00	20.58	23.90	19.36	22.11	49.02	63.16	54.22	42.33	23.80	26.95	29.76	30.34
1988–'89	26.56	20.03	24.42	14.54	20.88	40.00	75.04	51.78	39.12	26.55	26.24	29.75	29.38
1989–'90	26.09	18.91	22.66	18.83	21.33	32.76	57.53	41.24	41.72	28.37	22.95	29.78	28.47
1990–'91	25.39	18.26	20.77	15.14	19.32	24.04	32.93	27.61	33.17	25.48	17.88	24.38	23.13

Note : P–Piridi; VP–Vangalapudi; GP–Guntupalle; VPM–Veerannapalem; OA–Overall; BP–Brahmanaplle; SP–Sanjeevapuram; J–Jookal; R–Raigir; AN–Andhra Nagar; AP–Andhra Pradesh

significant increase in the yield per acre on the one hand and decline in labour cost due to less utilisation of labour. Added to this, the market price of agricultural produce has also increased significantly during the period under study. Thus, this decline in percentage of labour cost in the market value of produce should not be attributed to the expliotation of the agricultural labour but is the result of improvement in agricultural productivity.

Statutory Minimum Wages

a. Need for Fixation of Minimum Wages

The wages of labour will be determined by market forces on the basis of demand for labour and supply of labour. In underdeveloped countries, if market forces are given sole right to determine the wages of labour it amounts exploitation and unreasonable consideration as in many economies we find surplus of labour. Hence, there is need for statutory frame in which the wages of labour will be rational and logical to meet their needs which were expected from a human being living in a civilised society.

In this context, the Government has to take approperiate steps to regulate the wages of labour in economy, more so in agriculture sector. In this regard the Minimum Wages Act 1948 was enacted by the Government to fix minimum wages in farm sector.

b. Basis for Fixation of Minimum Wages

The problem of selecting the appropriate level for the minimum wages consists of striking a balance between the workers' recognised needs for maintaining a certain minimum living standard and the economic and social feasibility of ensuring them such a standard of living. Besides, the objective in determination of minimum wages should not only be fixation of wages which are fair but also to see that employment at existing levels is maintained and if possible increased. This can be achieved when the wages fixed are not very much out of line with wages in other comparable industries. Thus the broad criteria for fixation of minimum wages are considered to be[1]:

a) Minimum needs of the worker and his family
b) The capacity of the industry to pay: and

---

1. Internataional Labour Organisation, "*International Labour Conference, Report VII(1), Minimum Wage Fixing Machinery and Related Problems with Special Reference to Developing Countries*", Geneva, 1968.

c) The general level of wages in the region for comparable occupations.

The committees appointed in Andhra Pradesh made a thorough study of these factors before fixing the minimum wages. On the minimum needs of the worker and his family the First Committee has taken into consideration the views and information furnished by various people during the course of its tours and formulated the budget figures for a family keeping in view the norms laid down by the Indian Labour Conference. The subsequent Committees, following what is called 'theoretical method' have arrived at the minimum needs of the worker and his family.

Though no systematic attempt is made to assess the ability of the industry to pay a certain level of wage, all the Committees were of the unanimous view that the maximum wage fixed should not be too high to disturb the present pattern of employment in agriculture and encourage introduction of labour saving technology. The Committees have also taken into consideration the current level of wages paid in agriculture in different regions in the States and wages paid in comparable occupations outside agriculture.

It is not clear as to what weight is given to each of the factors considered earlier by different committees. However, one gathers the impression that the level of wages ultimately fixed are influenced by the relative bargaining power of the representatives of the employers and employees in the Committee rather than any other factor, since the wages fixed bear no similarity with estimates of any of the norms.

c. Implementation of Minimum Wages Legislation

The National Commission on Labour made a review of the Minimum Wages Act, as applied to agricultural labour, in 1969. It pointed out a number of deficiencies with regard to both fixation and enforcement. Yet, it came to the conclusion that 'the application of Minimum Wages Act, however defective it may be, at present will help agricultural labour'.[1] The main justification for this conclusion is the basic premise that 'notification of minimum wages under the legislation helps evolution of norms and will provide a basis for persons who are prepared to work in the interests of agricultural labour'.[2] Hence, the

1. Government of India, Ministry of Labour and Employment Rehabilitation, *'Report of the National Commission on Labour'*, 1969, pp.400-403.

2. Ibid, p.402.

Commission favoured improvements in procedures of fixation, revision and implementation of minimum wages. It recommended a number of steps towards achieving objective :

i. A periodic revision of minimum wages through constitution of tri-partitie committees for fixation or revision of minimum wages;

ii. Gradual extension of operation of Minimum wages Act beginning with low wage pocket areas to others;

iii. Wide publicity for wages fixed under the Act;

iv. Strengthening of field staff engaged in enforcement of Minimum wages and involving the village Panchayats in the task of implementation; and

v. Provision of such facilities by the State Government as are required to encourage the trade unions of agricultural labour.

The National Commission on Agriculture expressed doubts whether the fixation and revision of minimum wages have received the attention they deserve. It observed that in a number of cases, the minimum wages were fixed at an initially low level more than two decades ago and have been revised only infrequently since then.[1] Ineffective enforcement appears to explain the relatively higher level of prevailing wages in some states as compared to the minimum wages fixed. In the context of widespread demand for an upward revision of minimum wages it suggested that 'a realistic policy on minimum wages in the context of agricultural sector in India' keeping in view the heterogenity of the agricultural labour market is needed.[2] It is in consonance with this suggestion that the latest minimum wages committee for agricultural labour in Andhra Pradesh appears to have made its recommendations effective from 1991.

d. Revision of Statutory Minimum Wages 1961-'91

The statutory minimum wages payable to attached labourers and casual labourers in Andhra Pradesh have been revised six times as per the recommendations of six different committees during the period 1961-'91. Table 5.14 shows the changes in statutory minimum wages enforced for attached labourers and for different agricultural operations performed

1. Government of India, Ministry of Agriculture and Irrigation, '*Report of the National Commission on Agriculture*', Part xv, Agrarian Reform, New Delhi, 1976, pp.257-260.

2. Ibid, p.260.

Table 5.14 : Statutory Minimum Wages—1961 to 1991

Zones and Years	Daily Minimum Wages for Casual Labour				Annual Wage for Attached Labour
	PL	TR	WD	HR	
Zone—I					
1961	2.00	1.25	1.38	1.62	500
1968	3.00	2.00	1.50	2.00	*
1974	4.00	3.50	3.00	3.50	1,200
1983	12.00	10.00	9.00	10.00	2,400
1987	14.50	12.00	11.00	12.00	2,880
1991	23.40	21.00	19.25	21.00	5,040
Zone—II					
1961	1.75	1.00	1.25	1.37	400
1968	2.60	1.50	1.30	1.50	**
1974	3.50	2.75	2.50	2.75	1,000
1983	10.00	9.00	8.00	9.00	2,000
1987	12.00	10.80	9.60	10.80	2,400
1991	21.00	19.00	16.80	19.00	4,200
Zone—III					
1961	1.50	0.88	1.12	1.25	300
1968	2.25	1.25	1.00	1.25	***
1974	3.00	2.50	2.25	2.50	800
1983	8.00	8.00	7.00	8.00	1,600
1987	9.60	9.60	8.50	9.60	1,920
1991	16.80	16.80	15.00	16.80	3,360

Note : PL—Ploughing; TR—Transplantation; WD—Wedding
HR—Harvesting;
*—20–25 bags of 75 Kg or Cash equivalent
**—9 quintals of mager millets or cash equivalent
***—7 quintals of mager millets of cash equivalent.

by casual labourers. The entire State has been divided into three zones. The selected nine villages are covered by zones as follows :

Zone I : 1. Veerannapalem of Coastal Andhra, 2. Andhra Nagar of Telangana.

Zone II : 1. Piridi, 2. Vengalapudi, 3. Guntapalle of Coastal Andhra, 4. Brahmanapalle of Rayalaseema and 5. Rayagiri of Telangana.

Zone III : 1. Sanjeevapuram of Rayalaseema, 2. Jookal of Telangana.

In respect of attached labourers, the statutory minimum wage per annum has gone up from Rs.500 in 1961 to Rs.5,040 in 1991 in Zone I—an increase of ten times during the thirty year period. In respect of Zone II the annual statutory minimum wage had increased from Rs.400 in 1961 to Rs.4,200 in 1991—an increase of more than ten times. In respect of Zone III the minimum wage had similarly increased eleven times *i.e.*, from Rs.300 in 1961 to Rs.3,060 in 1991. It is to be noted that increase in minimum wage of attached labourers was more perceptable in the latest revision of in 1991.

The statutory minimum wages of casual labourers are given separately for four important agricultural operations viz., ploughing, transplanting, weeding and harvesting. The rates fixed for ploughing were found to be the highest followed by transplanting and harvesting in whose case, same rate is fixed from 1968 onwords. The rate payable for the weeding is found to be the lowest since the nature of the work is light compared to other operations. These wage rates had been revised six times during the thirty year period. Highest increase in wage rate during this period was found in respect of transplanting in all the three Zones. This was followed by weeding, harvesting and ploughing in that order. It may be noted, further that the rate of increase in minimum wage was the highest in the latest revision of 1991. The wage rates had gone up by 60 per cent to 80 per cent in this latest revision compared to the immediately preceeding revision of 1987.

e. Statutory Minimum Wages V Prevailing Wages

Attached Labourers

The prevailing annual money wages of attached labourers are compared with their statutory minimum wages for the period 1983-'84 to 1990-'91 in Table 5.15. It is heartening to note that the prevailing annual money wages were higher than the minimum wages in respect of all villages of Coastal Andhra and Telangana during the period under study. The gap between the two was largest in respect of Andhra Nagar followed by Guntupalle, Jookal and Vangalapudi. It was lowest in respect of Piridi. It may be further noted that the gap between the statutory minimum wage and the prevailing wage had by and large increased from year to year and reached the peak level by 1989-'90 and later narrowed down in respect of all the villages for 1990-'91 with the latest revision of minimum wages.

Casual Labourers

The prevailing wage rates of casual labourers for two important

Table 5.15 :Attached Labourers' Minimum Wages, Prevailing Wages and Difference in Between

YEAR	PIRIDI			VANGALAPUDI			GUNTUPALLE		
	MW	PW	D	MW	PW	D	MW	PW	D
1983–'84	2,000	2,200	-200	2,000	3,809	–1,809	2,000	4,768	–2,768
1984–'85	2,000	2,300	-300	2,000	3,577	–1,577	2,000	4,759	–2,789
1985–'86	2,000	2,400	-400	2,000	4,055	–2,055	2,000	4,789	–2,789
1986–'87	2,000	2,600	-600	2,000	4,500	–2,500	2,000	4,790	–2,790
1987–'88	2,400	3,000	-600	2,400	4,800	–2,400	2,400	4,800	–2,400
1988–'89	2,400	3,500	–1,100	2,400	5,000	–2,600	2,400	4,850	–2,450
1989–'90	2,400	4,000	–1,600	2,400	5,200	–2,800	2,400	4,900	–2,500
1990–'91	4,200	4,500	-300	4,200	5,500	–1,300	4,200	5,000	-800

Note : M–Minimum Wage; PW—Prevailing Wage; D—Difference.

(Contd...)

Table 5.15 : (Contd...)

YEAR	Veerannapalem			Jookal			Raigir			Andhra Nagar		
	MW	PW	D	MW	PW	D	MW	PW	D	MW	PW	D
1983–'84	2,400	4,000	–1,600	1,600	3,922	–2,322	2,000	3,022	–1,022	2,400	5,690	–3,290
1984–'85	2,400	4,200	–1,800	1,600	3,867	–2,267	2,000	3,078	–1,078	2,400	5,727	–3,327
1985–'86	2,400	4,350	–1,950	1,600	3,944	–2,344	2,000	2,958	958	2,400	5,907	–3,507
1986–'87	2,400	4,450	–2,050	1,600	4,100	–2,500	2,000	3,200	1,200	2,400	5,950	–3,550
1987–'88	2,880	4,500	–1,620	1,920	4,150	–2,230	2,400	3,400	–1,000	2,880	6,000	–3,120
1988–'89	2,880	4,700	–1,820	1,920	4,600	–2,680	2,400	3,600	–1,200	2,880	6,000	–3,120
1989–'90	2,880	5,550	–2,620	1,920	4,800	–2,880	2,400	4,000	–1,600	2,880	6,200	–3,320
1990–'91	5,040	6,000	–960	3,360	5,000	–1,640	4,200	4,500	–300	5,040	6,500	–1,460

Note : M–Minimum Wage; PW–Prevailing Wage; D–Difference.

agricultural operations viz; transplanting and harvesting have been compared with the statutory minimum wage rates for the period 1983-'84 to 1990-'91 in Table 5.16. As in the case of attached labourers, the statutory minimum wage rates fixed by the government were less than the prevailing wage rates of casual labourers for all the eight years and in respect of all the nine villages. The only exception is in respect of Piridi where the statutory minimum wage rate for transplanting for 1990-'91 was slightly higher than the prevailing wage rate of the same year. Further the gap between the minimum wage and prevailing wage had increased continuously in respect of all the villages upto 1989-'90. It was only the latest revision of 1990-'91 which narrowed down the gap between the two. But even then, the prevailing wage was higher by 20 to 50 per cent in respect of different villages for 1990-'91.

Incentives

Meaning and Significance

The 'term wage incentive' has been used both in the restricted sense of participation and in the widest sense of financial motivation. According to Hummel and Nickerson: "It refers to all the plans that provide extra pay for extra performance in addition to regular wages for a job."[1] According to the National Commission on Labour, "wage incentives are extra financial motivation. They are designed to stimulate human effort by rewarding the person, over and above the time rated remuneration, for improvements in the present or targeted results."[2]

"A wage incentive scheme is essentially a managerial device of increasing a worker's productivity. Simultaneously, it is a method of sharing gains in productivity with workers by rewarding them financially for their increased rate of output."[3] This definition is based on the principle that "an offer of additional money will motivate workers to work harder and more skillfully for a greater part of their working time, which will result in a stepped-up rate of output."[4]

---

1. O.P. Hummel and W.J. Nickerson, "Wage Incentive Plans" in *Industrial Engineering Handbook,* ed. by H.B. Maynard, 1963, p.64.
2. National Commisson on Labour, Report of the Study Group on Productivity and Incentives, 1969, p.39.
3. G.K. Suri, ed. *Wage Incentives : Theory and Practice*, 1973, p.19
4. G. K. Suri, "Role of Wage Incentives in Increasing Productivity," in *Industrial Relations Journal,* Vol.22, No.6, (November-December), 1971.

Table 5.16 : Minimum Wage Rate *vs.* Prevailing Wage Rates of Casual Labour

YEAR	PIRIDI				VANGALAPUDI				GUNTUPALLE			
	Transplanting		Harvesting		Transplanting		Harvesting		Transplanting		Harvesting	
	MW	PW	MW	PW	MW	PW	MW	PW	MW	PW	MW	PW
1983-'84	10.00	10.46	9.06	10.46	10.00	13.37	9.00	13.09	10.00	19.29	9.00	15.47
1984-'85	10.00	10.71	9.00	10.76	10.00	13.87	9.00	13.57	10.00	19.66	9.00	16.46
1985-'86	10.00	12.00	9.00	11.46	10.00	15.57	9.00	14.37	10.00	20.00	9.00	17.49
1986-'87	10.00	11.00	9.00	11.00	10.00	16.00	9.00	16.00	10.00	22.00	9.00	17.49
1987-'88	12.00	12.00	9.60	12.00	12.00	18.00	9.60	18.00	12.00	25.00	9.60	22.00
1988-'89	12.00	13.00	9.60	14.00	12.00	20.00	9.60	20.00	12.00	30.00	9.60	25.00
1989-'90	12.00	15.00	9.60	18.00	12.00	22.50	9.60	22.50	12.00	30.00	9.60	30.00
1990-'91	21.00	20.00	19.00	20.00	21.00	25.00	19.00	25.00	21.00	35.00	19.00	35.00

Note : M—Minimum Wage; PW—Prevailing Wage;

(Contd...)

Table 5.16 : (Contd..)

YEAR	VEERANNAPALEM				BRAHMANAPALLE				SANJEEVAPURAM			
	Transplanting		Harvesting		Transplanting		Harvesting		Transplanting		Harvesting	
	MW	PW	MW	PW	MW	PW	MW	PW	MW	PW	MW	PW
1983–'84	12.00	15.09	10.00	14.74	10.00	9.83	9.00	9.49	8.00	9.69	8.00	9.40
1984–'85	12.00	15.11	10.00	14.86	10.00	10.20	9.00	10.14	8.00	9.74	8.00	9.40
1985–'86	12.00	15.23	10.00	15.11	10.00	10.43	9.00	10.51	8.00	10.00	8.00	10.49
1986–'87	12.00	17.00	10.00	18.00	10.00	15.00	9.00	12.00	8.00	11.00	8.00	11.00
1987–'88	14.50	20.00	12.00	20.00	12.00	22.25	9.60	15.00	9.60	13.25	9.60	13.25
1988–'89	14.50	23.00	12.00	22.00	12.00	23.40	9.60	17.15	9.60	17.00	9.60	18.00
1989–'90	14.50	25.00	12.00	25.00	12.00	25.00	9.60	22.15	9.60	23.00	9.60	23.00
1990–'91	23.40	30.00	21.00	30.00	21.00	30.00	19.00	25.00	16.80	30.00	16.80	25.00

Note : M–Minimum Wage; PW–Prevailing Wage;

(Contd...)

Table 5.16 : (Contd..)

YEAR	JOOKAL				RAIGIR				ANDHRA NAGAR			
	Transplanting		Harvesting		Transplanting		Harvesting		Transplanting		Harvesting	
	MW	PW	MW	PW	MW	PW	MW	PW	MW	PW	MW	PW
1983–'84	8.00	10.49	8.00	10.49	10.00	12.83	9.00	12.03	12.00	16.51	10.00	16.14
1984–'85	8.00	10.49	8.00	10.49	10.00	12.89	9.00	12.03	12.00	17.66	10.00	16.14
1985–'86	8.00	10.57	8.00	10.57	10.00	13.57	9.00	12.89	12.00	18.29	10.00	16.86
1986–'87	8.00	11.00	8.00	12.00	10.00	14.00	9.00	13.50	12.00	19.00	10.00	17.25
1987–'88	9.60	12.00	9.60	12.00	12.00	15.00	9.60	14.00	14.50	21.00	12.00	18.30
1988–'89	9.60	15.00	9.60	15.00	12.00	17.00	9.60	16.00	14.50	23.00	12.00	20.00
1989–'90	9.60	17.00	9.60	20.00	12.00	19.00	9.60	18.00	14.50	25.00	12.00	25.00
1990–'91	16.80	20.00	16.80	25.00	21.00	22.00	19.00	20.00	23.40	30.00	21.00	30.00

Note : M–Minimum Wage; PW–Prevailing Wage;

While monetary incentives often appear as important motivators, many factors unrelated to money can also serve as "attention-getters" and 'encouragers of action'. Following are some examples of non-monetary incentives viz., *i)* job assignments; *ii)* the opportunity to communicate with and relate to others; *iii)* status symbols; *iv)* participative or free rein leadership in the decision making process; *v)* verbal 'praise' or publicised 'awards'; *vi)* awards recognising their seniority and *vii)* opportunities for participation.

In India, the role of incentives as a primary tool for motivating workers cannot be over emphasised. Besides, the necessity for raising the productivity of Indian Labour is also getting due attention. Different five-year plans have recommended the introduction of incentive schemes under certain conditions.

Incentives in Agriculture

Monetary incentives do not exist in agriculture as systematically and as extensively as they are found in industrial organisations. However, incentives here take the following forms.

Share-cropping system: This is considered as an age-old practice. Under this, the farmers meet the entire expenditure involved in agricultural operations and after realising this expenditure from the sale proceeds of the output, the income on selling the output will be shared between the farmer and the attached labourer. But the proportion in which it is shared differs from place to place.

Another form of incentive prevalent in agriculture is the piece rate system. It is widely practised in recent years with the advent of commercialisation of agriculture. In busy agricultural operations like sowing, transplanting, harvesting and thrashing, the work is often given to labour on piece rate basis.

Another mode of incentive is prevalent in areas where cotton is grown. When the annual income on the cotton output crosses a particular level agreed upon as a standard, the farmer provides some incentives to the labour in the form of utilitarian articles.

Incentives in Selected Villages

Against the above background it is thought appropriate to enquire into the incentives provided by farmers of selected villages to their labour.

Incentives to Attached Labourers

It is observed common in selected villages natural to offer certain incentives like *i.* additional wage for work during inconvenient hours/for overtime; *ii.* extra offerings in kind; *iii.* offering money for wine, cinema etc., so as to induce the attached labourers to work hard or to take more interest in work or to spend more time in their duty. The percentage of farmers offering these incentives is shown in Table 5.17. Eighty five per cent of farmers at State level were offering incentives to their attached labourers. Further all the farmers of Guntupalle and Raigir were in the habit of extending incentives to their attached labourers. The nature of incentives offered is also enquired into and shown in this table. Extra offerings in kind was the most important incentive offered by farmers of all the villages with the exception of Veerannapalem. This was followed by offering money for wine, cinema etc. Additional wage for work during inconvenient hours was significant only in two villages viz., Guntupalle and Raigir.

Incentives to Casual Labourers

The incentives offered by farmers to casual labourers are shown in Table 5.18. It was only in Rayalaseema, the practice of offering incentives to casual labourers was widely prevalent. While 67 per cent of farmers in Rayalaseema were offering incentives to casual labourers; only 17 per cent in Coastal Andhra; 20 per cent in Rayalaseema were

Table 5.17 : Incentives Offered by Farmers to Attached Labour—Farmers' Response

REGION AND VILLAGE		Nature of Incentive Offered		
		Additional Wage for work during inconvenient hours/over time	Extra Offerings in kind	Offering Money for wine, cinema etc.
COASTAL ANDHRA				
Piridi	90.48	9.52	71.43	85.71
Vangalapudi	90.91	--	91.91	18.18
Guntupalle	100.00	60.00	70.00	90.00
Veerannapalem	60.00	--	--	60.00
OVERALL	**89.36**	**17.02**	**65.96**	**68.08**
TELANGANA				
Jookal	77.78	22.22	66.67	11.11
Raigir	100.00	50.00	90.00	50.00
Andhra Nagar	66.67	13.33	53.33	33.34
OVERALL	**79.41**	**26.47**	**67.65**	**32.35**
ANDHRA PRADESH	***85.19***	***20.99***	***66.67***	***53.08***

Note : No Attached Labour in Rayalaseema Villages.

Table 5.18 : Incentives Offered by Farmers to Casual Labour—Farmers' Response

REGION AND VILLAGE	YES	Nature of Incentive Offered		
		Additional Wage for work during inconvenient hours/over time	Extra Offerings in kind	Offering Money for wine, cinema etc.
COASTAL ANDHRA				
Piridi	28.57	72.73	9.09	18.18
Vangalapudi	2.86	--	--	100.00
Guntupalle	7.11	36.84	31.58	31.58
Veerannapalem	17.14	33.33	16.67	50.00
OVERALL	**17.14**	**45.95**	**21.62**	**32.43**
RAYALASEEMA				
Brahmanapalle	80.00	40.00	27.50	32.50
Sanjeevapuram	57.14	40.74	40.74	18.52
OVERALL	**67.14**	**40.30**	**32.84**	**26.86**
TELANGANA				
Jookal	5.71	--	--	100.00
Raigir	17.14	33.33	66.67	--
Andhra Nagar	37.14	14.29	7.14	78.57
OVERALL	**20.00**	**18.18**	**22.73**	**59.09**
ANDHRA PRADESH	***29.21***	***38.10***	***27.78***	***34.12***

offering these incentives. The two important incentives offered were *i.*additional wage for work during inconvenient hours and *ii.* offering money for wine, cinema etc.

Adequacy of Incentives

The percentage distribution of attached labourers and casual labourers by their opinion on adequacy of incentives is shown in Table 5.19. It may be noted from this table that 50 per cent of attached labourers and 71 per cent of casual labourers were satisfied with the incentives offered.

Reasons for not providing incentives to casual labourers

It may be recalled that 83 per cent of farmers in Coastal Andhra, 33 per cent of farmers in Rayalaseema and 80 per cent of farmers from Telangana were not offering incentives to casual labourers. It is worth enquiring into the reasons for not providing incentives. Twothirds of these farmers replied that the incentives were not agreed upon at the time of taking up the work (Tabel 5.20). Other reasons mentioned by the

Tablw 5.19 : Percentage Distribution of Attached Labour and Casual Labour by their Opinion on Adequacy of Incentives

REGION AND VILLAGE	Adequate		Inadequate		Satisfactory		No Opinion		Total	
	AL %	CL %	AL %	CL %	AL %	CL %	AL %	CL %	AL %	CL %
COASTAL ANDHRA										
Piridi	50.00	--	--	--	50.00	100.00	--	--	100.00	100.00
Vangalapudi	--	--	75.00	--	25.00	--	--	--	100.00	100.00
Guntupalle	40.00	--	--	--	60.00	--	--	--	100.00	100.00
Veerannapalem	--	--	--	--	100.00	--	--	--	100.00	100.00
OVERALL	**28.57**	--	**21.43**	--	**50.00**	**100.00**	--	--	**100.00**	**100.00**
RAYALASEEMA										
Brahmanapalle	--	--	--	50.00	--	--	--	50.00	--	100.00
Sanjeevapuram	--	--	--	--	--	100.00	--	--	--	100.00
OVERALL	--	--	--	**25.00**	--	**50.00**	--	**25.00**	--	**100.00**
TELANGANA										
Jookal	--	--	--	--	75.00	--	25.00	--	100.00	100.00
Raigir	--	--	--	--	--	--	100.00	--	100.00	100.00
Andhra Nagar	--	--	25.00	--	50.00	--	25.00	--	100.00	100.00
OVERALL	--	--	**10.00**	--	**50.00**	--	**40.00**	--	**100.00**	**100.00**
ANDHRA PRADESH	***16.67***	--	***16.66***	***14.29***	***50.00***	***71.42***	***16.67***	***14.29***	***100.00***	***100.00***

Note : AL – Attached Labour CL – Casual Labour.

Table 5.20 : Reasons Given by Farmers' for not Providing Incentives to Casual Labour

REGION AND VILLAGE	Not agreed Upon	Financially Incapable	Unnecessary as they are not provided other Farmer	Unnecessary Incapable their Contribution	No Scope	Total
COASTAL ANDHRA						
Piridi	88.00	--	4.00	--	8.00	100.00
Vangalapudi	76.47	--	2.94	20.59	--	100.00
Guntupalle	67.86	7.14	3.57	21.43	--	100.00
Veerannapalem	62.07	13.79	3.45	17.24	3.45	100.00
OVERALL	**73.27**	**5.17**	**3.45**	**15.52**	**2.59**	**100.00**
RAYALASEEMA						
Brahmanapalle	25.00	50.00	--	25.00	--	100.00
Sanjeevapuram	33.33	46.67	--	13.33	6.67	100.00
OVERALL	**30.43**	**47.83**	--	**17.39**	**4.35**	**100.00**
TELANGANA						
Jookal	51.52	15.15	9.09	18.18	6.06	100.00
Raigir	82.76	3.45	--	10.34	3.45	100.00
Andhra Nagar	68.18	--	--	31.82	--	100.00
OVERALL	**66.67**	**7.14**	**3.57**	**19.05**	**3.57**	**100.00**
ANDHRA PRADESH	***66.37***	***10.31***	***3.14***	***17.04***	***3.14***	***100.00***

farmers are *i.* financial limitations; *ii.* unnecessary as they are not provided by the other farmers; *iii.* unnecessary compared to the labourers' contribution and *iv.* no scope for providing these incentives.

Fringe Benefits

Meaning and Significance

Fringe benefits are also known as non-wage benefits.[1] The term "fringe benefits" refers to the various extra benefits given to employees in addition to the compensation paid in the form of wages or salaries.[2]

1. S. Madhuri, "The Perspective of Non-wage Benefits", *Indian Journal of Industrial Relations,* Vol.12, No,4, (April, 1977), p.453.
2. Dale Yoder, "*Personnel Management Industrial Relations*" (New Delhi : Prentice-Hall of India Pvt., Ltd., 1972), p.652.

During the World War II period, certain non-monetary benefits were extended to employees as a means of neutralising the effect of inflationary conditions.[1] These benefits have grown considerably over the years to include housing, health education, recreation, credit, canteens, company stores, transport, retirement benefits, etc. It has been widely recognised that these benefits help employees in meeting some of their life's contingencies and enable them to meet their social obligations. Welfare of employee and his family members is an effective advertising and also a method of buying gratitude and loyalty of employees.[2] But while some employers provide these benefits over and above legal requirements to make more effective use of work-force[3], some confine themselves only to those benefits which are legally required. The primary effect of all these fringe benefits is to retain employee in the organisation on a long term basis.

Fringe Benefits in Agriculture Sector

The nature of fringe benefits provided to agricultural labour in India showed considerable difference. Thus, in the different regions of Uttar Pradesh these are variously gur, sattu and sharbat, chabena and ras, a mid-day meal or a handful of parched coarse grains. In Madras, ragi meal with tea or coffee is supplied in one region where as a similar coarse meal with tea or coffee supplied in another. The customary benefits in Mysore are a mid-day meal and in some cases coffee (in some parts of Madras) as well. Porridge made of rice or tapioca in the morning or a mid-day meal is supplied in Travancore-Cochin. A meal or breakfast and tea are allowed in Assam, a light breakfast or mid-day meal consisting of sattu or roasted grain in Bihar and rice porridge in the morning or a mid-day meal and muri (parched rice) in West Bengal are most common. In the Punjab, meals are suplied to men workers but seldom to women or child labourers. In PEPSU, these benefits consisted of two meals a day with a breakfast of two chapatis (bread) and lassi (curd) or tea twice a day. A meal and tea twice a day are allowed in Jammu and Kashmir. A mid-day meal is supplied in Saurashtra and Bombay.

---

1. M. Gangadhara Rao and P. Subba Rao, *Human Resource Management in Indian Railways* (Delhi : Manas Publications, Delhi, 1986), p.85
2. Pigors, Paul and Myers, Charless, A., 'Personnel Administration' McGraw-Hill, Tokyo, 1973, p.547.
3. Strauss, George and Sayles, Leonard,R., 'Personnel', Prentice Hall of India Private Limited, New Delhi, 1985, pp.187-188.

In Andhra Pradesh, as reported by Agricultural Labour Enquiry it is a common practice to provide fringe benefits such as mid-day meal, coffee or tea, Tobacco, firewood, a pair of new clothes and chappals. Besides, the attached labourers are allowed to collect the left out paddy from hay after threshing.

Fringe Benefits Provided in Selected Villages

In view of the above, it is thought appropriate to enquire into the fringe benefits provided to agaricultural labour in selected villages.

Benefits to Attached Labourers

The fringe benefits like food; fire wood; clothing; medical aid etc., are provided to attached labourers in selected villages. All these benefits, although provided now and then provide desirable impact on the relations between the farmers and attached labourers. At State level 53 per cent of farmers were providing food free of cost regularly to their attached labourers (Table 5.21). In addition to this another 17 per cent of farmers were providing food now and then. This was accepted by attached labourers also. At village level 95 per cent of farmers employing attached labourers from Piridi, cent per cent of farmers from Guntupalle and Veerannapalem provided food free of cost regularly to their attached labourers. The fire wood is provided either now and then or rarely by some of the farmers of Piridi, Vangalapudi and Guntupalle. Clothing was another important benefit provided to attached labourers by some of the farmers of Piridi, Guntupalle and Raigir. In very few cases and that too rarely medical aid is provided by some of the farmers of Piridi, Guntupalle and Raigir.

Benefits to Casual Labourers

The benefits provided to casual labourers are also enquired into contacting the farmers and casual labourers as could be seen in Table 5.22. Very few farmers provided the benefits like *i.* fire wood; *ii.* assistance in case of social ceremonies; *iii.* loans; *iv.* land without rent; *v.* free food; *vi.* medical aid etc. Among these benefits, fire wood was the most common item provided in the villages of Coastal Andhra. In Rayalaseema villages 'land without rent' was the most common benefit provided to casual labourers. Further free food was provided to casual labourers regularly in both the Rayalaseema villages by all the farmers. This practice is not found in Coastal Andhra villages.

Table 5.21 : Benefits Provided to Attached Labour—Response by Farmers and Attached Labour

REGION AND	Food		Fire Wood		Clothing		Medical		Others	
VILLAGE	F	AL	F	AL	F	AL	F	AL	F	AL
COASTAL ANDHRA	%	%	%	%	%	%	%	%	%	%
Piridi	95.24	100.00	--	--	9.56	60.00	--	--	42.86	60.00
	--	--	9.52	20.00	76.19	40.00	--	--	--	--
	--	--	47.62	20.00	--	--	57.14	20.00	85.71	60.00
Vangalapudi	45.45	--	--	--	--	--	--	--	9.09	--
	9.09	20.00	45.45	40.00	--	--	--	--	18.18	--
	18.18	20.00	18.18	--	--	20.00	--	--	9.09	--
Guntupalle	100.00	100.00	--	--	--	40.00	--	--	--	--
	--	--	--	20.00	100.00	60.00	--	40.00	--	--
	--	--	40.00	40.00	--	--	50.00	20.00	20.00	--
Veerannapalem	100.00	100.00	--	--	--	--	--	--	--	--
	--	--	--	--	--	--	--	--	--	--
	--	--	--	--	--	--	20.00	--	20.00	--
OVERALL	**85.11**	**75.00**	--	--	**4.26**	**25.00**	--	--	**21.28**	--
	4.26	**5.00**	**14.89**	**20.00**	**55.32**	**25.00**	--	**10.00**	**6.39**	--
	--	**5.00**	**34.04**	**15.00**	--	**5.00**	**38.30**	**10.00**	**46.81**	--

(Contd...)

Table 5.21 : (Contd...)

REGION AND VILLAGE	Food		Fire Wood		Clothing		Medical		Others	
	F	AL	F	AL	F	AL	F	AL	F	AL
TELANGANA	%	%	%	%	%	%	%	%	%	%
Jookal	11.11	--	--	--	--	--	--	--	11.11	--
	55.56	--	22.22	--	--	--	--	--	--	--
	11.11	100.00	11.11	--	--	--	--	--	--	--
Raigir	--	--	10.00	--	20.00	--	--	--	50.00	--
	30.00	20.00	--	20.00	20.00	60.00	10.00	--	--	--
	30.00	20.00	10.00	20.00	40.00	20.00	40.00	40.00	20.00	--
Andhra Nagar	13.33	--	6.67	--	6.67	--	--	--	33.33	--
	20.00	20.00	6.67	--	6.67	--	--	--	--	--
	--	--	6.67	--	6.67	--	6.67	--	--	--
OVERALL	**8.82**	--	**5.82**	--	**8.82**	--	--	--	**32.35**	--
	35.28	**10.00**	**2.94**	**5.00**	**14.71**	**15.00**	**2.94**	--	--	--
	11.76	**30.00**	**5.94**	**5.00**	**14.71**	**5.00**	**14.71**	**10.00**	**5.94**	--
ANDHRA PRADESH	***53.09***	***75.00***	***2.47***	--	***6.17***	***25.00***	--	--	***25.93***	--
	17.28	***15.00***	***9.88***	***25.00***	***38.27***	***40.00***	***1.23***	***10.00***	***3.70***	--
	4.94	***35.00***	***22.22***	***20.00***	***6.17***	***10.00***	***28.40***	***20.00***	***29.63***	--

Note : I. F—Farmers' Response; II. ALS—Attached Labourers' Response.
III. No Attached Labour in Rayalaseema Village.

Table 5.22 : Benefits Provided to Casual Labour-Response by Farmers and Casual Labour

REGION AND VILLAGE	Benefits	Farmers' Response		Casual Labourers' Response	
		Frequency	*No.*	*Frequency*	*No.*
COASTAL ANDHRA					
Piridi	Fire wood	Rarely	1	Rarely	1
	Assistance in case of social ceremonies	Rarely	1	--	--
Vangalapudi	Fire wood	Now/Then	3	--	--
	Loans	Rarely	2	Now/Then	1
	Land without Rent	--	--	Always	1
Guntupalle	Fire wood	Rarely	5	--	--
	Fire wood	Now/Then	1	--	--
	Land without Rent	--	--	Always	--
	Others	Rarely	1	--	--
	Others	Now/Then	5	--	--
Veerannapalem	Fire wood	Now/Then	2	--	--
	Loans	Now/Then	1	--	--
	Free food/Items	Now/Then	5	--	--
	Housing	Now/Then	2	--	--
	Medical	Now/Then	1	--	--
OVERALL	**Fire wood**	**Rarely**	**6**	**Rarely**	**1**
	Assistance in case of social ceremonies	**Rarely**	**1**	--	--
	Fire wood	**Now/Then**	**3**	--	--
	Loans	**Rarely**	**2**	--	--
	Land without Rent	--	--	**Always**	**2**
	Others	**Rarely**	**1**	--	--
	Others	**Now/Then**	**5**	--	--
	Loans	**Now/Then**	**1**	**Now/Then**	**1**
	Free food/Items	**Now/Then**	**5**	--	--
	Housing	**Now/Then**	**2**	--	--
	Medical	**Now/Then**	**1**	--	--
RAYALASEEMA					
Brahmanapalle	Land without rent	Always	3	Always	9
	Land without rent	Now/Then	1	Now/Then	1
	Loans	Now/Then	2	--	--
	Free food/Items	Always	35	Always	35
Sanjeevapuram	Land without rent	Always	1	--	--
	Free food/Items	Always	34	Always	31
OVERALL	**Land without rent**	**Always**	**4**	**Always**	**9**
	Land without rent	**Now/Then**	**1**	**Now/Then**	**1**
	Loans	**Now/Then**	**2**	--	--
	Free food/Items	**Always**	**69**	**Always**	**66**

(Contd...)

Table 5.22 : (Contd....)

REGION AND VILLAGE	Benefits	Farmers' Response Frequency	No.	Casual Labourers' Response Frequency	No.
ANDHRA PRADESH	Fire wood	Rarely	6	Rarely	1
	Assistance in case of social ceremonies	Rarely	1	--	--
	Fire wood	Now/Then	3	--	--
	Loans	Rarely	2	--	--
	Land without rent	Always	4	Always	11
	Others	Rarely	1	--	--
	Others	Now/Then	5	--	--
	Loans	Now/Then	3	Now/Then	1
	Free food/Items	Now/Then	5	--	--
	Housing	Now/Then	2	--	--
	Medical	Now/Then	1	--	--
	Land without rent	Now/Then	1	Now/Then	1
	Free food/Items	Always	69	Always	66

Note : No Benefits are Reported from Telangana Villages.

Indebtedness of Labourers

As rightly remarked by First Agricultural Labour Enquiry 1950-51, indebtedness is an age old malady among the rural population of India.[1] Their income from agricultural employment even when supplemented by income from other sources is hardly sufficient for subsistance. Frequent fluctuation and inadequacy of income as against inelastic family expenditure make borrowing inevitable. Unlike other sections of society, agricultural labour households are not privileged enough to rely on institutional agencies to meet their credit requirements. Hence, they are forced to depend upon non-institutional credit agencies. Indebtedness to non-institutional agencies determined the destiny of agricultural labour households in many ways. It restricts the freedom to choose his employer, limits his bargaining capacity in the wage market, and involves him in a host of obligations including the mortgage of the freedom of his family members. These borrowings at high rates of interest increase with geometric proportion especially because of the inability of the labourer to repay in time.

1. Government of India, *Agricultural Labour Enquiry, 1950-'51* : Report of Intensive Survey of Agricultural Labour, Employment, Underemployment, Wages and Leves Living (New Delhi : Ministry of Labour, 1954), I - All India.

Attached Labourers

Table 5.23 shows the source wise indebtedness of attached labourers. It could be observed from this table that 54 per cent of attached labourers were indebted and this percentage remained at more or less at the same level in Coastal Andhra and Telangana regions. At village level, the percentage of indebted attached labourers was highest in Guntupalle with 80 per cent followed by Vangalapudi, Veerannapalem, Jookal and Râigir with 60 per cent each. The average amount of indebtedness per indebted attached labour was nearly Rs.1,111 at state level. This was highest in Veerannapalem with Rs.1,833 followed by Guntupalle with Rs.1,450 Raigir and Andhra Nagar with Rs.1,400 each.

Sourcewise indebtedness shown in this table indicates that farmers constitute the most important source accounting for 81.70 per cent of total debt of attached labourers at State level. This percentage was further high with 91.49 in Telangana followed by Coastal Andhra with 71.23 per cent. At village level, farmers had accounted for the cent per cent of indebtedness of attached labourers in Raigir and Andhra Nagar. In all other villages, with the exception of Vangalapudi, farmers constitute the source for more than two thirds of total debt of attached labourers. The average amount of debt provided by the farmers was slightly higher in Telangana with Rs.1,228.57 followed by Coastal Andhra with Rs.1,042.50. At village level, the farmers of Guntupalle, Raigir and Andhra Nagar had extended maximum credit to the extent of Rs.1,400 each on an average per indebted attached labour. The next important source was Bankers with 13.82 per cent followed by village money lenders with 4.48 per cent. It may be noted,in this context, that bankers in Telangana had not extended any credit to the attached labourers. It was in Vangalapudi, bankers dominated the farmers in providing credit to attached labourers. The average amount due to bankers by attached labourers was highest in Guntupalle and Veerannapalem with Rs.800 each.

Casual Labourers

In respect of casual labourers, nearly 74 per cent of them were indebted at State level (Table 5.24). The percentage of indebted casual labour was very high in Rayalaseema with 90.00 per cent followed by Coastal Andhra with 62.57 per cent and Telangana with 59 per cent. At village level, the casual labourers of both the villages of Rayalaseema - Brahmanapalle and Sanjeevapuram were indebted to the extent of more than 88 per cent. In all other villages, the percentage of indebted casual labourers varied between 54 and 69.

Tablw 5.23 : Source-wise Indebtedness of Attached Labour

REGION AND VILLAGE	Farmers			Village Money Lenders			Bankers			Overall		
	A %	B Rs.	C %	A %	B Rs.	C %	A %	B Rs.	C %	A %	B Rs.	C %
COASTAL ANDHRA												
Piridi	20.00	200	66.67	--	--	--	20.00	100	33.33	20.00	300	100.00
Vangalapudi	20.00	40	36.36	20.00	20	18.18	20.00	50	45.46	60.00	37	100.00
Guntupalle	60.00	1,400	72.42	--	--	--	40.00	800	27.58	80.00	1,450	100.00
Veerannapalem	60.00	1,400	72.42	--	--	--	40.00	800	27.58	80.00	1,450	100.00
OVERALL	**40.00**	**1,042**	**71.23**	**5.00**	**20**	**0.17**	**30.00**	**558**	**28.60**	**55.00**	**1,065**	**100.00**
TELANGANA												
Jookal	40.00	800	66.67	20.00	800	33.33	--	--	--	60.00	80	100.00
Raigir	60.00	1,400	100.00	--	--	--	--	--	--	60.00	1,400	100.00
Andhra Nagar	40.00	1,400	100.00	--	--	--	--	--	--	60.00	1,400	100.00
OVERALL	**46.67**	**1,229**	**91.49**	**6.67**	**800**	**8.51**	--	--	--	**58.33**	**1,175**	**100.00**
ANDHRA PRADESH	***42.85***	***1,129***	***81.70***	***5.71***	***410***	***4.48***	***17.14***	***558***	***13.82***	***54.29***	***1,111***	***100.00***

Note : i) No Attached Labour in Rayalaseema Villages.

ii) A—Percentage of Attached Labour Indebted to this Source;
B—Average Amount of debt per Indebted Attached Labour;
C—Percentage Debt from this Source in the Total Debt.

iii) 'Overall' includes 'Others' also.

Table 5.24 : Source-wise Indebtedness of Casual Labour

REGION AND	Farmers			Village Money Lenders			Bankers			Overall		
VILLAGE	A %	B Rs.	C %	A %	B Rs.	C %	A %	B Rs.	C %	A %	B Rs.	C %
COASTAL ANDHRA												
Piridi	25.71	391	43.93	--	--	--	31.43	391	53.72	62.86	364	100.00
Vangalapudi	22.86	326	63.76	8.57	27	1.99	40.00	100	34.25	57.14	204	100.00
Guntupalle	34.29	246	32.68	5.71	16	0.36	25.71	629	62.69	65.71	392	100.00
Veerannapalem	45.71	828	86.97	2.86	114	0.75	14.29	237	7.79	68.57	635	100.00
OVERALL	**32.14**	**496**	**61.41**	**4.29**	**38**	**0.62**	**27.86**	**322**	**34.51**	**62.57**	**409**	**100.00**
RAYALASEEMA												
Brahmanapalle	88.57	1,459	100.00	--	--	--	--	--	--	88.57	1,459	100.00
Sanjeevapuram	91.43	506	87.51	--	--	--	8.57	1,071	12.49	91.43	579	100.00
OVERALL	**90.00**	**975**	**98.49**	--	--	--	**4.29**	**771**	**1.41**	**90.00**	**1,012**	**100.00**
TELANGANA												
Jookal	25.71	523	43.60	5.71	343	6.35	25.71	600	50.05	54.29	568	100.00
Raigir	31.43	749	65.32	22.86	500	31.74	5.71	71	1.13	60.00	600	100.00
Andhra Nagar	48.57	1,408	82.90	8.57	286	2.97	20.00	563	13.64	62.86	1,376	100.00
OVERALL	**35.24**	**997**	**70.55**	**12.38**	**426**	**10.60**	**17.14**	**527**	**18.14**	**59.05**	**843**	**100.00**
ANDHRA PRADESH	***46.03***	***832***	***90.90***	***6.03***	***304***	***1.75***	***19.05***	***387***	***6.87***	***73.97***	***712***	***100.00***

Note : i) A—Percentage of Casual Labour Indebtedness to this Source;
B—Average Amount of debt per Indebted Casual Labour;
C—Percentage Debt from this Source in the Total Debt.
ii) 'Overall' includes 'Others' also.

The average amount of debt per indebted casual labour is also calculated and shown in this table. It was Rs.712 at state level. The average amount of debt was very high in Rayalaseema with Rs.1,012 followed by Telangana with Rs.843 and coastal Andhra with Rs.409. At village level, the average amount of debt was highest in Brahmanapalle with Rs.1,459 followed by Andhra Nagar with Rs.1,376 and Veerannapalem with Rs.635.

The sourcewise indebtedness presented in this table shows that 46 per cent of casual labourers were indebted to farmers; 19 per cent of casual labourers to bankers and 6 per cent of casual labourers to village money lenders at State level. Farmers had extended credit to 90 per cent of casual labourers in Rayalaseema villages. In the other two regions, the percentage of casual labourers provided with credit by farmers varied from 23 per cent in Vangalapudi to 49 per cent in Andhra Nagar. Bankers followed by village money lenders constituted the second and third important sources of indebtedness.

The average amount of debt borrowed by casual labourers from their farmers was highest in Brahmanapalle with Rs.1,459 followed by Andhra Nagar with Rs.1,409 and Veerannapalem with Rs.828. Thus, the farmers constituted the major source in Vangalapudi and Veerannapalem of Coastal Andhra, Brahmanapalle and Sanjeevapuram of Rayalaseema and Raigir and Andhra Nagar of Telangana. Infact it was the only source available to casual labourers in securing financial assistance in times of need in Brahmanapalle of Rayalaseema. It is interesting to note that, bankers had come to play a significant role in providing credit to casual labourers. This was particularly so in villages like Piridi and Guntupalle of Coastal Andhra and Jookal of Telangana where more than 50 per cent of the total loans were borrowed from the bankers.

6

Agrarian Relations

The term "Agrarian Relations" refers to a dynamic and developing concept which deals with, in its widest sense, the complex of relations between peasants and agricultural workers and their unions; between peasants and the Government and between agricultural workers and the Government.

Agrarian relations do not constitute a simple relationship between peasant and worker, but are a set of personal and interdependent complexities involving historical, economic, social, psychological, demographic, technological, occupational, political, legal and other variables and accounts for and interdisciplinary approach to their study.[1]

1. If we make agrarian disputes (the absence of positive agrarian relations) the center of circle, it will have to be divided into various segments. A study of the conditions of the employment, comes under the purview of economics; their origin and development under history; the resultant social conflicts under sociology; the attitudes of their parties (peasants, workers and their unions), the Government and the press under social psychology; their cultural interactions under cultural anthropology; State policies bearing on the issues involved in the conflict under political science; the legal aspects of disputes under law; the issues arising out of international aid to the parties under international relations; the effectiveness with which labour policy is administered under public administration; the technological aspects (for example introduction of mechanisation of agricultural operations) of disputes under technology; and the quantitative assessment of losses incurred by the parties and the country's economy under Mathematics. It is obvious from these facts that agrarian relations do not function in a vacuum but are multidimensional in nature.

The creation and maintenance of good relation between the cultivators and agricultural labourers is the very basis on which the development of agriculture depends. It in turn seeks to enlist cooperation of the two patners in agriculture in the field of production and promotes agrarian peace. The health and orderly agrarian relations generate attitudes which promote progress and stabilise democratic institutions. Stable agrarian relations means a situation when requirements of peasants and labourers are discussed between them in a spirit of mutual trust and confidence and without causing frictions. For example, the farmer would like to develop stable relations with a view to getting a disciplined and conscientious work force for more work. This would reduce supervisory work as also enable better planning for production. The labourers on the other hand expects liberal thinking by the farmer and more human approach to its needs. This implies that the labourer must be assured of compensation package which is just and fair besides attractive perquisites. Stable agrarian relations also aims at reducing social and agrarian tensions. This is possible only when values of equality and egaliterianism are cherished.

It is proposed in this chapter to discuss certain aspects viz., Grievances, Discipline, Unionism, Conflicts and Consultation which influence agrarian relations.

Grievances

Meaning and Significance

A grievance is a sign of the employee's discontent with job and its nature. Beach defines a grievance as "any dissatisfaction or feeling of injustice in connection with one's employment situation that is brought to the notice of the management."[1]

The importance of grievance redressal is such that if an individual's grievances are unattended and unresolved, they will become collective disputes. A grievance ridden person has a tendency to communicate with other workers and thus spread the contagion.[2] Thus an efficient grievance management is an important and integral part of the human resource management.

A viable grievance system is the hall-mark of sound employer-employee relations. Industrial organisations, whether big or small, find

1. Dale S. Beach, *Personnel: The Management of Poeple at Work* (New York: Mcmillan Publishing Company, 1975), p. 583.
2. Keith Davis,"*Human Relation at work* (New York : Mc Graw-Hill Book Company, 1962), p.295.

it essential to develop adequate arrangements to deal with employee grievances. In small industrial units, since the relations are marked by informality and face to face contact, the aggrieved worker can directly approach his manager and report his grievances seeking their redressal. Big and complex organisations demand a different approach to treat grievance situations in view of their large size, formal organisation and complex bureaucratic set-up.[1]

Grievances among Agricultural Labour

Against the above background, grievances of agricultural labour in selected villages have been studied. The percentage of labour having grievances; nature of grievances; proportion of grievances favourably settled; satisfaction with grievance redressal are dealt with in this study. In addition, farmers' grievances against attached and casual labourers are also enquired into.

Attached Labourers

Table 6.1 shows the grievances of attached labourers in the seven selected villages of Coastal Andhra and Telangana regions. With the exception of Guntupalle, Veerannapalem and Jookal, all the attached labourers of the remaining four villages had grievances against farmers. While in Jookal, the percentage of attached labourers who had grievances was eighty; it was sixty each in Guntupalle and Veerannapalem.

The nature of grievances of attached labourers is also enquired into and presented in this table. While cent per cent of the grievances relate to wages in Piridi, Guntupalle and Veerannapalem; half or less than half relate to wages in the remaining four villages. The other important nature of grievances of attached labourers was unfavourable terms of employment in Andhra Nagar and heavy work in Vangalapudi and Jookal villages.

Attached labourers' Opinion on Proportion of Grievances Favourably Settled

It is also enquired as to the proportion of grievances favourably settled which is shown in Table 6.2. It could be seen from this table that two thirds of attached labourers of all the four villages of Coastal Andhra had expressed that only one fourth of their grievances were settled in their favour. It was only in Raigir that all the attached labourers had reported favourable settlement of grievances to the extent of one fourth of their

1. B.S.Murty, "Handling Employee Grievances: A Study of Rourkela," *Indian Journal of Labour Economies*, XVI, No.4, (January, 1974), pp.417-426.

Table 6.1 : Grievances of Attached Labour

REGION AND VILLAGE	Percentage of Attached Labour Who had Grievances	Percentage of Grievances Under Each Head to the Total Number of Grievances					
		Low Wages	Inadequate Benefits	Inconvenient Working Hours	Unfavourable Terms of Employment	Heavy Work	Total
COASTAL ANDHRA							
Piridi	100.00	100.00	--	--	--	--	100.00
Vangalapudi	100.00	33.33	--	--	--	66.67	100.00
Guntupalle	60.00	100.00	--	--	--	--	100.00
Veerannapalem	60.00	100.00	--	--	--	--	100.00
TOTAL	**80.00**	**76.47**	--	--	--	**23.53**	**100.00**
TELANGANA							
Jookal	80.00	20.00	--	--	--	80.00	100.00
Raigir	100.00	50.00	12.50	12.50	12.50	12.50	100.00
Andhra Nagar	100.00	44.00	--	--	33.33	22.23	100.00
TOTAL	**93.33**	**40.91**	**4.55**	**4.55**	**18.18**	**31.81**	**100.00**
ANDHRA PRADESH	***85.71***	***56.41***	***2.56***	***2.56***	***10.26***	***28.20***	***100.00***

Note : No Attached Labour in Rayalaseema Villages.

Table 6.2 : Percentage of Grievances Favourably Settled

REGION AND VILLAGE	Favourably Settled to the Extent of			
	0 %	25 %	50 %	Total %
COASTAL ANDHRA				
Piridi	--	60.00	40.00	100.00
Vangalapudi	40.00	60.00	--	100.00
Guntupalle	33.33	66.67	--	100.00
Veerannapalem	--	66.67	33.33	100.00
OVERALL	**18.75**	**62.50**	**18.75**	**100.00**
TELANGANA				
Jookal	75.00	25.00		100.00
Raigir	--	100.00		100.00
Andhra Nagar	60.00	40.00	--	100.00
OVERALL	**42.86**	**57.14**	--	**100.00**
ANDHRA PRADESH	***30.00***	***60.00***	***10.00***	***100.00***

Note : i) No Attached Labour in Rayalaseema Villages.

ii) No Cases under 75% and 100%

grievances. This indicates that the attached labourers had many unsettled grievances and these should be resolved as early as possible in the best interests of harmonious relations between farmers and attached labourers.

Casual Labourers

The grievances of casual labourers are also enquired into and shown in Table 6.3. More than 90 per cent of casual labourers had grievances in all the nine selected villages. While the highest percentage of casual labourers having grievances was found in Brahmanapalle and Raigir; it was lowest with 80 in Piridi.

The nature of grievances relates to low wages; inadequate benefits; inconvenient working hours; unfavourable terms and conditions; heavy work; delay in payment of wages and no proper treatment. More than half of the grievances in Coastal Andhra and Rayalaseema villages relate to low wages and it was slightly less than half in Telangana villages. The other important grievance was heavy work followed by unfavourable terms of employment.

Casual Labourers' Opinion on Proportion of Grievances Favourably Settled

More than half of the casual labourers reported that only 25 per cent of their grievances could be settled in their favour (Table 6.4). Less than one fourth of casual labourers reported that half of their grievances were settled in their favour. It is significant to note that more than one fifth of casual labourers reported that none of their grievances were settled in their favour. This is not a good indication and it certainly affects the agrarian relations.

Satisfaction with Grievance Redressal and Reasons thereof

It is heartening to note that more than three fourths of casual labourers were satisfied in all the villages with the outcome of grievance redressal (Table 6.5). As already reported, one fifth of casual labourers had complained that none of their grievances were settled in their favour. The reasons for this are enquired into and shown in Table 6.6. Most of the casual labourers with this dissatisfaction had expressed that the strength of farmers was more than that of labourers and this led to farmers dominating the labourers and thereby suppressing the grievances of latter. Other reasons for dissatisfaction were found to be biased third party's award and undue delay in settlement of the grievance.

Table 6.3 : Grievances of Casual Labour

REGION AND VILLAGE	Percentage of Grievances								
	CLG	*LW*	*IB*	*IW*	*UTE*	*HW*	*DPW*	*NPT*	*TOTAL*
COASTAL ANDHRA									
Piridi	80.00	67.57	2.70	5.40	8.11	13.57	2.70	--	100.00
Vangalapudi	94.29	52.38	2.38	--	9.52	33.33	--	2.38	100.00
Guntupalle	97.10	50.00	4.76	--	11.90	26.19	2.38	4.76	100.00
Veerannapalem	97.14	66.67	10.26	2.56	2.56	5.13	5.13	7.69	100.00
OVERALL	**92.14**	**58.75**	**5.00**	**1.88**	**8.13**	**20.00**	**2.50**	**3.75**	**100.00**
RAYALASEEMA									
Brahmanapalle	100.00	54.90	1.96	1.96	33.33	1.96	5.88	--	100.00
Sanjeevapuram	94.28	53.19	4.26	--	10.64	17.02	--	14.89	100.00
OVERALL	**97.14**	**54.08**	**3.06**	**1.02**	**22.45**	**9.18**	**3.06**	**7.15**	**100.00**
TELANGANA									
Jookal	97.14	35.71	4.29	--	22.86	28.57	8.51	2.86	100.00
Raigir	100.00	46.48	7.04	2.82	15.49	23.94	--	4.23	100.00
Andhra Nagar	97.14	47.06	15.69	3.92	9.80	15.69	1.96	5.88	100.00
OVERALL	**98.10**	**42.71**	**8.33**	**2.08**	**16.67**	**23.44**	**2.60**	**4.17**	**100.00**
ANDHRA PRADESH	***95.24***	***50.89***	***6.00***	***1.78***	***14.89***	***19.11***	***2.67***	***4.67***	***100.00***

Note : CLG—Casual Labourers who had Grievances; LW—Low Wages;
IW—Inconvenient Working Hours; UTE—Unfavourable Terms of Employment
HW—Heavy Work; IB—Inadequate Benefits;
DPW—Delay in Payment; NPT—No Proper Treatment

Table 6.4 : Percentage of Grievances Favourably Settled

REGION AND VILLAGE	Favourably Settled to the Extent of			
	0 %	25 %	50 %	Total %
COASTAL ANDHRA				
Piridi	7.14	50.00	42.86	100.00
Vangalapudi	15.15	63.64	21.21	100.00
Guntupalle	8.82	64.72	26.46	100.00
Veerannapalem	26.46	52.92	20.62	100.00
OVERALL	**16.28**	**56.59**	**27.12**	**100.00**
RAYALASEEMA				
Brahmanapalle	14.29	68.57	17.14	100.00
Sanjeevapuram	33.33	39.39	27.27	100.00
OVERALL	25.53	54.41	22.86	100.00
TELANGANA				
Jookal	11.76	64.70	23.53	100.00
Raigir	20.00	65.71	14.29	100.00
Andhra Nagar	47.06	44.12	8.82	100.00
OVERALL	**26.21**	**58.25**	**15.53**	**100.00**
ANDHRA PRADESH	***21.33***	***56.67***	***22.00***	***100.00***

Note : No Cases under 75% and 100%

Table 6.5 : Percentage Distribution of Casual Labour by their Satisfaction and Reasons for Dissatisfaction with the Outcome of Grievance Redressal

REGION AND VILLAGE	Satisfaction	Reasons for Dissatisfaction			
		Award is given by the third party with bias	*Strenght of Farmers is more than that of Labourers*	*Undue delay in Settlement*	*Total*
COASTAL ANDHRA					
Piridi	85.71	--	14.29	--	100.00
Vangalapudi	75.76	--	24.24	--	100.00
Guntupalle	88.23	2.94	8.83	--	100.00
Veerannapalem	73.53	--	17.65	8.82	100.00
OVERALL	**80.62**	**0.77**	**16.28**	**2.33**	**100.00**
RAYALASEEMA					
Brahmanapalle	80.00	11.43	8.57	--	100.00
Sanjeevapuram	87.88	--	12.12	--	100.00
OVERALL	**83.82**	**5.88**	**10.30**	--	**100.00**
TELANGANA					
Jookal	79.41	--	20.59	--	100.00
Raigir	91.43	--	5.72	2.85	100.00
Andhra Nagar	93.11	--	--	5.89	100.00
OVERALL	**88.35**	--	**8.73**	**2.92**	**100.00**
ANDHRA PRADESH	***84.00***	***1.66***	***12.34***	***2.00***	***100.00***

Table 6.6 : Farmers' Grievances against Attached Labour

REGION AND VILLAGE	Percentage of Grievances under Each Head								
	PAG	*A*	*LC*	*DMY*	*LCT*	*HDO*	*A/HHB*	*DH*	*LN*	*TOTAL*
COASTAL ANDHRA										
Piridi	85.71	35.71	30.95	11.91	--	--	--	11.91	9.52	100.00
Vangalapudi	72.73	--	55.56	--	11.11	33.33	--	--	--	100.00
Guntupalle	70.00	11.11	11.11	11.11	55.56	--	--	11.11	--	100.00
Veerannapalem	40.00	33.33	33.33	--	--	33.34	--	--	--	100.00
OVERALL	**74.47**	**26.98**	**31.75**	**9.52**	**9.53**	**6.35**	--	**9.52**	**6.35**	**100.00**
TELANGANA										
Jookal	77.78	--	18.18	9.09	18.18	9.09	9.09	36.37	--	100.00
Raigir	90.00	11.76	41.19	11.76	--	--	11.76	17.65	5.88	100.00
Andhra Nagar	80.00	7.69	34.62	3.85	19.23	19.23	3.85	3.85	7.69	100.00
OVERALL	**82.35**	**7.41**	**33.33**	**7.41**	**12.96**	**11.11**	**7.41**	**14.14**	**5.73**	**100.00**
ANDHRA PRADESH	***77.78***	***17.94***	***32.48***	***8.55***	***11.11***	***8.55***	***3.42***	***11.97***	***5.98***	***100.00***

Note: I) No Attached Labour in Rayalaseema Villages.

ii) PAG—Percentage of Farmers' Airing Grievances Against Attached Labour to Total Number of Farmers;

HDO—Highly Demand Oriented;
A/HHB—Arrogant/High Handed Behaviour;
LN—Laziness;
LCT—Low Commitment.

A—Absenteeism;
LC—Late Coming;
DMY—Discontinuation in the middle of the year
DH—Dishonest

Farmers' Grievances against Labourers

Farmers may also have some grievances against labourers; but for some reason or the other, they might be continuing their services. These grievances also disturb the harmonious relations between farmers and labourers. It is with this view, an enquiry into the farmers' grievances against labourers is made.

Against Attached Labourers

Table 6.6. shows that more than three fourths of farmers employing attached labourers had grievances against the latter. This percentage was slightly higher in the villages of Telangana compared to that of Coastal Andhra. It was only in Veerannapalem, only 40 per cent of farmers employing attached labourers had reported grievances against attached labourers.

The nature of grievances is also enquired into. They relate to absenteeism; late coming; discontinuation in the middle of the year; low commitment; highly demand oriented nature; arrogant/high handed behaviour; dishonesty and laziness. Nearly one third of grievances relate to late coming in all the seven villages. The next important grievance was dishonesty of attached labourers followed by their low commitment.

Against Casual Labourers

In the course of this enquiry, it has been brought to notice that farmers had grievances against casual labourers also. Nearly 80 per cent of farmers had grievances against casual labourers and this percentage was highest in Vangalapudi and Andhra Nagar with 97 each followed by Guntupalle with 91 (Table 6.7). The grievances of farmers were absenteeism; late coming; discontinuation in the middle of the work; low commitment; highly demand oriented nature; arrogant/high handed behaviour; dishonesty and laziness. Nearly 27 per cent of grievances relate to late coming; 14 per cent related to absenteeism followed by low commitment highly demand oriented nature with 13.09 per cent each and dishonesty with 11.64 per cent at State level. The same trend is more or less applicable in regions and individual villages.

Discipline

Meaning and Significance

No organisation, industrial or agricultural can prosper without discipline among its employees. Discipline has been a matter of utmost concern for all organisations.

Table 6.7 : Farmers' Grievances against Casual Labour

REGION AND VILLAGE	Percentage of Grievances under Each Head									
	PAG	*A*	*LC*	*DMY*	*LCT*	*HDO*	*A/HHB*	*DH*	*LN*	*TOTAL*
COASTAL ANDHRA										
Piridi	65.71	8.33	16.67	2.78	19.44	13.89	2.78	13.89	22.22	100.00
Vangalapudi	97.14	12.24	38.78	2.04	14.29	14.29	6.12	6.12	6.12	100.00
Guntupalle	91.43	7.45	20.90	2.99	14.93	13.43	16.42	13.43	10.45	100.00
Veerannapalem	68.57	13.95	20.93	4.65	18.60	13.96	2.33	6.98	18.60	100.00
OVERALL	**80.71**	**10.25**	**24.62**	**3.08**	**16.41**	**13.85**	**8.20**	**10.26**	**13.33**	**100.00**
RAYALASEEMA										
Brahmanapalle	80.00	30.36	32.14	--	8.93	7.14	7.14	7.14	7.14	100.00
Sanjeevapuram	60.00	23.73	27.12	1.69	1.69	13.56	8.47	13.56	10.18	100.00
OVERALL	70.00	26.95	29.57	0.87	5.22	10.43	9.83	10.43	8.70	100.00
TELANGANA										
Jookal	74.29	13.79	24.14	--	12.07	13.79	6.90	17.24	12.07	100.00
Raigir	71.43	12.20	29.26	2.44	9.76	4.88	4.88	19.71	17.07	100.00
Andhra Nagar	97.14	4.17	27.18	--	19.44	19.44	11.11	8.33	8.33	100.00
OVERALL	**80.95**	**9.41**	**27.06**	**0.59**	**14.71**	**14.12**	**8.23**	**14.12**	**11.76**	**100.00**
ANDHRA PRADESH	***78.41***	***13.93***	***26.63***	***1.67***	***13.09***	***13.09***	***8.11***	***11.64***	***11.64***	***100.00***

Note: i) PAG—Percentage of Farmers' Airing Grievances Against Attached Labour to Total Number of Farmers;
HDO—Highly Demand Oriented; A—Absenteeism;
A/HHB—Arrogant/High Handed Behaviour; LC—Late Coming;
LN—Laziness; DMY—Discontinuation in the middle of the year
LCT—Low Commitment. DH—Dishonest

Discipline refers to a condition or attitude, prevailing among the employees, with respect to rules and regulations of an organisation. Discipline in the broadest sense means,"orderliness, the opposite of confusion. It does mean a strict and technical observance of rigid rules and regulations. It simply means working, cooperating and behaving in a normal and orderly way, as any responsible person would expect an employee to do".[1]

Disciplinary rules regulate the behaviour of the employees in an organisation as the law regulates the behaviour of the people in the society. Moreover, most of the employees prefer to work under disciplined environment as fair rules protect the individuals and the organisation and enable the team work. Further, disciplinary measures ensure just and equal treatment to all employees, efficient two-way communication, encourages cooperation and build team pride.

A major purpose of disciplinary action is to ensure that employee behaviour is consistent with the firm's rules. Rules are established to further the organisation's objectives. When a rule is violated, the effectiveness of the organisation is diminished to some degree, depending on the severity of the infraction. For instance, if a worker is late to work once, the effect on the firm may be minimal. Consistently being late is another matter because it negatively affects both the productivity of the worker and the morale of other employees. Supervisors must realise that disciplinary action can be a positive force for the company when it is applied responsibly and equitably. The firm benefits from developing and implementing effective disciplinary policies. Without a healthy State of discipline, or the threat of disciplinary action, the firm's effectiveness may be severely limited. Disciplinary action can also help the employee become more productive thereby benefiting the employee in the long-run.

Discipline Among Agricultural Labour

There is every need for discipline even among agriculture labour. It is the discipline and commitment among work-force which determines the quality, the quantity and the cost of the production in agriculture. Usually persons with good conduct, behaviour and self control are preferred both as attached labourers as well as casual labourers. These virtues are highly valued particularly in case of attached labourers who

1. Earl R.Bramblett, "Maintenance of Discipline" *Management of Personnel*, Quarterly, I, No.1, Autumn, 1961, p.10.

is regarded almost a member of the family. He is entrusted with the responsibility of general supervision of the agricultural operations as also looking after the property of the farmer including the crop, agricultural implements, livestock etc. The farmer expects that he serves loyally as well as honestly. If the labourer indulges in any misconduct, like theft, or deriliction of duty, he is summoned to ascertain the truth. If the explanation of the labourer is not satisfactory, the matter is reported to village panchayath. The panchayath tries to ascertain the facts by hearing the versions of the both the parties and award punishment, commensurate with the nature of offence. In case of grave misconduct, the matter is refered to the police and at times the contract of the labourer is cancelled.

Against the above background, the indiscipline among attached labourers of selected villages is studied.

The farmers have been asked about the disciplinary behaviour of attached labourers working under them. The rate of indiscipline measured through the percentage of attached labourers involved in cases of indiscipline. This, along with the nature of indiscipline is shown in Table 6.8 for three years. The percentage of attached labourers involved in cases of indiscipline was 17.02 in Coastal Andhra and 29.41 in Telangana and 21.22 for the entire State. This percentage remained at the same level for all the three years of the study. Further at village level, the percentage was highest in Raigir with 40, followed by Guntupalle with 30 and Vangalapudi with 27. The lowest percentage was recorded in Piridi village with 9.52. The nature of indiscipline shows that most of the cases of indiscipline among attached labourers related to late coming followed by absence without permission. Very few cases related to either disobeying of orders or not doing the work properly.

Table 6.9 shows indiscipline among casual labourers for the three year period. The farmers of Piridi reported nil cases of indiscipline. The percentage of casual labourers involved in cases of indiscipline was highest in Guntupalle with 31.42 followed by Vangalapudi varying from 17 per cent to 29 per cent and Veerannapalem with 20 per cent to 23 per cent. The average percentage at State level varied between 16 and 17 - less than that of attached labourers. This percentage was highest in Coastal Andhra and lowest in Rayalaseema.

As in the case of attached labourers, most of the cases of indiscipline among casual labourers related to late coming followed by absence without permission and disobeying of orders.

Table 6.8 : Indiscipline among Attached Labour—Farmers' Response

REGION AND VILLAGE	YEAR	A	Nature of Indiscipline				
			B	C	D	E	Total
COASTAL ANDHRA							
Piridi	I	9.52	1	1	1	--	3
	II	9.52	1	1	1	--	3
	III	9.52	1	1	1	--	3
Vangalapudi	I	27.27	2	2	1	--	3
	II	27.27	2	2	1	--	5
	III	27.27	2	2	1	--	5
Guntupalle	I	30.00	2	--	--	1	3
	II	30.00	2	--	--	1	3
	III	30.00	2	--	--	1	3
Veerannapalem	I	--	--	--	--	--	--
	II	--	--	--	--	--	--
	III	--	--	--	--	--	--
OVERALL	**I**	**17.02**	**5**	**3**	**2**	**1**	**11**
	II	**17.02**	**5**	**3**	**2**	**1**	**11**
	III	**17.02**	**5**	**3**	**2**	**1**	**11**
TELANGANA							
Jookal	I	22.22	1	--	1	--	2
	II	22.22	1	--	1	--	2
	III	22.22	1	--	1	--	2
Raigir	I	40.00	3	2	1	1	7
	II	40.00	3	2	1	1	7
	III	40.00	3	2	1	1	7
Andhra Nagar	I	26.26	4	1	--	1	6
	II	26.26	4	1	--	1	6
	III	26.26	4	1	--	1	6
OVERALL	**I**	**29.41**	**8**	**3**	**1**	**2**	**15**
	II	**29.41**	**8**	**3**	**1**	**2**	**15**
	III	**29.41**	**8**	**3**	**1**	**2**	**15**
ANDHRA PRADESH	***I***	***22.22***	***13***	***6***	***3***	***3***	***26***
	II	***22.22***	***13***	***6***	***3***	***3***	***26***
	III	***22.22***	***13***	***6***	***3***	***3***	***26***

Note : i) No Attached Labour in Rayalaseema Villages.

ii) A—Percentage of Casual Labour involved in case of indiscipline;
B—Late Coming; C—Absence without permission;
D—Disobeying the orders; E—Not doing the work properly/spoilage.

Table 6.9 : Indiscipline among Casual Labour—Farmers' Response

REGION AND VILLAGE	YEAR	A	Nature of Indiscipline				
			B	C	D	E	Total
COASTAL ANDHRA							
Piridi	I	--	--	--	--	--	--
	II	--	--	--	--	--	--
	III	--	--	--	--	--	--
Vangalapudi	I	28.57	9	4	1	--	14
	II	17.14	8	3	1	--	12
	III	22.85	8	3	1	--	12
Guntupalle	I	31.42	5	2	1	3	11
	II	31.42	5	2	1	3	11
	III	31.42	5	2	1	3	11
Veerannapalem	I	22.85	6	5	2	--	13
	II	22.85	7	4	2	--	13
	III	19.99	6	4	2	--	12
OVERALL	**I**	**20.71**	**20**	**11**	**4**	**3**	**38**
	II	**20.00**	**20**	**9**	**4**	**3**	**36**
	III	**19.29**	**19**	**9**	**4**	**3**	**35**
RAYALASEEMA							
Brahmanapalle	I	8.57	2	1	--	2	5
	II	8.57	1	1	--	3	5
	III	8.57	2	1	--	2	5
Sanjeevapuram	I	2.86	--	--	1	--	1
	II	2.86	--	--	1	--	1
	III	2.86	--	--	1	--	1
OVERALL	**I**	**5.71**	**2**	**1**	**1**	**2**	**6**
	II	**5.71**	**1**	**1**	**1**	**3**	**6**
	III	**5.71**	**2**	**1**	**1**	**2**	**6**
TELANGANA							
Jookal	I	14.29	5	--	3	--	8
	II	14.29	5	--	3	--	8
	III	14.29	5	--	3	--	8
Raigir	I	11.43	2	--	1	2	5
	II	11.43	2	--	1	2	5
	III	11.43	2	--	1	1	4
Andhra Nagar	I	28.57	8	1	2	1	12
	II	17.14	7	1	2	1	11
	III	17.14	7	1	2	1	11

(Contd..)

Table 6.9 : (Contd..)

REGION AND VILLAGE	YEAR	A	Nature of Indiscipline				
			B	C	D	E	Total
OVERALL	I	18.10	15	1	6	3	25
	II	17.14	14	1	6	3	24
	III	17.14	14	1	6	2	23
ANDHRA PRADESH	*I*	*16.51*	*37*	*13*	*11*	*8*	*69*
	II	*15.87*	*35*	*11*	*11*	*2*	*66*
	III	*15.55*	*35*	*11*	*11*	*7*	*64*

Note : A—Percentage of Casual Labour involved in case of indiscipline;
B—Late Coming; C—Absence without permission;
D—Disobeying the orders; E—Not doing the work properly/spoilage.

Unionism

Origin Growth and Role of Trade Unions:

"A trade union is a continuous association for wage earners for the purpose of maintaining or improving the conditions of their working lives".[1]

Trade Unions are a product of industrial society. The main elements in the development of these unions in every country have been more or less the same. The setting up of large scale industrial units and the wide-spread use of new lines of production, changes in living and working environments of workers and concentration of industries in large urban centres have all created a new class of "Wage earners".

Trade unionism is the organised expression of the needs and aspirations of the working class. The principal functions of a trade union organisation are to protect the economic and social interests of its members and to work for the improvement of their standards of living through bargaining with employers and through organised pressure on the Government and other institutions in society.

Organised trade unionism in India could not develop till the end of the first world war. Prior to 1918, though some sporadic efforts were made at organising the working class, these did not had to any effective organisation. The first organised union of industrial workers in India,

1. Sydney and Beatrice Webb, *History of Trade unionism,* (1920), p.1.

Madras Labour Union,[1] was formed in 1918 by B.P.Wadia. Though it began as an industrial union of textile workers, in course of time it developed into a general union covering workers employed in different trades and industries of the Madras city. In two years immediately following the First World War, at least seven unions of a permanent type, including the Ahmedabad Textile Labour Association, sprang up. Gradually, in course of time, as a result of several influences, many unions at plant and industry level, regional and national level have come up. The growth of unionism is significant particularly during post independence period.

Trade unions now play an important role in the industrial and social life of the country. They have come to play a dynamic role in contributing to increased productivity and in accelerating the pace of industrial progress. Their usefulness can further increase and in fact, the union movement can be geared to subserve the national goals in the context, of planned economic development. This may be accomplished by properly conditioning their attitudes and instilling in them new values and strengthening their institutional aspects. Infact the Government's labour policy has been to involve trade unions in the formation and implementation of Five Year Plans.[2]

Unionism Among Agricultural Labour

It is well known that unionism among industrial labour has developed well and has taken strong roots unlike agricultural labour. These unions as powerful pressure groups, have been able to not only protect their rights but also improve their standards of living apart from promoting their interests socially and politically. The important factors which contributed for the growth of these unions are concentration of labour in industrial centres, regularity of employment, class consciousness and group consciousness, emerging of rank and file leadership apart from the outside political leadership etc. Whereas in case of agricultural labour, a set of factors inhibited the growth of strong unions. These factors

1. Though the union's founder President, B.P.Wadia viewed that the Madras Labour Union was a mere accident, taking the facts and circumstances of that time, it can be said that the union was not a mere accident, but an inevitable reaction to the post-war grave economic and social conditions of the Madras factory workers. S.D.Punekar, *Trade Unionism in India* (Bombay:NewBook Co.,Ltd.,),p.74.
2. Report of the National Commission on Labour, Government of India, New Delhi, 1969, pp.29-30.

include scattered nature of agricultural workers, their personal contact with and dependence on the landlord, lack of diverse cultures and religions or castes and want of identical goals, lack of any permanent work status with any particular employer, their small proportion to the number of employers, and the substitutability of hired labour by family labour.[1]

However, the failure of agricultural production system to improve the economic conditions of agricultural labourers[2] points to the lack of market mechanism which can ensure fair distribution of gains of productivity among those who contributed to it. The prospect of this had attracted State regulation of agricultural wages. But it is well known that wage regulation has been ineffective.[3] The ineffectiveness of the State regulation of wages on the one hand and the success of agricultural labour unions in some parts of the country in obtaining benefits[4] on the other have tended to build up a strong case for the unionisation of agricultural labourers.[5]

---

1. S.M. Pandey,"Problems and Prospects of Organising Agricultural Workers" in his ed. *Rural Labour in India* (New Delhi: Shri Ram Centres for Industrial Relations and Human Resources, 1976), pp.157-59.
2. It is held that despite a marked rise in farm productivity the real wages of agricultural labourers remained constant. Bardhan, Pranab K., "Green Revolution and Agricultural Labourers", *Economic and Political Weekly*, Special Number, 1970, pp.1240-41; N. Krishanaji, "Wages of Agricultural Labour", *Economic and Political Weekly*, September,25, 1971, p.A-150.
3. The National Commission on Labour commenting on the effectiveness of agricultural minimum wage legislation observed " our uniform experience has been that it has remained a dead letter in every State". Report of the National Commission on Labour, New Delhi: Government of India, 1969, p.400.
4. Thus the agrarian tension in Kuttanad region of Kerala created by the unionised workers was instrumental in the establishment of a tripartite body by the State to fix as also to review the wages and working conditions of the agricultural labourers. Oommen T.K.,"Agrarian Tension in a Kerala District: An Analysis", *Indian Journal of Industrial Relations*, 7, No.2 (October, 1971). Also Alexander K.C., "Emerging Farmer-Labour Relations in Kuttanad", *Economic and Political Weekly*, VIII, No.34 (Aug. 25, 1973) p.1556. Similarly, the organised pressure from agricultural labourers of East Tanjore district of Tamil Nadu caused a tripartite meeting which resulted in an increase in wages. C.Muthaiah, "Development of Landless Labourers: Role of Group Bargaining Power" (Unpublished), Quoted by Verma and Mukherjee s. "Unionising Indian Agricultural Workers: Problems and Prospects", *The Indian Journal of Labour Economics*, XVI, No.4, (January, 1974).
5. A. Aziz, "Unionising Agricultural Labourers in India: A Strategy", Indian Journal of Industrial Relations, 13, No.3, (January, 1978).

In the wake of the freedom movement, many socio-political organisations came into existence in the late twenties for the benefit of agricultural communities. These were known under various names such as 'Kisan Sabhas' 'Krishak Sabhas' and 'Peasant Unions'. In 1931, the Kisan Sabha in Bengal demanded abolition of 'Permanent settlement' and 'forced labour'. In 1935 the All India Kisan Sabha took shape. A mass peasant movement developed after the Second World War in some parts of the country led by local Kisan Sabhas. Thus peasant organisations spread to other parts of the country to protect the interests of the small farmer and labour from backward communities and tribes. It was only when agricultural labour emerged as a distinct class that agrarian movements and the attendant class relations acquired new meanings.[1] Labour movements mostly centred around such issues as land relations, wages, recruitment of labour, cultivator-labour relation etc. In fact they ultimately reflected on the very pattern of basic agrarian structure of society.

However, none of the efforts made so far has been able to bring together large sections of unorganised and scattered agricultural workers and weld them into a force for concerted action. But, with the development of agriculture, spread of education and political consciousness, agricultural labour will become more organised and conscious. It will naturally take time to make its existence felt.

The agrarian crisis that had been mounting-up in the late sixties had given an impetus to the unionisation among agricultural labourers. This could be partly attributed to the differentiation of peasantry, where poor peasants were pauperised and joined the ranks of proletariat.

There is a significant difference between the situation in the past and situation prevailing now. In the earlier times, the marketed surplus is low and agriculture is a leisurely occupation. Now agriculture has become a commercial proposition and the demand for labour has gone-up. The labourers are also realising that their services are needed by the peasants and therefore, they have been demanding a real wage that will suffice for their subsistence under the new dispensation where he had to seek employment as a wage labour. Hence the organisations have come up in different parts of the country to fight for their betterment.

In Andhra Pradesh the agricultural labourers had gone on strike for the first time in Mypadu of Nellore district. Later in 1930, another strike

1. Ani Lukose., *Labour Movements and Agrarian Relations* (Jaipur: Rawat Publications,1991) pp.1-3.

was reported at Potlapudi. The trend of labour going on strikes had been on the rise in 1935 where labourers had gone on strikes in 7 villages for wage increase. In 1938, these strikes were conducted in 22 villages while some of these were successful. However, there was no organisation in the proper sense directing the activities of agricultural labourers.

In 1934, an agricultural labour organisation was started in Nellore district. During 1935, organisation for agricultural labour had come-up in some taluks of Guntur, Krishna, West Godavari, East Godavari districts and the wage issues have been highlighted by these organisations. By 1941, district unions have come-up in Krishna, East Godavari and West Godavari districts.

A State level agricultural labour orgnaisation in Andhra State was inaugurated on 1st August, 1937 at Nellore under the presidentship of M.N.Roy. In 1938, a programme had been chalked out to lead the agricultural labour movement along class lines.

Organisation of agricultural labour unions at the State level was attempted by 1945 and a State level meeting of agricultural labourers was successfully held in 1947 at Jaggannapet in East Godavari district.[1]

In the early years of the struggle the main demands of the labour movement around enhancement of daily wages from two Annas to four Annas, stopage of atrocities on labour and the disuse of less standardised measures used for weighing jowar, paddy and other crops for payment of kind wages.

Later, the split in Communist Party (1964) gave rise to CPI and CPI(M). In Andhra Pradesh the CPI had formed the Bharatiya Khet Mazdoor Union (BKMU) in 1968 and highlighting different issues of labourers. Similarly the All India Agricultural Workers' Union, an affiliate of CPI(M) started its formal functioning in 1981 even though its State unit had been functioning at the State level even much earlier. The Naxalbari struggle and its aftermath had led to different CPI(ML) groups functioning in the State and some of these (ML) groups had been organising 'Ryotu Cooli Sangam' to highlight the demands of agricultural workers also apart from peasant demands. In 1970s, all these unions had become active in organising agricultural labourers in different parts of the State.

1. G.Yellamanda Reddy, Forty years struggle of State Agricultural Labour Union in Andhra Pradesh, *Cooli Dandu*, II, (October 1977), Vijayawada, p.2.

Unionism among Labour of Selected Villages

Attached Labourers

It has been enquired into whether there existed any formal trade union for attached labourers and in the absence of it, whether there was any informal group. The attached labourers, in their reply, unanimously told that they were aware of neither the existence of any formal union nor any informal group. Since the number of attached labourers in a village was very small there might not have been much scope for the formation of any formal union.

Casual Labourers

None of the casual labourers was aware of the existence of any formal union for agricultural labour. Consequently they were not members of any trade union. An enquiry about the existence of at least any informal group showed that only 16 per cent of the casual labourers from Coastal Andhra had confessed the existence of informal group. This percentage was very high in Piridi with 48.57 per cent. In Veerannapalem; in the villages of Rayalaseema and Coastal Andhra the casual labourers were not aware of the existence of informal group.

Farmers' opinion on Labour Unions

The farmers were asked about their awareness and desirability of labour unions. All the respondent farmers expressed that they were aware of the existence of unions for agricultural labour in some parts of the country. But only 27 per cent of them welcomed the formation of labour unions. This percentage was 19 in Coastal Andhra; 36 in Rayalaseema and 31 in Telangana (Table 6.10). At village level, more than 85 per cent of respondent farmers in Vangalapudi, Guntupalle and Veerannapalem of Coastal Andhra opposed labour unions. In other villages, this percentage varied from 54 to 83. The reasons for this opposition were also enquired into. Fifty three per cent of farmers felt, that the existence of labour unions would lead to more demands from labour. The other reasons for opposing unions are *i.* they result in more disputes, *ii.* they lead to worsening relations, *iii.* they cause less working hours, and *iv.* they cause one sided work.

The farmers' reasons for support of labour unions were also enquired into and shown in Table 6.11. It may be noted here that only 27 per cent of farmers supported the formation of labour unions. Among them most of the farmers supported the labour unions with the idea that they would result in fixed wages followed by regulation of employment

Table 6.10 : Percentage Distribution of Farmers by their Opposition for Unionization among Agricultural Labour and Justification Thereof

REGION AND VILLAGE	Percentage of Farmers Opposing Union for Agricultural Labour	Percentage of Farmers by Justification for Opposing Unionization				
		MD	RID	WR	LWH	OSW
COASTAL ANDHRA						
Piridi	54.29	54.29	--	--	--	--
Vangalapudi	88.57	·57.15	14.28	8.57	--	8.57
Guntupalle	97.14	57.15	8.57	11.42	5.72	14.28
Veerannapalem	85.71	57.15	11.42	--	8.57	8.57
OVERALL	**81.42**	**56.43**	**8.57**	**5.00**	**3.57**	**7.85**
RAYALASEEMA						
Brahmanapalle	62.86	51.42	5.72	5.72	--	--
Sanjeevapuram	65.71	48.58	8.58	2.86	2.86	2.86
OVERALL	**64.29**	**50.00**	**7.15**	**4.28**	**1.43**	**1.43**
TELANGANA						
Jookal	68.57	57.14	--	5.71	2.86	2.86
Raigir	54.29	40.00	2.86	2.86	2.86	5.71
Andhra Nagar	82.86	51.42	11.42	8.57	2.86	8.58
OVERALL	**68.57**	**49.52**	**44.76**	**5.71**	**2.86**	**5.71**
ANDHRA PRADESH	***73.01***	***52.69***	***6.99***	***5.00***	***2.86***	***5.39***

Note : MD – Moere Demands; RID – Results in Increase of Disputes; WR – Worsening Relations; LWH – Less Working Hours; OSW – One Sided work

and good relationship. The same trend existed at regional level also. At village level, it is interesting to note that 46 per cent of farmers from Piridi and Raigir, one-third of farmers from Brahmanapalle, Sanjeevapuram and Jookal supported the formation of labour unions.

The farmers also opposed the membership of their attached labourers and casual labourers in informal groups. It was only in Veerannapalem of Coastal Andhra and Jookal of Telangana that significant number of farmers supported the membership of attached labourers in informal groups. Similarly 29 per cent of farmers from Piridi and 20 per cent of farmers from Vangalapudi supported the membership of casual labourers in informal groups. The farmers, with the exception of five respondents from Vangalapudi, never met any union official.

Table 6.11 : Percentage Distribution of Farmers by their Support for Unionization among Agricultural Labour and Justification Thereof

REGION AND VILLAGE	Farmers' Support	Percentage of Farmers by Justification for Opposing Unionization				
		GWC	PR	GR	FW	RE
COASTAL ANDHRA						
Piridi	45.72	--	11.43	11.43	11.43	11.43
Vangalapudi	11.42	--	--	--	5.71	5.71
Guntupalle	2.86	--	--	--	2.86	--
Veerannapalem	14.29	--	--	8.57	2.86	2.86
OVERALL	**18.57**	--	**2.86**	**5.00**	**5.71**	**5.00**
RAYALASEEMA						
Brahmanapalle	37.14	5.71	8.58	5.71	11.43	5.71
Sanjeevapuram	34.29	2.86	2.86	5.71	14.28	8.58
OVERALL	**35.71**	**4.28**	**5.71**	**5.71**	**12.86**	**7.15**
TELANGANA						
Jookal	31.42	2.86	--	5.71	14.28	8.57
Raigir	45.71	5.71	5.71	11.43	14.28	8.58
Andhra Nagar	17.14	2.86	--	--	11.42	2.86
OVERALL	**31.43**	**3.81**	**1.91**	**5.71**	**13.33**	**6.67**
ANDHRA PRADESH	***26.67***	***2.22***	***3.18***	***5.39***	***9.85***	***6.03***

Note : GWC – Good Working Conditions; PR–Preserve the Rights; GR–Good Relationship FW–Fixed Wages; RE– Regulation of Employment.

Unionism among Farmers

It has been suggested often that farmers should combine themselves into a strong union to protect their interests. The opinion of respondent farmers on this suggestion is enquired into and is shown in Table 6.12. More than three fourths of farmers in all the regions have supported the idea of union. The nature of farmers' combine— *i.* whether it should be an informal group or *ii.* a formal association with regular membership in times of crisis or *iii.* a formal association deciding all matters of agricultural employment is enquired into. Most of the farmers from all the three regions and nine villages expressed that the farmers' combine should be in the form of an informal group.

The attached labourers were also asked about their opinion on the formation of farmers' union. Eighty per cent of attached labourers of Coastal Andhra and 87 per cent of attached labourers of Telangana opposed the formation of farmers' union. This shows that the attached labourers were afraid of the effects of combined strength of farmers. The trend is same in all the seven individual villages.

Table 6.12 : Percentage Distribution of Farmers by their Support for Organizing a Union for them and Its Nature

REGION AND VILLAGE	Percentage of Farmers Supporting Union for them	Nature of Farmer's Combine		
		Acting as an Informal Group	*Formal Association with regular membership in times of crisis*	*Formal Association deciding all matters of Agricultural Employment*
COASTAL ANDHRA				
Piridi	71.43	65.71	5.72	--
Vangalapudi	71.43	62.85	8.58	--
Guntupalle	80.00	80.00	--	--
Veerannapalem	77.14	77.14	--	--
OVERALL	**75.00**	**71.43**	**3.57**	--
RAYALASEEMA				
Brahmanapalle	77.14	74.28	--	2.86
Sanjeevapuram	85.71	100.00	--	--
OVERALL	**81.43**	**77.14**	--	--
TELANGANA				
Jookal	68.57	68.57	--	--
Raigir	77.14	77.14	--	--
Andhra Nagar	85.71	85.71	--	--
OVERALL	**77.14**	**77.14**	--	--
ANDHRA PRADESH	***77.14***	***75.25***	***1.58***	***0.31***

The casual labourers were also asked whether they support the existence of farmers' union. Table 6.13 shows the results of this enquiry. Eighty four per cent of casual labourers at State level had expressed aganist the formation of farmers' union. At regional level, 92 per cent of casual labourers in Coastal Andhra; 90 per cent in Rayalaseema and 70 per cent in Telangana were against the idea of formation of farmers' union. Most of the casual labourers had opposed this idea with the feeling that the farmers' union will lead to low bargaining capacity on their part and consequently low wages.

The State Governments, as a special measure, should provide such facilities as may be necessary to organisations of agricultural labour when these come into being. The type of encouragement which an industrial worker got in the twenties needs to be extended to agricultural labour now. The Assam Government for instance, has enacted the Assam Shramik Vahini Act (1959) to facilitate formation of voluntary association of workers and registration for better and regular supply of labour for execution of development works.

Table 6.13 : Casual Labourer's Acceptance of Farmer's Union

REGION AND VILLAGE	Yes %	No %	Total %
COASTAL ANDHRA			
Piridi	14.29	85.71	100.00
Vangalapudi	8.57	91.43	100.00
Guntupalle	8.57	91.43	100.00
Veerannapalem	--	100.00	100.00
OVERALL	**7.86**	**92.14**	**100.00**
RAYALASEEMA			
Brahmanapalle	11.43	88.57	100.00
Sanjeevapuram	8.57	91.43	100.00
OVERALL	10.00	90.00	100.00
TELANGANA			
Jookal	28.57	71.43	100.00
Raigir	45.71	54.29	100.00
Andhra Nagar	14.29	85.71	100.00
OVERALL	**29.52**	**70.48**	**100.00**
ANDHRA PRADESH	***15.56***	***84.44***	***100.00***

Conflicts and Consultation

Meaning and Manifestations

Conflict occurs at various levels-within a person, between members of a group and between groups. It has different implications for individual behaviour and work group behaviour. Whenever there are differences between the goals of separate groups or even several individuals in a group, conflict occurs.[1]

Conflict *per se* is neither bad nor contrary to good organisation. Disagreements and dissatisfactions can lead to reexamination of basic assumptions and practices, to the end that adjustments can be made to improve overall organisational effectiveness. Conflict is sometimes beneficial as it brings about social change as a consequence.[2] It also helps maintain the stability of the group by forcing groups to air their grievances and resolve their problems thus preventing unhealthy upheavals and illfeeling within and between groups. However we should also see the negative aspects of conflict which are dysfunctional. Strikes and lockouts

1. Arun Monappa, *Industrial Relations* (New Delhi: Tata Mc Graw-Hill Publishing Company Ltd., 1987) p.180.
2. A. Kornhauser, R. Dubin and A.M.Ross eds. *Industrial Conflict* (New York, Mc Graw-Hill, 1954), p.14.

bring about loss of production and profits to the owners, loss of wages to the workers, irregular supply of goods and services to the consumers, and aggregate loss in gross national product and income at the national level.

Industrial conflict assumes various forms, some overt while others not quiet. The ultimate manifestation of industrial conflict is a strike on the part of workers and a lockout on the part of managers/employers. The conflict is not confined to overt strikes or lockouts but there are other expressions of conflict which have significant effects on the working of an enterprise.[1] These forms of conflict include hostility, stresses and tension, absenteeism, work-to-rule, demonstration, morcha, gherao, etc.

Agrarian Conflicts

The eruption of agrarian conflicts in different parts of India has received the attention of scholars and administrators, and quite a few have expressed opinion on their causes. Since this phenomenon manifested in the wake of the green revolution, some scholars identified the accentuation of inequality aggravated by agricultural development as the principal cause of the discontent and unrest. On the basis of a study, Gananeshwar Ohja came to the conclusion that "in the race for technological improvement, substantial farmers are making better gains and that the gap between the big and small is widening. This is the dark shadow of the green revolution"[2] Martin E Abol found that "the concentration of the benefits of the 'Green Revolution' in the hands of relatively few cultivators, has already led to appreciable discontent in parts of rural India". For example, the agricultural labourers of Tanjore are not happy with the modest increase in their real wages, when they see owner-cultivators increasing their incomes several fold. Rural discontent, particularly among labourers and unsecured tenants, is being exploited by some political groups in West Bengal and Kerala as well as in other parts of the country.[3] Further, the ideological orientation of labourers is also responsible for conflicts in some parts of the country.[4] This agrarian

1. Kornhauser., op.cit., p.15.
2. Ganneshwar Ojha, "Small Farmers and High Yielding Variety Programme", *Economic and Political Weekly,* V, No.14, (April, 1971), p.605.
3. Martin E.Abel, "Agriculture in India in the 1970s", *Economic and Political Weekly,* V, No. 13, (28th March, 1970), p. A-9.
4. K.C. Alexandar, "The Nature and the background, Agrarian Unrest in Kuttanad, Kerala", *Indian Journal of Industrial Relations*, 11, No.1, (July, 1975), p.65.

unrest in different parts of India has been a problem of great prominence which has to be solved quickly and effectively.

It is heartening to note that no conflicts between the farmers and their labourers have been reported in the selected villages during the period under study.

Consultation

Meaning and Significance of Consultation

Consultation between employer and employee is the prerequisite for participative mangement.

Participation is not a unitary concept, but consists of interrelated elements which may be manifested in the decision making processes of an organisation in a wide variety of ways. Three elements central to the concept of participation are influence, interaction and information-sharing.[1] According to McGregor it is "a formal method providing an opportunity for every member of the organisation to contribute his brain and ingenuity as well as his physical efforts for the improvement of organisational effectiveness, as well as enhancing his own economic welfare[2].

It is conceded by all parties that association/participation of labour in management is an imperative necessity, for its seeks to promote democratic practices by replacing unilateral actions or even autocratic decisions. In India, the idea of promoting participative practices is a result of its encouragement by the Government and the direct and indirect pressure exerted by not only the unions and management but every thinking person. The objectives of the idea are: elevation of workers' status in industry; the promotion of democratic practices in the resolution of industrial relation problems, and the mobilisation of energy and intelligence of the workers and the management with a view to increasing efficiency.[3]

---

1. T. D. Wall and J. A. Lischeron, *Worker Participation: A critique of the literature and some fresh evidence* (London : Mc Graw-Hill Book Company Ltd., 1977), pp.36-37.
2. Douglas McGregor, *The Human Side of Enterprise* (New York : Mc Graw-Hill Book Company., 1960), p.113.
3. Kannappan Subbaiah, "Workers Participation in Management : A Review of Indian Experience," *Bulletin*, International Institute for Labour Studies, 1968.

Consultation between Farmer and Agricultural Labour

There is no gain saying the fact that consultation leading to participation is desirable in the agricultural sector too. But the form, content and extent of participation here is different from industrial sector. Since the relations between the farmer and agricultural labourer are bound with class and caste system, both the parties tend to percieve paraticipation from different angles. The farmer who is generally prerogative/consciouness, participation implies erosion of his traditional power and prerogatives. Thus he tends to be authoritative in his approach in taking decisions. The labour participation implies better voice in decision making and also distributive justice. Though he desires to have a share in decision making, the same is countered by the farmer's general sense of superiority and unilateral actions. As a result, participation becomes a marginal affair and usually revloves round such issues as preparation of seed beds, transplantation, weeding, manuring, harvesting and such other important operations.

Consultation in Selected Villages:

The consultation between farmers and labourers of selected villages is enquired into and the results are presented in Table 6.14. While seventy eight per cent of farmers were consulting attached labourers; only 51 per cent of farmers were consulting casual labourers on different aspects of agricultural work. The practice of consulting attached labourers was more in Vangalapudi and Veerannapalem of Coastal Andhra and Andhra Nagar of Telangana. In respect of casual labourers, this practice of consulting them was very much prevalent in Piridi of Coastal Andhra and Raigir of Telangana.

The labourers were also asked as to the consultation to get the version of farmers verified. It is heartening to note that 83 per cent of attached labourers agreed that the farmers were consulting them. But only 6 per cent of casual labourers expressed that there were consultations between them and farmers.

Tripartite Consultation

There should also be tripartite consultative bodies consisting of the representatives of agricultural labour, employers and State Government at the State and District levels to review periodically the conditions of agricultural labour, revise and enforce minimum wages, and take stock of the impact of development programmes on their employment. At present, the voice of even organised rural labour is feeble, and in several

Table 6.14 : Consultation between Farmers and Labour

REGION AND VILLAGE	Percentage of Farmers Consulting Labourers—Farmers' Response		Percentage of Labourers being Consulted by Farmers—Labourers' Response	
	Attached Labourers	Casual Labourers	Attached Labourers	Casual Labourers
COASTAL ANDHRA				
Piridi	70.00	71.43	100.00	42.86
Vangalapudi	91.67	51.43	60.00	--
Guntupalle	60.00	51.43	100.00	2.86
Veerannapalem	100.00	45.71	100.00	2.86
OVERALL	**76.00**	**55.00**	**90.00**	**12.14**
RAYALASEEMA				
Brahmanapalle	--	28.57	--	5.71
Sanjeevapuram	--	51.45	--	--
OVERALL	--	**40.00**	--	**2.86**
TELANGANA				
Jookal	66.67	48.57	100.00	--
Raigir	70.00	57.14	20.00	--
Andhra Nagar	93.33	51.45	100.00	5.71
OVERALL	**79.41**	**52.38**	**73.33**	**1.90**
ANDHRA PRADESH	***77.78***	***50.79***	***82.86***	***6.03***

Note : No Attached Labour in Rayalaseema Villages.

parts of the country it is non-existent. It should be the function of the Government to encourage the employers' and workers' organisation at the Central, State and District levels to come together for a meaningful dialogue on problems which crop up from time to time in regard to conditions of work of agricultural labour.

Farm Relations

Effects of Cordial/Strained Relations

Farmers

The prerequisite for the establishment of cordial relations is the firm belief of the parties in the disirability of harmonious relations. With the exception of one farmer in Vangalapudi of Coastal Andhra, all other respondent farmers expressed the need for harmonious relations with their labourers. Further all attached labourers also expressed their belief in cordial relations with farmers.

The effects of cordial and strained relations with labourers as opined by farmers were also enquired into and presented in Table 6.15. The positive effects have been identified as *i.* increased production and productivity *ii.* improved social relations *iii.* improved personal prestige and power and *iv.* peaceful work life. The negative effects of strained relations are found to be *i.* reduced production/productivity *ii.* disturbed social relations *iii.* tarnished personal image and *iv.* disturbed work life.

Forty two per cent of farmers felt that cordial relations will increase the production/productivity. Forty one per cent of farmers felt that it ensures peaceful work life. The same trend could be observed in regions as well as individual villages.

Forty three per cent of farmers felt that the strained relations will disturb social relations and another 42 per cent felt that it will reduce production/productivity. The farmers at regional level as well as in individual villages felt in the same manner about the negative effects of strained relations.

Attached Labour

The opinion of attached labourers regarding the effects of cordial and strained relations is also enquired into and shown in table 6.16. The positive effects of cordial relations are identified as *i.* more wages and benefits *ii.* good working conditions *iii.* improved social prestige and iv. peaceful work life. The negative effects of strained relations are found to be *i.* low wages and benefits *ii.* insecurity of employment *iii.* not possible to secure employment to other family members and iv. disturbed work life.

Thirty eight per cent of attached labourers have expressed that cordial relations would result in more wages and benefits; thirty four per cent of attached labourers felt that they would result in employment security. Both the regions and all the seven villages, with the exception of Raigir of Telangana, showed the same pattern.

Fifty five per cent of attached labourers were of the opinion that strained relations would result in low wages and benefits; twenty nine per cent of attached labourers felt that it would result in disturbed work life. In Telangana region, the second important negative effect is found to be the insecurity of employment.

Table 6.15 : Percentage Distribution of Farmers by their Opinion on Effects of Cordial/Strained Relations with Labour

REGION AND VILLAGE	Positive Effects of Cordial Relations					Negative Effects of Strained Relations				
	IP/P	ISR	IPPP	EPW	TOTAL	RP/P	DSR	TPI	RDW	TOTAL
COASTAL ANDHRA										
Piridi	37.50	17.19	7.81	37.50	100.00	33.33	15.79	7.02	43.86	100.00
Vangalapudi	29.73	8.10	5.41	56.76	100.00	28.00	36.00	4.00	32.00	100.00
Guntupalle	47.06	5.88	3.92	43.14	100.00	48.08	5.77	--	46.15	100.00
Veerannapalem	49.06	3.77	9.43	37.74	100.00	50.94	5.66	5.66	37.74	100.00
OVERALL	**41.46**	**9.27**	**6.83**	**42.24**	**100.00**	**40.09**	**15.57**	**4.25**	**40.09**	**100.00**
RAYALASEEMA										
Brahmanapalle	42.31	9.61	17.31	30.77	100.00	42.55	6.38	6.39	44.68	100.00
Sanjeevapuram	56.00	8.00	8.00	28.00	100.00	57.15	6.12	2.04	34.69	100.00
OVERALL	**49.02**	**8.82**	**12.75**	**29.41**	**100.00**	**50.00**	**6.25**	**4.17**	**39.58**	**100.00**
TELANGANA										
Jookal	40.54	5.41	2.70	51.35	100.00	42.86	--	2.85	54.29	100.00
Raigir	30.00	15.00	5.00	50.00	100.00	37.14	11.43	--	51.43	100.00
Andhra Nagar	41.46	12.20	2.44	43.90	100.00	41.03	10.26	2.56	46.15	100.00
OVERALL	**37.29**	**11.02**	**3.39**	**48.30**	**100.00**	**40.37**	**7.34**	**1.83**	**50.46**	**100.00**
ANDHRA PRADESH	***42.11***	***9.66***	***7.29***	***40.94***	***100.00***	***42.45***	***11.26***	***3.60***	***42.69***	***100.00***

Note : IP/P—Increases Production/Productivity; RP/P—Reduces Production/Productivity; ISR—Improves Social Relations; DSR—Disturbs Social Relations; IPPP—Improves Personal Prestige and Power; TPI—Tarnishes Personal Image; EPW—Ensures Peaceful Worklife; RDW—Results in Disturbed Worklife.

Table 6.16 : Percentage Distribution of Attached Labour by their Opinion on Effects of Cordial/Strained Relations with Farmers

REGION AND	Positive Effects of Cordial Relations							Negative Effects of Strained Relations				
VILLAGE	MWB	GWC	ISP	ES	EF	EPWL	TOTAL	LWB	IE	NPSEF	DWL	TOTAL
COASTAL ANDHRA												
Piridi	22.22	11.11	33.33	33.34	--	--	100.00	25.00	25.00	12.50	37.50	100.00
Vangalapudi	50.00	--	--	33.33	--	16.67	100.00	50.00	16.67	--	33.33	100.00
Guntupalle	57.14	14.29	--	--	28.57	--	100.00	28.57	28.57	--	42.86	100.00
Veerannapalem	40.00	--	--	50.00	--	10.00	100.00	50.00	--	--	50.00	100.00
OVERALL	**40.63**	**6.25**	**9.37**	**31.25**	**6.25**	**6.25**	**100.00**	**38.71**	**16.13**	**3.22**	**41.94**	**100.00**
TELANGANA												
Jookal	20.00	20.00	--	60.00	--	--	100.00	50.00	33.33	--	16.67	100.00
Raigir	40.00	40.00	--	20.00	--	--	100.00	80.00	20.00	--	--	100.00
Andhra Nagar	40.00	--	20.00	40.00	--	--	100.00	42.86	28.57	28.57	--	100.00
OVERALL	**33.33**	**20.00**	**6.67**	**40.00**	--	--	**100.00**	**55.56**	**27.78**	**11.10**	**5.56**	**100.00**
ANDHRA PRADESH	***33.30***	***10.64***	***8.51***	***34.05***	***4.25***	***4.25***	***100.00***	***44.90***	***20.41***	***6.12***	***28.57***	***100.00***

Note : i) No Attached Labour in Rayalaseema Villages.

ii) MWB—More Wages and Benefits; EPWL—Ensure Peaceful Work Life; GWC—Good Working Conditions; LWB—Low Wages and Benefits; ISP—Improves Social Prestige; IE—Insecurity of Employment; ES—Employment Security; NPSEF—Not Possible to Secure Employment to other Family members; EF—Employment for other Family members; DWL—Disturbed Work Life.

Casual Labour

In response to the enquiry, thirty two per cent of casual labourers felt that cordial relations will result in more wages and benefits; 27 per cent of casual labourers expressed that it would provide for employment security and slightly more than 18 per cent of casual labourers were of the opinion that cordial relations will result in peaceful work life (Table 6.17). The same trend is found in the three regions and in individual villages with the exception of Brahmanapalle, Jookal, Raigir and Andhra Nagar where other effects like good working conditions, improvement of social prestige were given more importance.

The negative effects of strained relations are also enquired into and presented in Table 6.17. As per this table, low wages and benefits life were mentioned as the major negative effects of strained relations. In Vangalapudi and Raigir villages, the casual labourers mentioned that it will not be possible to secure employment to other family members if strained relations exist.

Nature Of Relations During The Past Two Decades

The nature of relations between farmers and labourers in the last two decades is enquired into by eliciting the opinions of farmers, attached labourers and casual labourers.

a. Relations Between Farmers and Attached Labour

Farmers

Table 6.18 shows farmers' opinion on relation with attached labourers in the past two decades. It is distressing to note that 60 per cent of farmers were of the opinion that their relations were gradually worsening. This percentage was further higher in respect of Telangana with 71. It is interesting to note that while Piridi showed very low percentage of farmers having the opinion of gradually worsening relations; cent per cent of the farmers of the Veerannapalem village were of the opinion that their relations with attached labourers were gradually worsening.

The reasons for the above situation of worsening relations are also enquired into. Slightly more than one third of the farmers, in both the regions, had expressed that increase in awareness and individuality among labourers was responsible for worsening relations. The other two reasons for this State of worsening relations were increase in cost of living and decline in work consciousness and commitment.

Table 6.17 : Percentage Distribution of Casual Labour by their Opinion on Effects of Cordial/Strained Relations with Farmers

REGION AND	Positive Effects of Cordial Relations							Negative Effects of Strained Relations				
VILLAGE	MWB	GWC	ISP	ES	EF	EPWL	TOTAL	LWB	IE	NPSEF	DWL	TOTAL
COASTAL ANDHRA												
Piridi	26.39	11.12	8.33	20.83	12.50	20.83	100.00	25.81	30.65	24.19	19.35	100.00
Vangalapudi	19.23	7.69	1.92	38.46	1.92	30.78	100.00	20.00	51.11	26.67	2.22	100.00
Guntupalle	33.33	3.92	5.88	35.29	3.93	17.65	100.00	20.00	28.00	14.00	38.00	100.00
Veerannapalem	46.15	1.92	1.92	36.54	3.85	9.62	100.00	44.44	12.97	3.70	38.89	100.00
OVERALL	**30.84**	**6.61**	**4.84**	**31.72**	**6.17**	**19.82**	**100.00**	**27.96**	**29.86**	**17.06**	**25.12**	**100.00**
RAYALASEEMA												
Brahmanapalle	42.86	16.33	14.29	18.36	2.04	6.12	100.00	39.58	20.83	4.17	35.42	100.00
Sanjeevapuram	33.33	5.26	1.76	22.81	12.28	24.56	100.00	39.22	21.57	9.80	29.41	100.00
OVERALL	37.74	10.38	7.55	20.75	7.55	16.03	100.00	39.39	21.21	7.08	32.32	100.00
TELANGANA												
Jookal	15.38	9.62	19.23	21.15	--	34.62	100.00	48.08	13.46	3.85	34.62	100.00
Raigir	39.47	13.16	7.89	31.59	--	7.89	100.00	41.67	36.11	16.67	5.56	100.00
Andhra Nagar	35.14	32.41	10.81	16.22	--	5.40	100.00	47.22	36.11	8.33	8.33	100.00
OVERALL	**28.35**	**17.32**	**13.39**	**22.83**	--	**18.11**	**100.00**	**45.97**	**26.61**	**8.87**	**18.55**	**100.00**
ANDHRA PRADESH	***31,74***	***10.43***	***7.83***	***26.74***	***4.78***	***18.48***	***100.00***	***35.71***	***26.96***	***12.45***	***24.88***	***100.00***

Note : i) MWB—More Wages and Benefits; EPWL—Ensure Peaceful Work Life; GWC—Good Working Conditions; LWB—Low Wages and Benefits; ISP—Improves Social Prestige; IE—Insecurity of Employment; ES—Employment Security; NPSEF—Not Possible to Secure Employment to other Family members; EF—Employment for other Family members; DWL—Disturbed Work Life.

Table 6.18 : Percentage Distribution of Farmers by their Opinion on Relations with Attached Labour in the Past Two Decades and the Reasons for Worsening Relations

REGION AND VILLAGE	Farmers' Opinion				Farmers' Reasons for Worsening Relations		
	GI	GW	NC	TOTAL	IAIL	ICL	DWCC
COASTAL ANDHRA							
Piridi	10.00	19.04	70.00	100.00	9.52	4.76	4.76
Vangalapudi	--	81.81	10.00	100.00	54.54	27.27	--
Guntupalle	--	70.00	30.00	100.00	50.00	20.00	--
Veerannapalem	--	100.00	--	100.00	60.00	20.00	20.00
OVERALL	**4.76**	**53.18**	**35.71**	**100.00**	**34.04**	**14.89**	**4.25**
TELANGANA							
Jookal	--	77.78	22.22	100.00	44.45	22.22	11.11
Raigir	--	80.00	20.00	100.00	50.00	50.00	--
Andhra Nagar	--	60.00	40.00	100.00	26.67	13.33	20.00
OVERALL	--	**70.59**	**29.41**	**100.00**	**35.30**	**23.53**	**11.76**
ANDHRA PRADESH	***2.48***	***60.49***	***37.03***	***100.00***	***34.56***	***18.53***	***7.40***

Note : i) No Attached Labour in Rayalaseema Villages.

ii) GI—Gradually Improving; GW—Gradually Worsening; NC—No Change; IAIL—Increased Awareness and Individuality Among Labour; ICL—Increase in Cost of Living; DWCC—Decline in Work Consciousness and Commitment.

Attached Labourers

The attached labourers are also asked about their relations with farmers in the past two decades and their replies are given in table in 6.19. More than two thirds of attached labourers had subscribed to the view of farmers by expressing that their relations were gradually worsening. It is to be noted that the percentage of attached labourers with this opinion was 93 in Telengana while in Coastal Andhra it was only 50. Thus half of the attached labourers of Coastal Andhra were with the view that there was no change in their relations with farmers in the past two decades. But at village level cent per cent of attached labourers of Vangalapudi, Jookal and Raigir had subscribed to the view of worsening relations.

The reasons for worsening relations are also enquired from the attached labourers. It may be noted from Table 6.19 that their opinions on the cause of worsening relations are more or less equally divided. Thus more exploitation by farmers; increase in general awareness; increase in cost of living; low wages and benefits were found to be important reasons for this situation.

Table 6.19 : Percentage Distribution of Attached Labour by their Opinion on Relations with Farmers in the Past Two Decades and the Reasons for Worsening Relations

REGION AND VILLAGE	Attached Labourers' Opinion			Attached Labourers' Reasons for Worsening Relations					
	GW	NC	TOTAL	IGA	ICL	EF	DWCC	LWB	DWC
COASTAL ANDHRA									
Piridi	--	100.00	100.00	--	--	--	--	--	--
Vangalapudi	100.00	--	100.00	20.00	--	20.00	--	60.00	--
Guntupalle	20.00	80.00	100.00	--	--	--	--	--	20.00
Veerannapalem	80.00	20.00	100.00	20.00	40.00	--	20.00	--	--
OVERALL	**50.00**	**50.00**	**100.00**	**10.00**	**10.00**	**5.00**	**5.00**	**15.00**	**5.00**
TELANGANA									
Jookal	100.00	--	100.00	20.00	--	60.00	20.00	--	--
Raigir	100.00	--	100.00	20.00	40.00	40.00	--	--	--
Andhra Nagar	80.00	20.00	100.00	20.00	20.00	--	20.00	20.00	--
OVERALL	**93.33**	**6.67**	**100.00**	**20.00**	**20.00**	**33.33**	**13.33**	**6.67**	--
ANDHRA PRADESH	***68.57***	***31.43***	***100.00***	***14.28***	***14.28***	***17.15***	***8.58***	***11.42***	***2.86***

Note : i) No Attached Labour in Rayalaseema Villages.

ii) GW—Gradually Worsening; NC—No Change; IGA—Increase in General Awareness; ICL—Increase in Cost of Living; EF—Exploitation by Farmers; DWCC—Decline in Work Consciousness and Commitment; LWB—Low Wages and Benefits; DWC—Deterioration in Working Conditions.

b. Relatioins between Farmers and Casual Labour

Farmers

The farmers are also asked about the relations with casual labourers in the past two decades. Table 6.20 shows their opinion on the State of relations and the reasons thereof. Eighty three per cent of farmers had accepted that these relations with casual labour were gradually worsening and only 15 per cent saw no change. The same situation prevailed at regional level. At village level, the only exception was Piridi where two thirds of farmers saw no change in their relations with casual labourers. The important reasons for worsening relations were found to be increase in awareness and individuality and decline in work consciousness and commitment among casual labour and increase in cost of living. The same trend applied at regional and State levels.

Table 6.20 : Percentage Distribution of Farmers by their Opinion on Relations with Casual Labour in the Past Two Decades and the Reasons for Worsening Relations

REGION AND VILLAGE	Farmers' Opinion				Farmers' Reasons for Worsening Relations				
	GI	GW	NC	TOTAL	IAIL	ICL	EF	BWCC	RAL
COASTAL ANDHRA									
Piridi	5.71	28.57	65.72	100.00	11.43	2.86	2.86	5.71	5.71
Vangalapudi	--	100.00	--	100.00	28.57	22.86	8.57	32.43	8.57
Guntupalle	--	97.14	2.86	100.00	74.28	--	--	17.14	5.72
Veerannapalem	--	91.43	8.57	100.00	20.00	42.86	2.85	25.72	--
OVERALL	**1.43**	**79.28**	**19.29**	**100.00**	**33.57**	**17.14**	**3.57**	**20.00**	**5.00**
RAYALASEEMA									
Brahmanapalle	5.71	71.43	22.86	100.00	48.58	14.28	--	5.71	2.86
Sanjeevapuram	--	94.29	5.71	100.00	51.43	22.86	--	8.57	11.43
OVERALL	**2.86**	**82.86**	**14.29**	**100.00**	**50.00**	**18.57**	--	**7.14**	**7.14**
TELANGANA									
Jookal	--	88.57	11.43	100.00	48.58	5.71	--	22.86	11.42
Raigir	--	88.57	11.43	100.00	54.28	11.43	2.86	11.43	8.57
Andhra Nagar	2.86	88.57	8.57	100.00	45.72	17.14	--	17.14	8.57
OVERALL	**0.95**	**88.57**	**10.48**	**100.00**	**49.53**	**11.42**	**0.95**	**17.14**	**9.53**
ANDHRA PRADESH	***1.59***	***83.17***	***15.24***	***100.00***	***42.53***	***15.56***	***1.90***	***16.19***	***6.99***

Note : i) GI–Gradually Improving; GW–Gradually Worsening; NC–No Change; IAIL–Increased Awareness and Individuality Among Labour; ICL–Increase in Cost of Living; EF–Exploitation of Farmers; DWCC–Decline in Work Consciousness and Commitment. RAL–Rising Aspirations of Labourers

Casual Labour

The opinions of casual labourers on their relations with farmers during the last two decades are shown in table 6.21. As in the case of farmers, most of the casual labourers (75 per cent) were of the opinion that their relations with farmers were gradually worsening. This percentage was 68 in Coastal Andhra; 79 in Rayalaseema and 82 in Telangana. The most important reason for these worsening relations, as expressed by casual labourers was exploitation by farmers followed by increase in cost of living and increase in awareness among labour.

Table 6.21 : Percentage Distribution of Casual Labour by their Opinion on Relations with Farmers in the Past Two Decades and the Reasons for Worsening Relations

REGION AND	Casual Labour Opinion				Casual Labour Reasons for Worsening Relations					
VILLAGE	GI	GW	NC	TOTAL	IAIL	ICL	EF	BWCC	LWB	DWC
COASTAL ANDHRA										
Piridi	11.43	11.43	77.14	100.00	2.86	2.86	5.71	--	--	--
Vangalapudi	5.71	9.143	2.86	100.00	11.43	11.43	25.71	28.58	14.28	--
Guntupalle	--	85.71	14.29	100.00	14.29	14.29	25.71	5.71	8.57	17.14
Veerannapalem	--	82.86	17.14	100.00	8.58	28.57	34.28	--	8.58	2.85
OVERALL	**4.28**	**67.86**	**27.86**	**100.00**	**9.29**	**14.29**	**22.86**	**8.57**	**7.85**	**5.00**
RAYALASEEMA										
Brahmanapalle	--	88.57	11.43	100.00	14.28	28.85	37.15	2.86	8.57	2.86
Sanjeevapuram	--	68.57	31.43	100.00	14.28	14.28	37.15	2.86	--	--
OVERALL	--	**78.57**	**21.43**	**100.00**	**14.28**	**18.58**	**37.18**	**1.43**	**5.71**	**1.42**
TELANGANA										
Jookal	--	71.43	28.57	100.00	14.29	14.29	20.00	11.43	5.71	5.71
Raigir	--	88.57	11.43	100.00	11.43	14.28	42.86	11.43	5.71	2.86
Andhra Nagar	--	85.71	14.29	100.00	14.28	17.14	28.58	17.14	5.71	2.86
OVERALL	--	**81.90**	**18.10**	**100.00**	**13.30**	**15.23**	**30.48**	**13.34**	**5.71**	**3.80**
ANDHRA PRADESH	***1.90***	***74.92***	***23.18***	***100.00***	***11.74***	***15.58***	***28.58***	***8.58***	***6.66***	***3.80***

Note : i) GI—Gradually Improving; GW—Gradually Worsening; NC—No Change;
IAIL—Increased Awareness and Individuality Among Labour; ICL—Increase in Cost of Living; EF—Exploitation of Farmers;
DWCC—Decline in Work Consciousness and Commitment. LWB—Low Wages and Benefits; DWC—Deterioration in Working Condtions.

Measures for Improving Relations

As already indicated above, the relations between farmers and labourers were worsening during the past two decades. In view of this, the respondent farmers, attached labourers and casual labourers are asked about the measures to be taken for improving relations.

Farmers

The responses of farmers are shown in Table 6.22. Nearly 36 per cent of respondent farmers felt that attached labourers are to be educated regarding the need for work consciousness and commitment. In respect of casual labourers, nearly 33 per cent of farmers felt that they should be educated about the need for work consciousnes and commitment. Twenty seven per cent of farmers stated that the values of honesty and decent behaviour are to be inculcated among attached labourers. This suggestion is given by the same percentage of farmers in respect of casual labourers also. Another 15 per cent of farmers mentioned that political parties are to be kept away from the scene to improve their relations with attached labourers. But in respect of casual labourers, the percentage of farmers who gave this suggestion is only eight per cent. The suggestion of strengthening existing arrangements for consultation and communication is given by 13 per cent of farmers in respect of attached labourers and by twenty five per cent of farmers in respect of casual labourers. The same trend could be observed at regional level and also in individual villages with the exception of minor differences in the percentage of farmers mentioning different suggestions for improving relations with labourers.

Labourers

The sugestions given by attached labourers and casual labourers for improving relations with farmers are also enquired into and presented in Table 6.23. Thirty four per cent of attached labourers and 31 per cent of casual labourers suggested that educating labourers will go a long way in improving relations. Sixteen per cent of attached labourers and 21 per cent of casual labourers had expressed that greater consultation and communication will be very much useful in improving relations between farmers and labourers. Other suggestions given by attached labourers and casual labourers are *i.* educating farmers *ii.* strengthening of unions *iii.* institution of appropriate grievance handling mechinary *iv.* government legislation for regulation of wages and working conditions etc. At regional level, strengthening of unions is found to be an important suggestion offered by attached labourers and casual labourers next to educating labourers in Telangana. The casual labourers of Rayalaseema had given more importance to consultation and communication than any

Table 6.22 : Measures Suggested by Farmers for Improving Relations with Labour

REGION AND VILLAGE	ELCC		IVHD		PPAS		ECCS		GLWE		OTHERS		TOTAL
	AL	CL	AL	CL	AL	CL	AL	CL	AL	CL	AL	CL	AL/CL
COASTAL ANDHRA													
Piridi	28.57	30.23	32.14	34.88	21.43	20.93	7.14	9.30	3.57	--	7.14	4.66	100.00
Vangalapudi	54.55	23.53	--	39.22	--	3.92	9.09	29.41	9.09	3.92	27.27	--	100.00
Guntupalle	43.75	34.54	18.75	23.64	25.00	20.00	6.25	21.82	9.09	--	6.25	--	100.00
Veerannapalem	33.33	27.66	--	19.15	--	12.76	66.67	36.17	--	4.26	--	--	100.00
OVERALL	**37.39**	**29.08**	**20.69**	**29.08**	**17.24**	**14.29**	**10.34**	**24.49**	**3.45**	**2.04**	**6.90**	**1.02**	**100.00**
RAYALASEEMA													
Brahmanapalle	--	36.36	--	15.91	--	2.27	--	22.73	--	13.63	--	9.10	100.00
Sanjeevapuram	--	39.13	--	19.57	--	--	--	30.43	--	10.87	--	--	100.00
OVERALL	--	**37.78**	--	**17.78**	--	**1.11**	--	**26.67**	--	**12.22**	--	**4.44**	**100.00**
TELANGANA													
Jookal	12.50	30.43	62.50	32.61	12.50	2.17	12.50	10.87	--	15.22	--	8.70	100.00
Raigir	44.44	34.78	44.44	34.78	--	--	11.11	30.44	--	--	--	--	100.00
Andhra Nagar	35.71	38.63	21.43	20.45	14.29	4.55	28.51	31.82	--	4.55	--	--	100.00
OVERALL	**32.26**	**34.56**	**38.71**	**29.41**	**9.68**	**2.21**	**19.25**	**24.26**	--	**6.62**	--	**2.94**	**100.00**
ANDHRA PRADESH	***35.96***	***32.70***	***26.97***	***29.78***	***14.61***	***7.58***	***13.48***	***24.88***	***2.25***	***5.69***	***6.74***	***2.37***	***100.00***

Note : i) No Attached Labour in Rayalaseema Villages.

ii) ELCC — Educating Labour regarding the need for work Consciousness and Commitment;
IVHD — Inculcating Values of Honesty and Decent Behaviour among labour;
PPAS — Political parties are to be Away from Scene.
ECCS — Existing Consultation and Communication to be Strengthen;
GLWE — Government Legislation for regulating Wages, working conditions and terms of Employment.

iii) 'Others' include 'Institution of appropriate grievance handling machinery' 'Constitution of Board' and 'Responsible Unionism to be developed'.

Table 6.23 : Measures Suggested by Labour for Improving Relations with Farmers

REGION AND	EL		EF		US		IAGHM		GCC		GLRWC		OTHERS		TOTAL
VILLAGE	AL	CL	AL	CL	AL	CL	AL	CL	AL	CL	AL	CL	AL	CL	AL/CL
COASTAL ANDHRA															
Piridi	14.29	31.08	14.29	21.62	--	1.35	--	5.41	42.86	21.62	--	1.35	28.58	17.57	100.00
Vangalapudi	--	26.79	--	7.14	--	10.71	40.00	--	60.00	12.50	--	26.79	--	16.07	100.00
Guntupalle	33.33	25.49	16.67	15.69	--	19.61	--	5.88	16.67	19.61	--	9.80	33.34	3.92	100.00
Veerannapalem	66.66	26.67	16.67	17.78	--	4.44	16.67	--	--	22.22	--	6.67	--	22.22	100.00
OVERALL	**29.17**	**27.87**	**12.50**	**15.93**	--	**8.41**	**12.50**	**3.10**	**29.17**	**19.03**	--	**10.62**	**16.67**	**15.04**	**100.00**
RAYALASEEMA															
Brahmanapalle	--	25.00	--	17.86	--	--	--	--	--	35.71	--	10.71	--	10.72	100.00
Sanjeevapuram	--	37.74	--	5.66	--	1.89	--	--	--	28.30	--	--	--	26.41	100.00
OVERALL	--	**31.19**	--	**7.93**	--	**0.92**	--	--	--	**32.11**	--	**5.50**	--	**18.35**	**100.00**
TELANGANA															
Jookal	50.00	41.67	--	2.07	50.00	22.92	--	--	--	12.50	--	10.42	--	10.42	100.00
Raigir	28.57	30.35	14.29	17.86	42.86	14.29	14.29	--	--	23.21	--	8.93	--	5.36	100.00
Andhra Nagar	42.86	40.43	--	10.64	--	12.77	28.57	--	--	6.38	14.29	17.02	14.29	12.76	100.00
OVERALL	**45.00**	**37.08**	**5.00**	**10.60**	**30.00**	**16.56**	**15.00**	--	--	**14.57**	**5.00**	**11.92**	--	**9.27**	**100.00**
ANDHRA PRADESH	***34.09***	***31.48***	***9.09***	***13.37***	***13.64***	***9.26***	***13.64***	***1.44***	***15.91***	***20.58***	***2.27***	***9.88***	***11.37***	***13.99***	***100.00***

Note : i) No Attached Labour in Rayalaseema Villages.

ii) EL — Educating Labour; EF—Educating Farmers;
US — Union to be Strengthened; AGHN—Institution of Appropriate Grievance Handling Machinery;
GCC — Greater Consultation and Communication; GLRWC—Government Legislation for Regulation of Wages and Working Conditions.

iii) 'Others' include 'Inculcating values of honesty and decent behaviour on the part of farmers, 'Political parties are to be away from scene, and 'Constitution of Board.

other step. At village level certain deviations from that of State and regional level could be observed. In Vangalapudi 40 per cent of attached labourers suggested institution of appropriate grievance handling mechinery. In the same village 27 per cent of casual labourers had suggested government legislation for regulation of wages and working conditions. Fifty per cent of attached labourers and 23 per cent of casual labourers in Jookal were for strengthening of unions to improve their relations with farmers. Similarly in Raigir also, largest percentage of attached labourers (43 per cent) suggested the need for strengthening the unions. In Andhra Nagar, twenty nine per cent of attached labourers were in favour of institution of appropriate grievance handling mechinary.

Future Plans

In view of the changing trends in agrarian relations, the farmers, attached labourers and casual labourers are asked about their future plans.

Farmers

Table 6.24 shows future plans of farmers in view of the worsening relations with attached labourers and casual labourers. Sixty per cent of farmers were of the view that they would comply with the demands of attached labourers and casual labourers to some extent. Around 20 per cent of farmers felt that they would depend on labour of other villages. Other future plans of farmers, although not so significant, are i. shifting to capital intensive crops; ii.resort to mechanisation of agricultural operations ; iii. giving away the lands on lease and iv. selling away the lands and starting other economic activities. The farmers of Telangana have given second rank to the plan of shifting to capital intensive crops. This plan is expressed by significant number of farmers from Jookal village.

The opinion of attached labourers and casual labourers regarding the future employment plans in view of the worsening relations with farmers are elicited and presented in Table 6.25. Eighty six per cent of attached labourers strongly replied that they would continue as attached labourers. Seventy per cent of casual labourers also expressed that they would continue as casual labourers inspite of worsening relations. The same trend could be observed at regional level also in respect of both attached labourers and casual labourers. Thirty one per cent of casual labourers from Piridi, 34 per cent of casual labour from Brahmanapalle and 23 per cent of casual labourers from Andhra Nagar have also expressed readiness to start their own cultivation on lease basis. Twenty three per cent of casual labourers from Veerannapalem, on the other hand, indicated that they would start their own business.

Table 6.24 : Future Plans of Farmers in View of Changing Trends in Agrarian Relations with Labour

REGION AND VILLAGE	DLOV		CDSE		SEIC		RMAO		GLL		SLSE		TOTAL
	AL	CL	AL	CL	AL	CL	AL	CL	AL	CL	AL	CL	AL/CL
COASTAL ANDHRA													
Piridi	4.76	2.70	76.19	72.97	9.52	8.11	--	8.11	9.52	8.11	--	--	100.00
Vangalapudi	27.27	23.91	54.55	58.70	--	6.52	18.18	8.70	--	--	--	2.17	100.00
Guntupalle	50.00	31.11	50.00	40.00	--	30.33	--	2.22	--	6.67	--	6.67	100.00
Veerannapalem	100.00	36.17	--	46.80	--	--	--	4.26	--	4.26	--	8.51	100.00
OVERALL	**29.79**	**24.57**	**57.45**	**53.72**	**4.26**	**6.86**	**4.26**	**5.71**	**4.26**	**4.57**	--	**4.57**	**100.00**
RAYALASEEMA													
Brahmanapalle	--	24.49	--	51.02	--	--	--	--	--	14.29	--	10.20	100.00
Sanjeevapuram	--	28.57	--	63.27	--	--	--	--	--	2.04	--	6.12	100.00
OVERALL	--	**26.53**	--	**57.15**	--	--	--	--	--	**8.16**	--	**8.16**	**100.00**
TELANGANA													
Jookal	--	--	55.56	60.46	33.33	32.56	--	--	11.11	2.33	--	4.65	100.00
Raigir	20.00	7.83	70.00	76.32	10.00	10.53	--	--	10.00	5.26	--	--	100.00
Andhra Nagar	--	2.63	66.67	81.58	6.67	10.53	--	--	13.37	--	6.67	5.26	100.00
OVERALL	**5.88**	**3.10**	**64.71**	**66.67**	**14.71**	**17.05**	--	--	**11.76**	**2.33**	**2.94**	**3.10**	**100.00**
ANDHRA PRADESH	***19.75***	***18.62***	***60.49***	***60.21***	***8.64***	***8.67***	***2.47***	***2.55***	***7.41***	***4.85***	***1.23***	***5.10***	***100.00***

Note : DLOV — Dependence on Labour of Other Villages; CDSE—Compliance to their Demands to Some Extent.
SCIC — Shifting to Capital Intensive Crops. RMAO—Resort to Mechanisation of Agricultural Operations;
GLL — Giving the Lands on Lease; SLSE—Selling the Lands and Starting other Economic Activities.

Table 6.25 : Percentage Distribution of Attached Labour and Casual Labour by their Future Plans

REGION AND	Attached Labourers' Response					Casual Labourers' Response					
VILLAGE	CALF	CALFI	CC/RP	SOCT/CS	TOTAL	CC/RP	SOB	GEI	SOCT/CS	CCL	TOTAL
COASTAL ANDHRA											
Piridi	100.00	--	--	--	100.00	2.86	2.86	5.71	31.43	57.14	100.00
Vangalapudi	60.00	--	20.00	20.00	100.00	--	5.71	5.71	8.58	80.00	100.00
Guntupalle	60.00	--	--	40.00	100.00	5.71	8.57	11.43	11.43	62.86	100.00
Veerannapalem	100.00	--	--	--	100.00	2.86	22.86	2.86	17.14	54.28	100.00
OVERALL	**80.00**	--	**5.00**	**15.00**	**100.00**	**2.86**	**10.00**	**6.43**	**17.14**	**63.57**	**100.00**
RAYALASEEMA											
Brahmanapalle	--	--	--	--	--	--	2.86	--	34.28	62.86	100.00
Sanjeevapuram	--	--	--	--	--	2.86	5.71	11.43	5.71	74.29	100.00
OVERALL	--	--	--	--	--	**1.43**	**4.29**	**5.71**	**20.00**	**68.57**	**100.00**
TELANGANA											
Jookal	80.00	20.00	--	--	100.00	--	--	11.43	11.43	77.14	100.00
Raigir	100.00	--	--	--	100.00	2.86	--	--	14.28	82.86	100.00
Andhra Nagar	100.00	--	--	--	100.00	--	--	--	22.86	77.14	100.00
OVERALL	**93.33**	**6.67**	--	--	**100.00**	**0.95**	--	**3.81**	**16.19**	**79.05**	**100.00**
ANDHRA PRADESH	***85.71***	***2.86***	***2.86***	***8.57***	***100.00***	***1.90***	***5.40***	***5.40***	***17.46***	***69.84***	***100.00***

Note :
CALF – Continue as Attached Labour forever;
CALFI – Continue as Attached Labour until freed from Indebtedness;
GEI – Getting Employment in Industry;
SOCT/CS– Starting Own Cultivation on Tenant basis/Crop Sharing basis;
CC/RP – Conversion into Casual/Rikshaw Puller;
SOB – Starting of Own Business;
CCL – Continue as Casual Labour.

7

Evaluation and Suggestions

The analytical observations presented in earler chapters make it necessary to offer certain suggestions at macro and micro levels.

Planning Process

Inspite of crucial and pervasive role of agriculture in Indian Economy, its two main partners— farmers and labourers are not paid that much attention as they deserve. While 75 per cent of farmers are marginal and small farmers with less than two hectares of holding; more than 50 per cent of agricultural labour are below the poverty line. Both of them are unorganised, voiceless and have no lobby. At the same time, they are victims of market forces, big farmers, politicians and even the village money lenders. The efforts made during the last 40 years of planning have not significantly improved their economic position. Further, the plans have not recognised the agricultural labour as a 'resource' and this resource cannot fructify without the complement of land and other assets. The planning has been largely confined to production and growth areas. In the context of surplus agricultural labour, meticulous planning at macro and micro levels should have been emphasised with regard to human resource utilisation, development and employment generation.

The emphasis in the shortrun may be on provision of employment coupled with basic social services like health, education, nutrition etc., In the longrun efforts are to be made to augment income, earning capacities of rural communities by encouraging non-farm activities also. A conducive climate for private initiative towards self employment will have to be established. Suitable and attractive incentives like house sites, agricultural lands etc. may be offered to encourage the manpower to move from surplus areas to deficit areas which will have a favourable effect on demand-supply relationship and consequently on wage rate.

In the planning process itself, the cultivators and labourers should be encouraged to participate actively and this helps them to assert their rights and monitor the activities to avoid wastage and leakages in implementation of different programmes. The role of Panchayat Raj bodies, Voluntary agencies, cooperative and workers' organisations, should be recognised in the planning process and mechanism should be evolved to strengthen them.

Employment Generation

The Indian agriculture is faced with problem of surplus labour. As already observed in Chapter 5, the casual labour could get employment for less than half of the year. The agricultural operations are seasonal in character with unemployment and under employment prevailing outside the sowing and harvesting seasons. Besides, there is a large, marginal and small farmers who remain idle for a significant period of the year. There is a every need for diversifying the employment opportunities in the agricultural sector. This would necessitate identifying and determining the extent of removable agricultural labour surplus. It is suggested that the rural industrialisation with agrobased industries and other non-farm activities might solve the problem of agricultural underemployment and unemployment. Added to this, the cropping pattern might need to be changed and intensive farming be promoted. This might increase the agricultural production and productivity and generate further employment opportunities. Thus, there is an urgent need to provide incentives to promote intensive farming with improved methods of production and develop non-farm activities.

The government had launched a number of special programmes of employment generation in the rural areas. Some of the important schemes are *i.* Crash Scheme of Rural Employment (CSRE), *ii.* The Food For Work Programme (FFWP), *iii.* Employment Gurantee Scheme (EGS), *iv.* The National Rural Employment Programme (NREP), *v.* Rural Landless Employment Guarantee Programme (RLEGP), and the recently introduced, *vi.* Jawahar Rozgar Yojana (JRY). But the implementation and results of these schemes are not satisfactory as reported by offcial and non-official evaluations. The performance of Employment Guarantee Scheme launched by Maharastra Government is reported to have been successfully operating and has proved to be an important employment generation scheme. The Government of Andhra Pradesh may make an attempt in formulating a scheme of employment generation on these lines, particularly in drought prone areas of Rayalaseema and Telangana.

Decasualisation of Employment

The employment in agriculture is mostly of casual nature. Further, the process of casualisation of labour is increasing continously as indicated by the phenomenal increase in the proportion of casual wage labour to total wage labour. Consequently the agricultural labourer is prone to many hardships like indebtedness, low standard of living, etc. To overcome these problems, steps to decasualise the employment may be initiated. A tripartite board labelled as Agricultural Labour Employment and Welfare Board may be constituted at State level, District level and also at Village Panchayat level with equal representation from farmers, labourers and Government.

The Board will register the potential labour force of each village under its juridication. The agriculturist whenever there is need for labour, sends requisition for the supply of required number of labour. In turn the cultivator pays, the wages to the Board directly.

The Board may undertake broadly the following functions :-

1. Registration of agricultural labour force.
2. Fixation of daily wage rate.
3. Fixation of days of minimum guranteed wage in a season.
4. Allocation of work to labour on the basis of rotation.
5. Collection of wages from the agriculturist for the employed days.
6. Raising of fund from the farmers, labourers, Government and Voluntary agencies.
7. The fund so raised may be utilised for paying wages under guaranteed employment; and for providing welfare benefits to labour, including maternity benefits and old age pension.

This may be experimented on a trial basis in one district each in all the three regions.

Indebtedness

As already observed, the amount of indebtedness among agricultural labour is very high and the two important sources are farmers and money lenders. Very few agricultural labourers are approaching, schedule banks and other cooperative agencies for loan at the time of need. The Government should take measures to bring awareness among the labourers about the facilities of loans provided by these agencies. Further, the Government should encourage the agricultural labour to have their own cooperative credit and welfare societies.

Besides the above measures, the strategy of providing gainful employment and increase in income may be pursued to reduce indebtdness.

Social Security Measures and Welfare Fund

At State level, Agriculture Labour Welfare Fund may be constituted by collecting levy on agricultural products. This fund may be used for providing social security in times of unemployment, sickness, disablement, old age, maternity etc. It may also be used to provide welfare amenities like housing, education and recreation.

Besides the above, the insurance companies may come forward to extend to benefit of group insurance to agricultural labourers and premium may be paid by the Government.

Unionism

As already observed in Chapter 7, the unionisation among farmers and labour is absent in selected villages and is insignificant at State level due to pecularities of farmer and labour and also of the agricultural activity. In this, connection, the Government may take necessary steps in support of unionism. The farmers and labour may be educated and encouraged about the need for forming a union to protect and promote their interests. The social service agencies and voluntary organisations have to play vital role in making the farmers and labour aware of the benefits of unionisation.

Legislative Framework

A separate legislation may be enacted for agricultural labour covering the provisions of existing Industrial Disputes Act and Trade Union Act with the objective of encouraging the formation and working of unions, reducing tensions and to establish hormonious relations between farmers and labourers. This legislation may encourage collective bargaining, mutual settlement of disputes and immediate redressal of grievances. Another legislation comprising of welfare and social security provisions may be enacted exclusively for agricultural labour.

Need for Training in New Methods

The increase in agricultural productivity is the need of the hour. This is possible only by improving the productivity of both farmers and labourers. Adequate training facilities to both in the new methods of farming technology are to be provided from time to time for this purpose.

From Conflict to Cooperation

It is needless to mention that the planned progress in agriculture sector can be achieved only through harmonious and constructive relations between the farmers and labourers. However, of late, cases of tensions and conflicts between the farmers and labourers are reported from different states from time to time. Under these circumstances efforts will have to be made to change the attitudes and perceptions of the farmers and labourers through suitable education programmes and thereby remove suspicion and hatred and establish mutual trust and cooperation between the parties. The national literacy programme launched in recent years has an important role to play in this regard. Implementation of practices of effective human resource management is the ultimate step to establish peace, harmony and constructive cooperation in rural India.

Bibliography

Books

Aggarwal, P.C. "Some observations on Changing Agrarian Relations in Ludhiana, Punjab", in *Changing Agrarian Relations In India*. Hyderabad: National Institute of Community Development, 1975.

Akhilesh, K. B. and Nagaraj, D.R. *Human Resource Management : 2000*. Bombay : Wiley Eastern Limited, 1990.

Alavi, Hamza. "Peasants and Revolutions", in A.R.Desai *ed. Rural Sociology in India.* Bombay: Popular Prakashan, 1975.

Alexander, K.C. "Changing Labour-Cultivator Relations in South India", *in Changing Agrarian Relations in India.* Hyderabad: National Institute of Community Development, 1975.

Ansari, N. *Socio - Economic Profile of Agricultural Labourers in the Boundlkhad region of U.P.* Allahabad : Reseach Project sponsored by Govind Ballabh Pant Science Institute, 1986.

Anjaneya Swamy, G. *Agricultural Enterprenurship in India.* Allahabad: Chugh Publications, 1988.

Aziz, Abdul. *Organising Agricultural Labourers in India: A Proposal.* Calcutta: Minerva Associates, 1980.

Bailey, F.G. *Caste and Economic Frontier.* Manchester: Manchester University Press, 1975.

Bandopadhyay, D. "A Tale From Telangana", in Aravind Das. *ed., Agrarian Relations in India.* New Delhi: Manohar Publications, 1979.

Bean, R. *ed., International Labour Statistics*. New York: Routledge, 1989.

Beteille, Andre. *Studies in Agrarian Social Structure*. London: Oxford University Press, 1974.

Bhalla, G.S. *Changing Agrarian Structure In India*. Meerut : Meenakshi Prakashan, 1974.

Bhaskara Rao, V. *Agrarian and Industrial Relations in Hyderabad State*. New Delhi: Associate Publishing House, 1985.

Booth, Anne and Sundrum R.M. *Labour absorption in Agriculture*. Oxford: Oxford University Press, 1984.

Carl K. Eicher., Lawrence W. Witt, *ed. Agriculture in Economic Development*. Bombay: Vora & Company, Publishers Pvt., Limited, 1970.

Chandra, Bipan. "Peasantry and National Integration" in K.N.Panikar, *ed. National and Left Movements in India*. New Delhi: Vikas Publishing House, 1980.

Cole, G. D. H. *The World of Labour*. London: George Bell and Sons, 1913.

Commons, John R. et al. *History of Labour in the United States Vol.I*. New York: The Macmillan Company, 1919.

Connel, J. and Lipton, M. *Assessing Village Labour Situations in Developing Countries*. London: Oxford University Press, 1977.

Dalton, Dennies. " The Gandhian View of Caste, and Caste After Gandhi", in Philip Mason, *ed. Indian and Cylon: Unity and Diversity*. New York: Oxford University Press, 1967.

Das Arvind N. and Nilakant, V. *Agrarian Relations in India*. New Delhi: Manohar Publications.

Dasai, A. R. "Economic Life of the Rural People", in A.R.Dasai, *ed. Rural sociology in India*. Bombay: Popular Prakashan, 1969.

Dasgupta, Biplab. *The New Agrarian Technology and India*. Bombay: The Macmillan Company, 1977.

Dhanagare, D.N. *Peasant Movement in India*. Bombay: Oxford University Press, 1983.

Etienne, Gilbert. *Studies in Indian Agriculture*. California: University of California Press, 1968.

Farmer, B. H. *Green Revolution.* London: The Macmillan Press, 1977.

Hari Singh, M. *Agricultural Workers' Struggle in Punjab.* New Delhi : People's Publishing House, 1980.

Huizer, Gerrit. *Peasant Movements and their Counterforces in South-east Asia.* New Delhi : Marwah Publications, 1980.

International Labour Office. *Industrial Relations in Asia.* Geneva : International Labour Office, 1976.

Krishna, Daya. *Indian Farmer at Crossroad.* New Delhi : Swan Publishers, 1980.

Kropp, Erhand. *The Use of Labour for the Formation of Agricultural Real Capital.* New Delhi : Manohar Publications, 1980.

Mathies, L. Robert and Jackson, H. John. *Personnal/Human Resource Management.* New Delhi : Tata McGraw Hill Publish ing Company, 1982.

Malaviya, H.D. "Agrarian Unrest After Independence" in A.R. Dasai ed. *Rural Sociology in India.* Bombay : Popular Prakashan, 1969.

Mencher, Joan, P. *Agriculture and Social Structure in Tamil Nadu.* New Delhi : Allied Publishers Pvt. Ltd., 1978.

Mitrany, David. *Marx Against the Peasant.* London : George Weidenfeld and Nicolson, 1951.

Mondy R Wayne and Noe M Robert. *Human Resource Management,* Fourth ed. Boston : Allyn and Bacon, 1990.

Monoppa, Arun. *Industrial Relations.* New Delhi : Tata McGraw-Hill Publishing Company Limited, 1982.

Murthy, B.S. *Profile of Indian Trade Unions.* New Delhi : B.R. Publishing Corporation, 1986.

Nitish, R.De,. 'India's Agrarian Situation : Some Aspects of Changing the Context' in Aravind Das ed. *Agrarian Relations in India.* New Delhi : Manohar Publications, 1979.

Oommen, M.A. 'Land Reforms and Agrarian Change' in M.A. Oommen ed. *Kerala Economy Since Independence.* New Delhi : Oxford and IBH Publishing Company, 1979.

Paramahamsa, V.R.K. ed. *Changing Agrarian Relations In India.* Hyderabad : National Institute of Community Development, 1975.

Ramesh, K. *Human Relations in An Indian University.* New Delhi : Ajanta Books International, 1991.

Rastyanikov. *Agrarian Evolution in a Multiform Structure Society Experience of Independent India.* London : Routledge and Kegan Paul, 1981.

Ratnawat, B. P. *Agriculture Manpower and Economic Development.* London : Yale University, 1975.

Sen, Bandhudas. *The Green Revolution In India.* New Delhi : Wiley Eastern Pvt. Ltd, 1974.

Seshadri, K. 'A Look Into the Peasant Struggles in Andhra Pradesh' in K.N. Panikkar ed. *National and Left Movement in India.* New Delhi : Vikas Publishing House, 1980.

Siddiqi, M. H. *Agrarian Unrest in North India : The United Provinces 1918-1924.* New Delhi : Vikas Publishing House, 1978.

Sinha, Arun. "A Labour Goes to Court' in Aravind Das ed. *Agrarian Relations in India.* New Delhi : Manohar Publications, 1991.

Subba Rao. P. and Rao, V.S.P. *Personnel/Human Resources Management.* New Delhi : Konark Publishers Pvt. Ltd., 1990.

Webbs. *Industrial Democracy.* New York : Green and Company, 1920.

Windmuller P. John, et at. *Collective Barganing in Industrial Market Economics : A Reappraisal.* Geneva : International Labour Office, 1987.

JOURNALS

Alexander, K.C. Emerging Farmer-Labour Relations in Kuttanad. *Economic and Political Weekly,* VIII, No.24 (August, 1973).

Alexander, K.C. Some Characteristics of Agrarian Social Structure of Andhra Pradesh. *Social Action,* 27 No.2 (April-June, 1977).

Alexander, K.C. The Dynamics of Peasant Organisations in South India. *Social Action.* I No. 28, (January-March, 1981).

Aziz, Abdul. Unionising Agricultural Labourers : A Strategy. *The Indian Journal of Industrial Relations.* I.13, No.3, (January, 1978).

Balagopal K. Agrarian Revaluation, not Wage Increases, *Economic and Political Weekly.* No.37, (September 10, 1988).

Bardhan, Pranab. Variations in Agricultural Wages. *Economic and Political Weekly.* VIII, No.21, (May, 1973).

Barik, Bishnu C. Rural-urban Migration and Economic Development : A Case Study of Oriya Agricultural Labourers in Surat. *Man and Development.* 6(3) (Septermber, 1984).

Basant Rakesh. Attached and Casual Labour Wages Rates. *Economic and Political Weekly,* 9 (March 3, 1984).

Bharti Indu. Bihar : Farce of Farm Wages Hike. *Economic and Political Weekly.* No.28, (1990).

Bhardwaj, J.L. and Mishra, C.S. Rising Trends in Wage Rates of Agricultural Labourers : A Study. *Kurukshetra* 34(4) (January, 1986).

Bose. P. K. Proletarianization of Agricultural Labourers : A Sociological Study of Some Villages in Bengal. *The Indian Journal of Labour Economics.* (January, 1978).

Charyulu, U.V.N. Social Legislation for Agricultural Labour : Trends in Implementation, *Social Action.* 30, No.3, 8, No.7(February, 1980).

Chauhan, J.B. Singh. Agricultural Labour in India. *Social Change.* 13(3) (September 1983).

Dhaliwal, R.S. and Grewal, S.S. Impact of Agricultural Development on Farmer-Labourer Relationship. *Economic Affairs.* 28(1) (January-March, 1983).

Frisvold, George and Mines Richard and Perloff M. Jaffrey. The Effects of Job Site Sanitation and Living Conditions on the Health and Welfare of Agriculture Workers. *American Journal of Agricultre Economics.* 70, No.4 (November 1988).

George, Alex. Social and Economic Aspects of Attached Labourers in Kuttanad Agricultures. *Economic and Political Weekly.* (Supplement) 22, No.52 (26 December 1987).

Jose, A.V. Agricultural Wages in India. *Economic and Political Weekly.* (Supplement), 23, No.26 (June 29, 1988).

Joseph, K.V. Rising Agricultural Wages Rates : A sign of Kerala's Economic Prosperity. *Indian Labour Journal.* 29,No. 4 (April, 1988).

Myer, R.M. and Paul, R.R. An Analysis of Wage Trend and Wage Structure of Agricultural Labour in Punjab. *Manpower Journal.* 19, No.1 (April-June, 1983).

Pandey, R.K. and Other. Agricultural Field wages in Orissa : An Economic Study. (October-December, 1988).

Parmer, B.D. Spatial Wage Differentials in Agriculture : A Case of Saurashtra Region. *Indian Journal of Labour Economics.* 28, Nos. 1-2 (April-July, 1985).

Parmar, B.D. Trend in Agricultural Wages in Şaurashtra Region. *Indian Journal of Industrial Relations.* 21, No.4(April, 1986).

Ramesh Chandra. Minimum Wages in the Eastern Region. *Administrator.* 34, No.2 (April-June, 1989).

Reports

Government of India, Agriculture Labour Enquiry 1950-'51 : Report on Intensive Survey of Agricultural Labour, Employment, Underemployment, Wages and Levels of Living (New Delhi : Ministry of Labour, 1954).

Government of India, Second Agricultural Labour Enquiry 1956-'57 (New Delhi : Labour Bureau, Ministry of Labour and Employment, 1960).

Government of India, Rural Labour Enquiry, 1963-'65, Final Report (Simla : Labour Bureau, Department of Labour and Employment, 1973).

Government of India, Rural Labour Enquiry, 1974-'75, Final Report (Chandigarh : Labour Bureau, Ministry of Labour, 1979).

Govenment of India, Report on the Second Agricultural Labour Enquiry 1956-'57, Vol. III, Andhra Pradesh (New Delhi : Labour Bureau, Ministry of Labour and Employment, 1961).

Government of India, Report of the National Commission on Labour (New Delhi : Ministry of Labour and Employment and Rehabilitation, 1969).

Government of India, Report of the National Commission on Agriculture, Part-II, Policy and Strategy, University of Agriculture and Irrigation (New Delhi : 1976).

Government of India, Report of the Minimum Wages Committee for Employment in Agriculture, Chairman : Prof. G. Parthasarathy (New Delhi : Home Department, 1973).

Report of the Royal Commission on Labour in India, (London, 1931).

Labour Problems in India, (General Report), ILO, 1950.

World Agriculture Census Report 1990-'70 : Andhra Pradesh, Bureau of Economic and Statistic, Hyderabad.

Index